Joe Maddy of Interlochen

JOE MADDY
of INTERLOCHEN

By Norma Lee Browning

Foreword by Van Cliburn

HENRY REGNERY COMPANY

CHICAGO · 1963

Dedicated to the Memory of
My Father . . .
Who opened the door.

Music

When music sounds gone is the earth I know,
And all her lovely things even lovelier grow;
Her flowers in vision flame, her forest trees
Lift burdened branches stilled with ecstasies.

When music sounds out of the waters rise
Naiads, whose beauty dims my waking eyes.
Rapt in strange dream burns each enchanted face,
With solemn echoing stirs their dwelling place.

When music sounds all that I was I am,
Ere to this haunt of brooding dust I came,
While from Time's woods break into distant song
The swift winged hours as they hasten along.

Walter De la Mare

Author's Note

WHEN I was in pigtails and tooting a tenor saxophone in my school band in Missouri, my most cherished dream was to spend a summer at a fabulous place in the Michigan northwoods which I knew only as Interlochen.

Interlochen was a magic word to all of us who played in school bands and orchestras. We didn't know much about Interlochen except that it was a summer camp 'way up north in the pine country where, if we had been lucky enough to go, we could have played music all summer long. To most of us it was a dream beyond reach. Those were the depression years, and few of our parents could afford summer camps for their children.

I'll never forget the day my father came home carrying a big black case, almost as big as I was. Inside was a brand new shiny tenor saxophone, to me the most beautiful thing I had ever seen.

I remember the worried, questioning look on my mother's face. My father told her not to worry, he would get it paid for some way. The saxophone cost a hundred and fifteen dollars. My father was a railroad man in a railroad town hard hit by the depression. He had three children to feed and clothe, and that sum seemed a fortune to him even when times were good. I will never know how he managed to pay for the saxophone, but I do know that it became the brightest thing in my life during those years when clouds didn't always have a silver lining.

I paid for my lessons by selling seeds from big bins in a hardware store, working part time in our town's small Five and Ten, and helping my music teacher collect old overdue bills from parents who wanted their children to have lessons but could barely afford them.

One summer a girl clarinetist in our band and orchestra was offered a scholarship at Interlochen. She was the first of our group and the first from our town really to *see* this wonderful place that the rest of us could only dream about, and she came back so aglow, so enraptured that I made a secret resolution to practice harder until I, too, was good enough to get a scholarship.

Alas, no one had told me then the facts about saxophones, symphony orchestras, and music scholarships. My music teacher gently broke the news to me that the saxophone's usefulness was limited and that I shouldn't get my hopes up for a scholarship. He also told me as tactfully as possible that I could write better than I could play the saxophone, and he suggested that I concentrate on writing rather than music as a professional career.

Eventually I did trade my saxophone for a typewriter. And then, many years later, my husband and I were traveling on a writing assignment in northern Michigan when suddenly ahead of us loomed a big roadside sign that rang a bittersweet bell in my memory. It said: "INTERLOCHEN. HOME OF THE NATIONAL MUSIC CAMP." The sign opened the floodgates of nostalgia. The name Interlochen still held the irresistible magic it once had in a long ago corner of my youth.

"We've *got* to go there," I said to my husband. "I have to see if it's what I used to dream it might be."

We turned off the highway and down the pine-forested road. The more worldly and grown-up part of me felt that this was probably quite silly. Nothing in one's life as an adult is ever as Utopian as it seemed in childhood. But I *had* to see this enchanted place which had bewitched me all through those tenor sax days.

We entered the rustic gates of Interlochen just as Howard Hanson, the famous composer and conductor, was raising his baton for the first strains of his "Romantic Symphony." A white moon hung like a thin cradle over the peak of the rough-hewn, outdoor Interlochen Bowl. Beyond was the lake shimmering with moonlight, and the whole magnificent setting of towering Norway pines was ablaze with music. The audience was sitting on row after row of hard-backed wooden benches, a vast sea of faces transfixed with enchantment in the deepening twilight. And on stage was the orchestra, more than a hundred young boys and girls playing their hearts out in a great moving symphony, a performance not only technically competent but full of depth and perception that would have been extraordinary in performers twice their age.

I knew then that here was a dream spun not only from the gossamer of childhood. And when the concert was over I turned half dazed to the person sitting next to me and asked, "Say, who runs this place?"

He replied, "Maddy. Joe-Maddy," as though it were all one word, and we made our way through the departing crowds in search of a man named Joe-Maddy.

That was the summer of 1941.

Assignments since then have taken us to faraway places to meet countless unusual and gifted people. But each summer we are drawn irresistibly back to Interlochen. Why? We know very little about music. But there's a man—or is he a legend?—and they call him Joe-Maddy of Interlochen.

My tenor saxophone didn't make the grade, and no typewriter can ever catch up with Joe-Maddy of Interlochen, but anyone who has ever watched a miracle, or loved a child, will understand Joe-Maddy's gift to our time.

NORMA LEE BROWNING

Autumn, 1962

TABLE OF CONTENTS

Foreword

By Van Cliburn

SUDDENLY each summer on the lake shores of northern Michigan a living truth is rekindled. I have felt its glow all the way around the world, across continents and across borderlines that let down their barriers only for those who know the universal password.

In Berlin, Moscow, Helsinki, Munich, Vienna, I have watched in wonder, and often with a throb in my throat, as the glorious music of Brahms or Beethoven or Tschaikowsky or Richard Strauss suspended national enmities and softened the look in men's eyes.

I am no politician. I am a pianist, an American from Kilgore, Texas, who has had the privilege and the responsibility of playing for many peoples of the world. And of this I am sure: If there is a universal language, it is music.

Nowhere in the world, in my opinion, is there a place—or a man—turning out more musical missionaries for peace than Dr. Joseph Maddy's summer music camp at Interlochen, Michigan. On my concert tours I am constantly meeting former Interlochen students. Interlochen is a magic word in the music world and I had felt its impact long before I became personally acquainted with it.

In the winter of 1961 while I was in Chicago making a recording, my mother telephoned me to ask a special favor. Would I

agree to play a benefit concert at Interlochen the following summer? I knew, of course, that Interlochen was the home of the
National Music Camp. And though I was well aware of its fine
reputation and influence on American youth, I frankly was not
enthusiastic over the idea of a summer camping trip. I would
have to interrupt a concert tour for the benefit performance.
And I was scheduled to leave for another European tour that
summer; I simply could not afford the time.

But my mother, who taught me until I was seventeen and
who is passionately interested in her own pupils as well as all
young people, is also a very persuasive woman, and she has a
sixth sense about such things. Several of her own pupils had
attended Interlochen. And she had just met Dr. Joseph Maddy
who, she told me, had come all the way to Kilgore to invite me
to Interlochen. My mother is an excellent buffer for me, a strict
disciplinarian, and not given to burdening me with extra work
in the middle of a concert tour. She said, "Please, won't you
do this for Dr. Maddy? I just have a good feeling about it."
It was her sixth sense in action.

I didn't know Dr. Maddy. The telephone bill was mounting.
I finally compromised, with great reluctance. "I'll do it for you,"
I said.

That summer, just before the music camp opened, Dr. Maddy
telephoned me to discuss the program. He said the students
wanted me to play the *Tschaikowsky B Flat Minor Concerto,*
and he told me I would be accompanied by a hundred-and-
eighty-piece high school orchestra.

After recovering from the shock, I managed to inquire, "Did
you say one hundred and eighty?"

"That's right," he said matter-of-factly.

"What are you going to use for amplification—for sound?" I asked, thinking of one piano amidst the din of nearly two hundred amateur musicians.

"Oh, don't worry about a thing," Dr. Maddy replied. "Everything will be all right."

Between then and the time I arrived at Interlochen I was frantic. I had never had occasion to play with a high school orchestra. Never had I been accompanied by a throng of young student musicians. So it was with the greatest trepidation and bewilderment that I sat down for our first rehearsal, taking my place at the piano in front of those earnest and silent hundred and eighty youngsters in their blue corduroy uniforms.

When it was finished, I knew that here was something quite extraordinary. These young musicians, still in their teens, would do credit to some of our professional symphony orchestras. I felt like sitting down and immediately writing recommendations for some of them.

We played the Tschaikowsky that summer; and the following summer, 1962, I needed no persuasion to interrupt a busy schedule once more and return to Interlochen for another benefit concert. This time they especially chose the *Rachmaninoff Third Piano Concerto* because it is difficult and rarely played. I knew it would be a challenge to these young players, and I thought they would enjoy playing it. With only one week of rehearsals before I arrived, and only two rehearsals with me, those youngsters came through as if they had been seasoned troupers. It was one of the most memorable experiences of my professional career.

If I live to be ninety I will never forget the way they played. I doubt whether any other high school orchestra has performed the *Third Rachmaninoff*. Yet the youngest member of that Inter-

lochen orchestra was only thirteen. He was a little second violinist and looked barely out of swaddling clothes. Five others were
fourteen, and the oldest one was only eighteen. Believe it or not,
there was no supplementation by even one faculty member. Our
concertmaster, or first violinist, was a pretty eighteen year old
girl from Wooster, Ohio—Paula Dodez. The first oboe player,
Philip Alexander, of Conroe, Texas, and Nancy Howe, the first
flutist from Iowa City, Iowa, had solo wind passages which
joined the piano in its cadenzas; for all I predict a fine musical
career. Nancy was only seventeen and Philip a year older when
they played the *Rachmaninoff Third* with me, and we had played
the *Tschaikowsky* together the summer before. Incidentally,
next summer we will play the *Brahms Second Piano Concerto*.

But how can one express the wonder of Interlochen? No one
can truly translate it for others. I can only say that in a world
which deals so much, for expedience's sake, in tinsel and material
values, there is something fine and wholesome and splendid and
altogether overwhelming in the euphony of sixteen hundred
young boys and girls delighting in the wonders of great music.
Any man who can do this for young people bears the mark of
genius, and a nation fortunate enough to have an arts center like
Interlochen can look to the future with hope.

For it is not in the least necessary that all young people with a
talent for music become professional musicians. It matters little
whether or not Interlochen students use their musical training
professionally in their later life. They had been trained, with
discipline and trust, for leadership in life as well as in the arts.
And somehow you can always spot them. They may be doctors,
lawyers, businessmen, or civic leaders. They're usually prominent in their communities, performing in local orchestras or

chamber music groups and helping guide the cultural life of the community.

I think what has impressed me most about Interlochen is that it is so uniquely American—a music center for youth operating within a framework that gives daily expression to the God-fearing ideals and traditions held by our forefathers. It always fills me with indignation to hear anyone call America a cultural wilderness. Part of the reason we have acquired this reputation is because of our political persuasion not to have any interference from a central government. Our cultural achievements have traditionally come about mainly under private auspices, and this is good. I feel it is very much to the credit of the American people that they can contribute to the cultural life of their communities without government subsidies. I am not for government support of the arts. The national workshop of music at Interlochen is, of course, a privately sponsored institution operating without the helping hand of government, local, state, or national. And its over-all theme, boldly emphasized in every facet of this mammoth organization of music for youth, is strictly and refreshingly American. It is simply: in order to make progress one must keep working.

These young musicians learn very quickly that today's achievement does not assure tomorrow's success. The orchestra, for example, holds competitive examinations each week to determine each player's ability and qualifications to hold his position. Age and tenure make no difference. When a fifth chair player thinks he is good enough to challenge a second or first chair player he may do so, and the best man wins. A player may move up or down only one or two or maybe a dozen chair positions at a single competitive tryout, depending on his ability—and probably the length of time he has practiced the previous week. It may be a nerve wracking procedure, but the young musicians soon learn a lesson that they definitely must know before embarking on life's greater competitions.

Equally important, after the weekly competitions are over and the coveted chair positions are won, it then dawns on these youngsters that the winning of their goal was not the end but only the beginning. For next week they must strive for greater objectives.

For most of these youngsters their first love is music. Their enthusiasm, their energy, and their consequent skill evoke the attitude of seasoned professionals, but without the professional's ofttimes blasé or jaded world-weariness. No finishing school has dampened their enthusiasm. No critic has made them cautious. The spirit of the invincible conqueror is with them, and when they look at you, they look not only with their eyes, full face, but with their hearts, and a smile and a maturity quite uncommon for teenagers. This was one of my most memorable impressions on my first visit to Interlochen, and I noticed it again, even more acutely, during my return. These youngsters look back at you full in the face, in the eyes. They never appear cowed or timid or shy like so many this age. They are gracious, mature, and human. I think music does this for them.

You will never find the young musicians at Interlochen discussing music in a spirit of pseudo-intellectual snobbery to impress others. They're discussing it because they love it. And they sing and play and practice music from dawn to dusk partly because it's the rule of the school—but chiefly because they want to.

No guest artist or conductor ever appears on the Interlochen concert stage in the usual formal attire, white tie and tails. It is traditional for guest artists to wear the Interlochen uniform. The boys wear blue corduroy trousers and the girls wear blue knickers. They wear blue shirts on weekdays, white shirts on Sunday.

I never thought I would live to see the day when I would play a concert in corduroys and shirtsleeves! The outdoor Interlochen stage is the only place I have ever performed not in full formal concert attire. I can't tell you what the audiences—and they were huge—thought, but I can tell you how I felt. The workshop spirit of Interlochen was so *present,* and the seriousness of those young people was so inspiring that formal concert dress could not have made the performance more dignified, for it already had achieved its own dignity.

In this spirit Interlochen has become a special corner of America that is kindling sparks in the youth of our land, and even in distant parts of the globe. For its influence is felt throughout the world: former students appear as far away as the Vienna and Munich Youth Symphony Orchestras; they contribute notably to our fourteen hundred professional orchestras; and they hold first chair positions in many of the world's major symphonic groups. Other music camps have mushroomed, patterned after Interlochen. One of these, the Transylvania Music School at Brevard, North Carolina, was founded by a former Interlochen student.

With my own feeling for music and for all people who share it, I have no hesitancy in saying that America should be proud and grateful for this vital training ground where our nation's youth learns not only music but universal values. Interlochen is a proving ground of responsibility, endurance, and growth. It is a significant example in our time of youth at its best, and of individual, competitive freedom. Too much of this has vanished from the American scene. We should cherish these young people who can look you straight in the eye, and at the same time I take great pleasure, as we all should, in saluting this extraordinary man, Dr. Joseph Maddy, whose dreams and pioneering spirit keep the thread of music and youth fastened to the stars.

"I'm No Genius, By Gum"

IN THE summer of 1962 there was an unusual air of tranquility about Interlochen's Joe Maddy. He was embroiled in no major skirmishes. He wasn't fighting with anyone—not for the moment. He was at peace temporarily with his trustees, the Chamber of Commerce, and Mr. James C. Petrillo. In fact in the summer of 1962 it looked as though Joe Maddy of Interlochen had finally ARRIVED.

Things were beginning to take shape for him the way he always knew they would. He had found a Santa Claus to finance some of the holes he was always digging. Come September, by gum!, he was going to open his new year around school. Not many would dare to dream so bold a dream, but Joe Maddy of Interlochen was a man whose dreams knew no limits, and whose indignation was stirred by those who tried to restrain him.

In the summer of 1962 Joe Maddy was celebrating his thirty-fifth year as a musical Pied Piper in the woods of Northern Michigan near the old lumberjack town with the tinkling name of Interlochen. In late June each summer the quiet green pine forests burst into musical fireworks, for Interlochen was the home of that remarkable phenomenon known as Joe Maddy's National Music Camp. In thirty-five years Joe Maddy's little empire of music had grown from a hundred and fifteen students to more than two thousand. Many of his friends felt he had gone far enough. He should relax and stop dreaming. After all, he *was* seventy years old. But each time anyone suggested that after all these years he really *should* take a vacation, he bristled.

In his own mind he was only beginning. At seventy Joe Maddy still had the bounce of a fifteen-year-old. He never walked—he sprinted, like a pole vaulter in training. No one could keep up with him. He rarely sat down and it often annoyed him to see others sitting unless they were also engaged in some productive work such as playing music. Under his dark bushy brows were sharp bright eyes that could flash fire or melt a heart of flint—as he willed. He could be crisp and crackling, or gentle and fey as a wood sprite, but he was made of some inner fiber as tough and tensile as piano wire, and people who got in his way somehow quite quickly got out. Joe's impact could be as jarring as a Kansas cyclone.

No one back in his home town of Wellington, Kansas, would be the least bit surprised to hear that Joe Maddy had finally made it to the White House. After all, why shouldn't he? He had spent most of his seventy years demonstrating that he could do anything he set out to do, by gum! This was Joe's favorite expletive —by gum—and he always ran the words together as one, BY-GUM, in much the same way that he ran his own name together to sound like JOE-MADDY. In a sense the two were synonymous. It was Joe-Maddy By-gum who in the summer of 1962 finally had the money in the bank to start his new school. It was Joe-Maddy By-gum who had lured the brilliant young pianist Van Cliburn to Interlochen two years in a row for benefit concerts. And it was Joe-Maddy By-gum, from Wellington, Kansas, who could soon say that he had finally made it all the way to the White House.

There it was in black and white, the invitation from First Lady Mrs. Jacqueline Kennedy for Joe Maddy to bring his music camp orchestra to the nation's capital. It didn't matter to Joe that the state of Michigan was too poor at the moment to finance the trip to Washington for his young musicians, as he had hoped. He would get the money some way to pay their fare. It didn't matter to him that someone in the White House knew so little about the Midwest that the invitation was almost missent to a music camp in North Dakota. All problems which were even remotely connected with Interlochen had a way of working themselves out by some supernatural law which only Joe understood. People who had known Joe for years and witnessed his uncanny miracles could only say, with unceasing wonderment, "Well, there goes Joe Maddy waving that old magic horseshoe again. It works every time."

There was no doubt that Joe would somehow find someone to pay for the trip.

Early in May, before camp opened, Joe flew to Washington to meet with Mrs. Kennedy's social secretary, Miss Letitia Baldridge. The Interlochen concert was to be held on the White House lawn on August sixth. Miss Baldridge was prepared to do all she could to help.

"How many instruments will we have to rent?" she asked.

"We don't use other people's instruments," Joe said. "Our kids have their own. We have six symphony orchestras, five hundred pianos, twenty-two harps . . ."

"What about music stands?" Miss Baldridge asked, possibly startled by the notion of twenty-two harps to choose from, but thinking the White House could perhaps furnish something.

Joe assured her the young players had those too. All that was needed from the White House, he mentioned casually, was a specially constructed acoustical shell for the orchestra and a special platform for his ballet dancers.

Miss Baldridge was intrigued. Orchestras had been invited to play on the White House lawn before, but never a ballet group. She was not one, however, to be defeated by problems.

"What kind of platform would be suitable?" she asked.

One about thirty by forty feet, Joe told her, and covered with something smooth like battleship linoleum. The dancers also would need a dressing room to change from camp uniforms to costumes.

Joe had seen at once that the White House lawn was not the most ideal place for a symphony concert. There were noisy jets swarming overhead. However, as he told himself, he could select music with a good deal of brass, and rearrange the seating positions so the strings would be heard. He also made a mental note to bring four harps instead of two. He wanted his musicians to be heard to the best advantage, with a minimum of interference from the upper hemisphere.

At the Sunday morning religious services at the beginning of the 1962 camp season Joe spoke to an assembly of more than two thousand students, faculty, and visiting parents.

His message was in the best Maddy tradition.

He first quoted from Brahms and then from vital statistics. The United States, he said, was spending ten thousand times as much for war as for peace—forty-eight billion annually for military preparation. Music and the arts, he declared, were also weapons—weapons for peace—and he cited the experiences of an American student orchestra from the Eastman School of Music playing in Communist Leningrad the previous year. At the end of the Eastman program, he related, the orchestra played *The Stars and Stripes Forever.* The Russian audience stood, applauding and shouting, compelling the orchestra to repeat the number for seven encores. Joe Maddy proudly told his Interlochen audience that half of those Eastman touring orchestra players were former Interlochen students. He fervently declared, "We at Interlochen are doing our share to promote peace in this world. When one American orchestra can do this, think what we could do with a dozen, or a hundred!"

Someone irreverently whispered, "How in hell is he going to pay for that new hole . . . ?"

Joe Maddy's mania for hole digging had been for years a matter of major concern to the more conservative members of his faculty and staff, his Board of Trustees, and especially to George Mackmiller, his devoted but chronically pessimistic camp treasurer. The holes always eventually turned into handsome new buildings, and that was the problem—the hole in the ground usually matched a hole in the budget. It was a standing joke among the staff that Dr. Joe was always out digging a new hole before the last one was paid for.

Nearly everyone who knew Joe had long ago accepted the fact that he was some species of genius with all the prerogatives of a genius. But there were also those who felt that he needed a gentle restraining hand at times.

George Wilson, band conductor and vice-president of the little music empire, sometimes found it necessary to remind others, "We are working with a genius, you know, and we are fortunate because it isn't everyone who is privileged to work with a true genius. But we must try to remember—all geniuses have a common denominator: they see only the vision, not the details."

Joe Maddy's visions, it was generally agreed, were always in the realm of chasing million dollar butterflies with a nickel. And in spite of the skeptics, he had attained some measure of success. At the opening of the 1962 season, for example, a small boy with trumpet in hand, had been overheard complaining bitterly to his departing mother, "But Mom, you told me this was a music *camp*, not a *school*. Every place I turn, I bump into a building." The boy, of course, was soon consoled by the informality of Interlochen and the abundance—the astonishing and incredible abundance—of beautiful music in all those buildings.

But it was true that Interlochen as old-timers knew it had changed from a camp to a campus. Along Faculty Row there were modern cement-block dormitories named "Brahms," "Beethoven," and "Mozart," and they even had modern plumbing, heat, and hot water—and flower bordered green lawns. But it wasn't always like that. Trombone teacher Sigurd Swanson could remember the time, not too many years earlier, when he was routed from bed in the middle of the night by a leak in the plumbing which had caved in his roof. Melba Bram, a trumpet player and administrative assistant to the music camp, could recall summers in which she had spent half her time chasing bats from the rafters. It was all changed now. The bats were gone. The plumbing was replaced. No more six in a line waiting for a cold water shower.

The woodland campus actually had street signs: "Percy

Grainger Lane," "John Philip Sousa Avenue," "Frederick Stock Drive," "Howard Hanson Walk." Young campers gazed in wonder at the new uptown streetlights that had been installed along the wooded paths. And it was rumored there was more yet to come. . . .

In Joe Maddy's opening speeches of the 1962 season he kept repeating that this was going to be the finest summer yet. He had been saying the same thing for thirty-five summers, but now, possibly for the first time in all those years, his trustees offered no pessimistic comment. On their bookshelves, as on all of the music camp's bookshelves, was a brand new volume which Joe was urging everyone to read. It was written by a Chicago multi-millionaire and philanthropist, W. Clement Stone, who in his own world was as much of a legend as Dr. Joe Maddy. Mr. Stone had a magic touch with money and a magnificent obsession for giving. In his quiet way he went around giving little hundred-thousand-dollar gifts to those he felt were doing good work for a good cause, and asking nothing in return except that they keep on vigorously with what they were doing. Nice things always happened to those whose abilities Mr. Stone had discovered. He had recently discovered Joe Maddy and had showered him with enough cash to cover some of his deficits.

Typically, Joe at once went out and dug the biggest hole of his career. Nor, probably, was Mr. Stone disquieted by this move. Mr. Stone's book was called *Success Through A Positive Mental Attitude,* and no phrase could better have described Joe's own habitual outlook.

In his opening speeches Joe urged everyone to go out and see the latest digging—the fact was they could hardly avoid dropping into it—and he explained that it was soon to be a large auditorium-gymnasium with four bowling alleys on the lower level. The building would be used mainly for a music and arts auditorium, he said, but to content the state of Michigan's school accreditation officials, he also had to have a gymnasium for his new year-around Interlochen Arts Academy. And he was including bowling in the gymnastics curriculum because he had happened to run across a fine bargain in bowling lanes—at two hundred dollars each.

Parenthetically Joe mentioned that he had also picked up seventy-five pairs of snowshoes at a dollar and twenty-five cents a pair from the government surplus warehouse. He felt these might come in handy for his winter activities at his school.

"Now," he crackled, fixing his gaze upon Alden Dow, the school's architect, "I hope Mr. Dow can come up with building plans as fast as I come up with the money, because in the next ten years I expect to spend ten million dollars making the Interlochen Arts Academy the greatest school in the world. We're going to revolutionize the whole educational system. . . ."

George Mackmiller sat poker-faced as Joe outlined his latest dreams, but there was no doubt what he was thinking. "The Academy isn't even open yet. The bills aren't paid and here he is buying bowling lanes and snowshoes and talking about ten million dollars."

Mackmiller—or Mack, as everyone called him—was a Phi Beta Kappa, a deacon in the First Presbyterian Church, and for twenty years he had been the frustrated bookkeeper for the Genius of Interlochen who always insisted on spending tomorrow's money yesterday. Mack hadn't yet met Mr. W. Clement

Stone but he did feel that Joe Maddy was carrying positive thinking a little too far. If Joe had cared to ask him—though no possibility was more remote—Mack would have said there were more pressing details that required attention and money, such as paying the hamburger bills and other current debts. And there was the pending problem of transporting the music camp students to the White House.

These, however, were small matters compared to the still unpaid-for hole digging. There was still a three hundred thousand dollar debt for the Brahms, Beethoven, and Mozart dormitories. There was also still the unpaid balance on the Van Cliburn Lodge. Van Cliburn's 1961 benefit concert had netted the camp twelve thousand dollars. This money was earmarked for a rental guest lodge, the income to be used for piano scholarships for students. And before the '61 season closed, big cranes were scooping out the twelve thousand dollar hole which, as usual, got out of hand and wound up as a two-garage, double-decker duplex guest lodge costing twenty-six thousand dollars. And no one could understand how two little piano students from Texas could be enrolled on Van Cliburn scholarships in 1962—before the Cliburn lodge was ready for occupancy, or earning scholarship income, or even paid for.

But everyone knew this was the way Joe Maddy had operated for thirty-five years, and it was too late to stop him now.

With the proceeds from Van Cliburn's 1962 benefit concert Joe was buying a new grand piano. Mack could worry about the bills.

There was also the handsome new Stone Student Center—named for the school's new benefactor. Outside, a big shiny new marker recently had been erected proclaiming Interlochen an official historical site in the state of Michigan. Here, on a former hunting ground of the Ottawa Indians, the marker read, was the home of the National High School Orchestra. For many years the camp headquarters had been in a ramshackle old firetrap that once had been a lumber-camp hotel. The new student center, which only recently had replaced the old hotel, also wasn't quite paid for yet. But this, too, was Mack's headache.

Staff members could not guess how even the carpeting would be paid for in the new Liberal Arts Building, much less the building itself. Long accustomed to teaching in Interlochen's chilly rustic cottages they were overwhelmed by the Liberal Arts classrooms in the spectacular star-shaped, concrete-domed structure which Alden Dow had designed for the Arts Academy. And Alden Dow was already at work on designs for the auditorium-gymnasium, a new science building, and a multi-million dollar center for the performing arts. Joe had the signs posted beside each hole in progress, marking the site of each building, and he was now needling Dow to finish the plans.

Poor Mack. It had been *his* dream that the music camp might someday get on a pay-as-you-go basis.

"If we had done that," Joe told him, "we'd still be struggling along with one or two shacks."

"But they would both be paid for," said Mack.

Mack was one of the few non-musicians at Interlochen. He admitted that he didn't know which end of the fiddle to blow. But he did know that the camp's infrequent windfalls were always spent long before they actually arrived. He complained grievously that it was impossible to balance the books for a man who operated on intuition instead of on facts and figures. But once Joe's mind was made up, everyone's impression was that he did not wish it to be confused by facts. As Mack once said, "If all the bricks and stones in the universe, including the great pyramids, were to fall at one time, they would not by one iota disturb Joe Maddy's frame of mind."

Periodically Mack reminded Joe that they ought to have a hundred thousand dollar minimum bank balance for operating expenses at all times. Joe appreciated Mack's attention to details. He thought Mack made a splendid camp treasurer, and he regarded him as a loyal and dedicated worker. But he thought it was perfectly silly to leave money lying idle in banks when it could be used for a new building or new musical equipment for his campers. "Mack's only trouble," he often said, "is that he's too dedicated. He worries too much about details."

Once when Mack reproached him for signing checks amounting to seventeen thousand dollars in overdrafts, Joe retorted, "I'm running this camp, and I'll *run* it, by gum." As an after thought, he added, "You worry too much, Mack. There'll be enough in the bank to cover these checks Monday morning." And of course there was. Joe frequently had to remind Mack of what happened back in the nineteen thirties. "Remember, the banks failed and we didn't. Our credit is ace high with all of them."

In moments of desperation Mack found solace in abandoning his adding machine for a line or two of creative prose. Only a few knew of the secret file containing dittoed copies of *Mack's Gems,* as they were called, which reflected the history of his own day-to-day gloomy thoughts on the future of Joe Maddy's million-dollar dreams.

In June of 1959 Mack wrote this memo to himself:

"Should a stranger to the quagmire of baffling and bewildering intricacies which so well characterize the financial maze in which the National Music Camp operates, be asked to carry on because of the incapacity of the present camp treasurer, there might be a long period before the railroad is operating smoothly again. . . .

"There has been expended here a hell of a lot more blood, sweat and tears than cement blocks, nails and lumber."

In November, a heavy bill-paying month, his dittoed gem was eloquently succinct:

"Extraordinary tranquility and equanimity have been exercised and maintained while the edifice crumbled."

His position and outlook were summed up in a little verse which he labeled simply *Mack's Poem*:

> I'm not allowed to run the train,
> The whistle I can't blow.
> I'm not the one who designates
> How far the train will go.
> I'm not allowed to blow the steam
> Or even ring the bell,
> But let the damn train jump the track
> And see who catches Hell.

At the opening of the 1962 camp season, Joe gave Mack a copy of *Success Through a Positive Mental Attitude* and urged him to read it. "Everyone has been telling me for thirty-five years I'm going to sink this camp," he said. "Well, by gum, I haven't yet. And by now, people ought to know I'm not going to."

There were a few—but only a few—who felt that after thirty-five years Joe Maddy was beginning to mellow. As one said, "He has recently shown himself willing, when the evidence is almost overwhelming, to concede a point. But not often."

He still had his own inflexible notions about how to teach

music, and he still had a habit, which some of his teachers found exasperating, of bouncing in on them unexpectedly to see if they were following his rules. Notably missing from his 1962 faculty was one teacher he had caught teaching while perched in sitting position on a high stool. Joe's theory was that teachers ought to be on their toes. He didn't want them sitting on desks or stools, and he wasted no time in making decisions when anyone ran afoul of his rules.

Solutions to all problems, in fact, always seemed to Joe to be simple, well defined, and clear-cut, leaving no room for argument. A script writer from his radio department, for example, once consulted him about a program—one of his taped NBC *Best From Interlochen* series featuring music and a guest speaker. When the radioman told Joe that the program was running three minutes too long and asked tentatively, "Where should we cut the music?" Joe replied without batting an eye, "You can't cut the music. Just eliminate the speaker." And he went on with the next matter of business.

This was Joe Maddy, the man everyone accepted as the "genius of Interlochen." Everyone, that is, except Joe. By 1962 Joe decided he'd better set the record straight. At the dedication of his new Liberal Arts Building—nothing pleased Joe more than dedicating a new building—Stanley Kresge from Detroit introduced Joe to the audience, as everyone always did, as the "genius of Interlochen."

Joe promptly corrected him. "I don't like that word," he said. "I'm no genius. I just looked the word up in the dictionary, by gum, and it doesn't fit me. . . ."

Even those who worshiped at Joe's shrine had to admit that he was often reckless in his public relations. They could only hope that Stanley Kresge would overlook Joe's touchiness. After all, it was the Kresge Foundation which supplied some of the funds to start the building Joe was about to dedicate. . . .

Most of Joe's Interlochen staff felt they were underpaid. They liked to say that Joe ran his camp on dedicated slave labor, but they knew that Joe himself worked harder than any of them. Many wondered audibly what it was that drew them back year after year. But deep down they knew. As Maynard Klein, the camp's long-time choral director once said, "Sometimes I wonder what I'm doing here working a ninety hour week when I could be home fishing and drinking mint juleps. But there's something electrifying about four hundred young voices singing the *Berlioz Requiem* in a festival choir. And besides, how do you say 'No' to a man like Joe Maddy?"

It was part of Joe's bumptious, rebellious nature that he was immune to the devotion some held for him. It never made him egotistical or seemed to turn his head. No one knew better—or cared less—that his dreams were once considered the mark of a crackpot rather than a genius. Joe knew that for years there were many who looked on him as a fanatic, of a more or less wholesome variety it is true, but an impractical dreamer with no head for business. Yet, from a shoestring beginning financed by a borrowed fifteen thousand dollars, he had built a five million dollar non-profit enterprise—and Joe knew that it was all going to be paid for someday.

He knew there were a few musicians who whispered behind his back that Joe Maddy didn't really know how to conduct. Yet he went right on conducting. As early as 1932 music historian Augustus Zanzig* credited Joe with organizing and conducting more orchestras than anyone else in the world. And at seventy,

* *Music and American Life, Present and Future* by Augustus D. Zanzig. Oxford University Press. 1932.

long past the age when most conductors have the stamina to conduct, Joe was still cracking his basswood baton on the conductor's stand. Moreover, his flocks of starry-eyed youngsters loved it. They didn't seem to mind working hard for Dr. Maddy, and they usually turned in superb performances.

Music educators had chuckled back in the days when Joe Maddy, with a ninth grade education, decided to become a music educator. Joe knew this. Yet, in the summer of 1962 he could boast more plaques, trophies, citations, certificates, and honorary degrees for his contribution to music education than he knew how to handle. He had accepted them all with appropriate pride and respect. But one thing bothered him enormously. With four honorary doctorates he still couldn't adjust to being called *Dr.* Joe, as some called him, or *Dr.* Maddy. He vastly preferred plain Joe Maddy, the name his mother had given him, and the name by which he was best known throughout the music world. If his Interlochen campers chose to call him *Dr.* instead of Mr. Maddy, there wasn't much he could do about it, but the truth was that it was many years before Dr. Joe Maddy would even hire anyone with a doctorate for the Interlochen faculty.

He always said, "If they've spent all that time getting degrees, they haven't had time to learn how to teach." He preferred professional musicians as teachers. Joe always enjoyed reminding others, "I didn't get educated. Therefore, I don't have to quote any psychologists or follow anyone's lead but my own."

2

For years the people of Traverse City, Interlochen's nearest large town, had looked on Joe Maddy with a jaundiced eye. Little they cared that he was a musical genius. All they knew was that a sprightly, rambunctious little man had set up camp in the woods sixteen miles away for a batch of school kids with musical instruments. They seemed like nice, normal youngsters when they came into town on Monday afternoons with their chaperones, but to an outsider sometimes they did look a little odd in those blue corduroy knickers.

No one knew exactly what that man Maddy was up to, and from the first the citizenry of all the neighboring communities looked on his so-called "music camp" as an unstable, impractical, fly-by-night operation. It was no wonder, for everyone knew that Joe Maddy had no money to operate his camp. They couldn't help knowing. At every concert they were exhorted to "drop a dollar in the blanket"—to help save the enterprise from bankruptcy. Joe's money-begging blankets caused no less consternation to concert-goers in the early years than his extravagant hole digging later.

His blanket act was introduced by a young man from Chicago named John Minnema. Joe had hired him as a tympani teacher and then discovered that he wasn't as good on the tympani as some of his students. But Minnema did have a flair for showmanship, so Joe appointed him concert manager in charge of soliciting donations from audiences. He turned out to be quite good at this.

Minnema became known as the music camp's "blanket man." At the ticket booth, after each concert started, the ticket sellers would stretch brown army blankets across the counters, tacking them to the opposite wall of the shanty to form a catch-all for the coins they hoped would be tossed in. Minnema would step up to the stage at the end of the concert and urge everyone to show his appreciation by dropping something extra in the blanket. Concert admission in those days was only twenty-five cents.

Minnema always asked the audiences for a dollar for the blanket, but he rarely got more than half-dollar coins.

One night Minnema tricked the audience with an old carnival trick which many found unamusing, but it worked. He stepped up to the podium and announced, "I've heard a rumor that every single person here tonight is going to drop a dollar in the blanket. Is that true?"

He paused. Then, "Now, I'll tell you what I'm going to do. I'm going to ask everyone here who intends to drop a dollar in the blanket tonight to stand up. Come on, now, all those with a dollar for the blanket—stand!"

Then, on cue, the orchestra struck up "The Star Spangled Banner." The audience, of course, stood.

Meantime, Minnema hurried off to the ticket booth and scattered a bundle of dollar bills over the blanket as an inducement. Quite a few concert-goers that night felt obliged to follow the dollar-dropping example.

Minnema's most valuable service to the camp, however, was in helping Joe sell debentures to businessmen in Traverse City to pull the camp out of bankruptcy. Later he settled in Traverse City and opened a music store, and for many years he supplied Joe with as many second-hand pianos as he could find for the music camp.

Through the years Traverse City adjusted slowly to Joe Maddy. Behind his back most of the townspeople usually referred to him either as Beggar Joe or Fighting Joe. Joe felt that the community should do more to support his camp, and since he did not hesitate to express himself vocally, tempers sometimes flared. However, the "civilians" of Traverse City usually came out on the short end of their battles with the one-man army from Interlochen. They soon learned that nothing could stand in the way of Joe Maddy's music camp. Some would never forgive him for opposing the jet air base which they were counting on to bring an economic boom to the community. Joe wanted no jets drowning out Interlochen's music. He got the air base abandoned. He raised a ruckus when a convict labor camp began moving into the area. He would have no convicts straying into his camp grounds. The prison camp was relocated.

With what some citizens saw as unreasonable stubbornness, he refused to bring his bands into town to march in the Cherry Festival Parade. Actually he had been advised by a local doctor against bringing the children in for the parade because of the risk of polio. He would not endanger the health of his young musicians for the sake of a commercial promotion.

In the eyes of some of the townspeople, Joe was just plain ornery. As some expressed it, "You might as well save your breath as argue with that man. It's water off a duck's back."

But in the summer of 1962 things were comparatively peaceful between Joe and the "civilians," who after three decades had pride, affection, and even occasional understanding for their obstreperous fellow citizen. Department stores which once sold only red, green, brown, and black corduroy now openly displayed bolts of blue. This signified at least a temporary truce with the former piccolo player from Wellington, Kansas, who would wage warfare at the drop of a chord on anyone who tried to halt the progress of music.

True, there were still a few sparks flying in the cold war. Joe was still annoyed that the town's new junior college had been named Northwestern Michigan College and was referred to in the local press as N.M.C. He felt that he had a twenty-five year prior claim to these initials for his National Music Camp, and he had taken the matter up with the Chamber of Commerce.

He was further piqued that the community gave more financial support to the college than to the music camp. Joe had come a long way since his dollar-in-the-blanket days. In fact, he only recently had deposited Mr. Stone's check for three hundred and fifty thousand dollars at one of the local banks. The Traverse City *Record Eagle* reported the transaction, whereupon the town's other bank asked Joe about depositing some of the money with them. Joe obligingly withdrew one hundred and seventy-five thousand from Bank number one and deposited it with Bank number two. In appreciation the second bank gave Joe a thousand dollar contribution for his music camp—without being asked.

Joe then went back to the first banker, told him of the contribution, and asked whether he wanted to match it. A plain refusal would have been enough to annoy Joe. But the banker also made the mistake of explaining, "We have just contributed a thousand dollars to Northwestern Michigan College. That's all we can afford." And this despite the fact that the bank had handled millions of dollars of music camp money over a span of thirty-five years.

Joe never hesitated to take his business elsewhere if he could not get what he wanted at the right price from local merchants. In spite of this and also despite the fact that some felt he had hurt the local economy by knocking out the jet air base, no one could deny that his camp poured money into the community. Al Kidder's optical business quadrupled during the concert season, with campers needing new lenses and repairs on their glasses. Local farmers prospered from Interlochen orders during strawberry, raspberry, and sweet corn season. The local Tru-

Fit Trousers Company toted up six to seven thousand dollars annually, making fifteen hundred pairs of blue corduroy pants and knickers for camp uniforms. And local dairies hit a bonanza by supplying five thousand half-pints plus a hundred gallons of bulk milk daily to the camp.

As a customer, Interlochen sometimes presented problems, as dairyman Charles Feibing learned. Feibing, probably to get the camp's business, came up with the idea of a special design for his individual, half-pint milk cartons. The design was to depict the campers in uniform with their instruments. Everyone was aghast when the first cartons arrived showing the campers in the wrong uniform. On the milk cartons they were wearing shorts instead of knickers.

The music campers protested. Some even refused to drink their milk. Joe Maddy, of course, promptly ordered the error corrected. Feibing, however, already had thousands of the milk cartons on hand. He continued to use them. But his business, as well as his state of mind, suffered from the vociferous complaints against the picture on his cartons. Finally, in 1962, the carton was re-designed and everyone was relieved. The musicians pictured on the milk carton were shown wearing knickers. Their real-life counterparts therefore began happily drinking their milk. And dairyman Feibing was reinstated in Joe Maddy's good graces.

There were many signs in the summer of 1962 that the Grand Traverse Bay area was beginning to regard Joe Maddy as a man who had finally arrived. When one of Joe's staff members suggested that it might be diplomatic to stage a *Traverse City Night* and invite leading citizens, Joe made no objection. The invitation drew a surprising number of community leaders and their families. It seemed as if the long camp versus community tussle might be over. There was growing rapport, for instance, between Joe and the local Rotary Club. He occasionally took in an ensemble group to furnish music for their luncheons. And the Rotarians reciprocated with a special "Rotary Night" at Interlochen. More and more of the "civilians" were beginning to discover the camp, after thirty-five years. From what they were reading in the papers it appeared that Joe was doing something for the community, economically as well as culturally.

Even the Chamber of Commerce temporarily had no quarrel with a man who could bring Van Cliburn to the woods of Northern Michigan two years in a row, and who had an invitation to play a concert on the White House lawn.

But clearly Joe's biggest *coup* in the eyes of most of the local citizens was coming up with the donation from that Chicago philanthropist. Civic leaders beseeched him to ask his benefactor for a contribution to Northwestern Michigan College. College officials sought his advice on fund raising. The general reaction of the townspeople to the camp's sudden affluence was, "Give us the man's address and help us get donations from him for the college."

Yes, after thirty-five years Joe Maddy had "arrived" on the home front. It was probably the most unexpected achievement of his career.

In January, 1963, Joe Maddy was awarded the Distinguished Citizen of the Year citation by Traverse City Chamber of Commerce.

"We're Going to the White House..."

WE'RE in deep trouble," said Betsy Thornton, executive housekeeper for the music camp. Her deep trouble concerned an item associated almost synonymously with Dr. Joe and his music campers—the uniform, the blue corduroy slacks for the boys and below-the-knee buttoned knickers for the girls.

Betsy revealed that after one washing of Dr. Joe's brand new pair of corduroys, they had fallen apart. Wouldn't he like to change the uniform—now and at last, after all these years?

He would not.

Dr. Joe instructed her to find another company to supply the camp corduroys.

Betsy was indeed in deep trouble.

The standard corduroy trousers for the boys were no problem. But finding a company to make the knickers was like looking for a needle in Carlsbad Caverns. Sears and Roebuck, who once made the camp uniforms, had given up because they didn't want to bother with the knickers. Neither did anyone else. When Betsy first took over the camp's housekeeping chores in 1942, she had suggested to Dr. Joe that he put the girls in something more modern and up-to-date—for example, pedal pushers.

After that interview, however, she refrained from bringing the subject up—until the day Dr. Joe's new uniform fell to pieces. Then, once more she broached the subject but she might have known—somewhere and somehow the knickers must be produced.

"It's tradition," she sighed. "That's something you just don't discuss with Dr. Joe."

But she knew one thing for sure—she could not possibly get new corduroys before the Washington trip. She could only hope that none actually fell apart during the White House concert.

The Interlochen camp uniforms always had been a subject of major concern, second only to Dr. Joe's hole digging, to everyone but Joe himself and the young musicians who wore them. Faculty and staff members generally learned to accept the corduroy uniform, but there were occasional problems. One summer, for example, Joe hired Noble Cain, a well known but temperamental choral conductor and composer, to teach at Interlochen. Mr. Cain arrived full of verve and enthusiasm—until he queued up for his corduroys.

He tried them on, took one look at himself and said, "I'll be damned if I'll wear this monkey suit for anyone."

He changed back into his traveling suit and took the first train out, leaving Joe high and dry for a choral conductor.

When Joe Maddy started his music camp in 1928, the popular fashions for outing trips were billowy bloomers for ladies and plus-fours for men. Co-educational summer camps were unheard of at the time, and among other things Joe was charged with in the early days was starting a "den of immorality" in the Northwoods.

He needed a camping costume for his young people that would reassure his critics. However, he thought bloomers were among the homeliest costumes ever invented. He finally decided on knickers, a modified version of bloomers, as a compromise both practical and becoming. When slacks and pedal pushers came in style, Joe was more determined than ever to keep knickers for his girl campers. The knickers covered a multitude of musical and anatomical problems. A girl cellist, for example, could park her cello between her knees with ease and modesty. In her tailored and comfortable knickers she was far more attractively dressed for rehearsals than in tight-fitting slacks.

Joe Maddy had chosen corduroy for the uniforms for excellent reasons. The material was inexpensive, washable, and warm. In northern Michigan even in mid-summer there were more chilly days than warm ones. The campers wore white shirts on Sundays, blue shirts on week days. When it was cold they wore red sweaters; and when it was warm they played their concerts in shirt sleeves. This was Interlochen tradition. This was the way it had been for thirty-five years. And this was the way it was going to stay—by gum!—as long as Joe Maddy was running the camp.

His young musicians loved the uniforms. In corduroy no one could tell the difference between the millionaire's son and the farmer's boy. But audiences who didn't know Interlochen were sometimes shocked to see both conductor and musicians playing an important concert in corduroy trousers, knickers, and shirtsleeves. Joe usually announced to out-of-town audiences, on those rare occasions when his orchestra played away from home, that the uniforms existed for purposes of democracy.

"Any prestige they get at Interlochen," he declared, "comes from performance, not from costumes."

And the first thing he always did with guest artists as soon as they arrived on the camp grounds was to march them over to Betsy Thornton's department to be outfitted in corduroys. No guest artist or conductor at Interlochen ever appeared on the stage in formal concert attire.

By the summer of 1962, however, the corduroys had become a controversial issue in some circles. Early in the season Alden Dow, the architect, was having lunch with Dr. Joe and Mrs. Maddy in the student center dining room. Joe Maddy had never allowed separate dining rooms or reserved sections for faculty and distinguished guests. Thus the huge dining hall was as usual teeming with busy, enthusiastic, preoccupied youngsters, some singing as they hurried through the cafeteria line, others talking excitedly of challenges, auditions, tryouts, and the trip to Washington.

Mr. Dow, who was certainly no stranger to Interlochen, seemed lost in his own puzzled thoughts as he studied the campers, and then he asked a question which only the strong of heart would have dared to put to Joe.

"Tell me," he said, "do you have a concert uniform for these youngsters for their White House concert?"

"Sure," Joe snapped. "Camp uniform."

"You mean these corduroys?" asked Dr. Dow.

"Sure. And blue shirts and red sweaters."

Mr. Dow ventured cautiously, "Don't you think you should have concert uniforms for the White House?"

Without missing a bite, Joe asked:
"Why?"
His imperturbable tone left no room for an answer.

2

It was "Bloody Friday" at Interlochen.

Marta Olarte, a little twelve year old girl with a flashing smile and spitfire eyes, had arrived at camp a week late—from Bogota, Colombia.

Marta played the trumpet, and she played well enough to win a national competition in Colombia for a scholarship to study in the United States. Marta's father had taught her to play the trumpet, and in Bogota she played regularly with the National Police Symphonic Band. Her father played saxophone in the same band. Marta had not wanted to enter the national competition. She knew that many of the entrants were much older and, she felt, much better players than she, but her father advised her to try. And a jury of national symphony orchestra players picked Marta as the winner over twenty other finalists.

But a week before she was to leave Colombia for Interlochen, Marta's family decided she would have to give up her scholarship. They could not afford to pay her transportation to the United States. Her scholarship was only for tuition.

An eleventh-hour long distance conference between Dr. Joe and Guillermo Espinosa, chief of the music division of the Pan American Union in Washington, resulted in a grant from the Fairfield Foundation and the Inter-American Music Council to pay Marta's fare.

And so Marta arrived, knowing scarcely a word of English.

Her cabin mates and teachers got out translation books to talk to her—but how could they tell Marta about Bloody Friday? How indeed could you tell *anyone* about Bloody Friday. . . ?

Every Friday was Bloody Friday at Joe Maddy's music camp. That was tradition. It was also Joe Maddy's reminder that his music camp was a work camp, not a play camp. It was the time for survival of the fittest, the one day of the week that every camper referred to simply but with excitement as Bloody Friday, or "challenges." It was the day any student in any of the camp's bands or orchestras could improve his position, if he was good enough, simply by challenging the player ahead of him.

The camp's tradition of "challenges" was the outgrowth of Joe Maddy's own youthful annoyance at being held back to last chair viola because of his age in the days when he had been the youngest member of the Minneapolis Symphony Orchestra.

His music camp was so big now that bands and orchestras had to be organized on various age levels: for junior, intermediate, high school, and college campers. But no one was ever held back to his own age division. Each young performer had his day on Bloody Friday to challenge his way up to first chair—and even right out of his own age group into the next one, if he could play well enough. There was nothing complex about challenges. They reflected Joe's philosophy about an American way of life, which in his mind could stand rejuvenation in a great many places besides Interlochen. And when people asked him, as they often did, "But is such stiff competition good for these children?" Joe became vehement.

The truth was, no one was more eager for Bloody Friday than the young musicians themselves. They couldn't wait to get into the fray. Everyone congratulated both the winners for winning and the losers for trying, and everyone knew that come next Bloody Friday the winners might wind up in the back seat in the battle of musical chairs.

Besides motivating the students to practice, practice, practice, the challenges held more suspense for them and for everyone watching than perhaps any other wonder of Interlochen. The organizational pattern of the challenge system was simple. Each Friday the separate sections of the various bands and orchestras— the strings, wind instruments, brass, percussion, and so on— would meet separately for rehearsal with their sectional teacher or conductor.

There might be fifty violins on the Interlochen Bowl stage, forty clarinets on Kresge stage, thirty trombones in the band shell, twenty trumpets on the flat roof of the Minnesota Building, all waiting for their chance to challenge.

The teacher-conductor of the violins, for example, taps for order and asks, "Are there any challenges today?"

A girl in the second row raises her hand and says, "I challenge Jim for second chair."

"Very well," the conductor says, riffling through the music on the stand before him. "In the Tschaikowsky, page six, the following bars," and he brackets a difficult passage.

The one challenged plays first, then the challenger.

When both are finished, the conductor says, "Heads down." All heads are bowed while the kids' hands go up in a vote for the one who played best.

The conductor says simply, "Challenger wins. Move up!" And challenger and challenged exchange places.

Joe's idea in permitting the young players to do their own

judging and voting was to eliminate the possibility of any accusa-
tions of "teacher's pet." He soon found that the students were
their own most severe critics. They would even vote against their
best friends if they felt someone else deserved the chair. But far
from creating jealousies and endangering youthful friendships
as some might have anticipated, challenges gave the youngsters
an even stronger common bond in their world of music. No loser
was ever really left out of the game, for he could always try
again next week—and, more important, he still had the friendship and respect and admiration of his fellow campers for being
a *good* loser.

On Bloody Friday the youngsters were learning, perhaps without always realizing it, that there are immutable laws of life and
music which are closely interwoven.

They were learning that music is adventure and exploration,
that it requires courage, perseverance and hard work, that a good
teacher can do much, but the actual work must always be the
student's own. They were learning self-reliance, a quality that has
become more and more rare in an age of groupishness; but in
music each player is on his own. In a sense they were learning
Dr. Joe Maddy's philosophy that music is freedom with discipline, that tyranny is death to music, that control must be self-
control. They were learning that music has its laws of technique
and proper order, but more important are its laws of inspiration,
understanding, penetration. In life the laws on the statute books
—against robbery and murder, for instance—are obeyed by the
majority. Far rarer is the obedience to the invisible laws—kind-
ness, compassion, unselfishness. Camp life at Interlochen was—
and is—a daily practice of the unwritten laws of music, bringing
with it a sensitivity to unwritten laws of all kinds.

Perhaps more important than anything else—at least to Joe Maddy—was that these young people were absorbing some of his own deep but often inarticulate feeling. Joe rarely *talked* about this; he didn't need to. To him music was an expression that is deeper than language, a language of the emotions that affects both the performer and the composer more than all the other arts, an expression that summons a spiritual response, a deeper drive, an insatiable hunger for more. Music, Joe always said on those rare occasions when he did talk about it, has a tendency to draw people away from anything cruel.

"Musicians," he once remarked, "are never cruel. If you ever find one in jail, it won't be for anything connected with cruelty."

And this was why it didn't matter so much to Joe Maddy when people called him a fanatic or claimed he was an "ornery cuss" or a "genius" or whatever the appelation of the moment might be. What mattered most to him was that children learn to love music, and the happiest day of the week for him, as for many campers, was Bloody Friday with all its joyous, spontaneous, insatiable drive of the youngsters for music. Joe knew that children like this would never be either cowardly or cruel.

A great deal of chair switching always took place on Bloody Friday. A player could move up or down as many as fifteen chairs at one session. And this was just what happened when Marta Olarte, the twelve year old scholarship student from Bogota, finally learned what Bloody Friday was all about.

Marta had to take last chair in the trumpet section of the intermediate band when she first arrived at camp from her native Colombia because she came a week late and missed the first Bloody Friday tryouts.

With her scanty knowledge of English and her lack of experience with anything remotely approaching the challenge system in other orchestras, she sat wide-eyed and bewildered at all the head bowing, hand raising, and changing of positions. She had seen nothing like this in Bogota.

At Interlochen the music campers were not compelled to challenge and on some Bloody Fridays they preferred not to—if, for example, they had shirked their practicing—but each one was given the opportunity if he wanted it.

The problem with Marta was how to make her understand what she could do and why. All the other young trumpet players, as well as her instructor, wanted to help the girl who had come all the way from South America.

But Marta couldn't understand the word "challenge."

Finally someone hit on the word competition.

"Oh, *competicion, competicion,* si, si," cried Marta, beaming.

She grasped her trumpet and pointed it to the boy sitting the first chair up from her, squealing excitedly, *"Competicion."*

In a few seconds she had his chair. Then she pointed to the next one up, and the next. One by one she outplayed fifteen of the seventeen trumpet players in her section, and moved up from last chair to second in one challenge session. The entire band, including all the losers, stampeded Marta with applause and adulation.

Bloody Friday in the miniature music kingdom of Interlochen holds none of the adult world's ingrown prejudices and pretenses. Race, religion, wealth or social position have no relation at all to chair positions in the camp bands and orchestras. The youngsters vote their own music rivals up and down in their chairs solely on the basis of how well they play. Darwyn Apple, a talented young Negro violinist from Detroit, held his position as concertmaster through two Interlochen seasons by vote of his music student colleagues. He was concertmaster of the camp's High School Philharmonic Orchestra in 1961 and of the University Symphony Orchestra in 1962.

Another Negro boy who survived Interlochen's Bloody Friday challenges and came out on top was Jimmy Gholson from Washington, D.C. Jimmy played clarinet and he held onto his first chair in the symphonic band for the full eight weeks, and in the high school symphony orchestra for six weeks during the 1962 season. He was first chair clarinetist in the orchestra that went to the White House.

In fact, the fiercest competition in the Bloody Friday battles of the 1962 season was the one that was being fought for positions—any position—in the White House concert orchestra.

Interlochen had grown enormously in thirty-five years. It was now known as one of the world's largest fine arts schools. But its focal point always had been and still was Joe Maddy's National High School Symphony Orchestra. The music camp, in fact, was established as a summer home for that orchestra, which in 1928 numbered only one hundred and fifteen students.

By 1962 it would not have been stretching a point too far to say that each of Joe's separate music and arts organizations at Interlochen—the assorted bands, orchestras, operettas, choral and ballet groups, plus departments of drama and speech, art and ceramics, radio-TV, electronics, and related activities—probably outnumbered the original hundred and fifteen students at his music camp. And by 1962 his High School Symphony Orchestra alone was so big that it had to be split into two orchestras, numbering about a hundred and fifty players in each.

Nothing would have pleased Joe more than to take a three

hundred piece orchestra to the White House, but there were enough problems involved in transporting a hundred young musicians and their instruments, including seven-foot harps and people-size string basses; fourteen ballet dancers and their costumes—the costumes would require almost as much room as the dancers; a crew of librarians, stage hands, and chaperones; crates of music, music stands, and, of course, personal luggage.

All of this, plus cymbals, xylophone, four-foot chimes, a bass tuba, and five sets of percussion and tympani Joe expected to crowd into two ninety-eight passenger chartered DC-7's.

When a few of these vital statistics reached the airline officials, they earnestly advised Joe to keep his orchestra down to one hundred. And with Joe's stage and acoustical requirements for the White House lawn, Miss Baldridge might not have been so cooperative about a three hundred piece orchestra when the most she had ever coped with for White House concerts was seventy.

Thus, when Joe announced, regretfully, at the opening of his 1962 season that only a hundred of his High School Symphony players could go to Washington, the students plunged into the most vigorous battle of musical chairs in camp history.

Many supplemented their rehearsals and classwork with two or three private lessons a week in hopes of winning a place in the White House orchestra.

Others fought to keep the chairs they already had.

First chair positions, of course, were the most coveted and the majority of these were held by students in their third or fourth season at Interlochen.

Erica Goodman from Toronto, Canada, for example, had held her place as first harpist with the High School Symphony for two seasons—though she was only fourteen years old. She had started at Interlochen when she was nine. Pretty eighteen year old Paula Dodez from Wooster, Ohio, was hanging onto her chair as first violinist and concertmaster. Cathy Meints, seventeen, from Hinsdale, Illinois, was first in the cello section. Nancy Howe, eighteen, from Iowa City, Iowa, was first flutist and Philip Alexander, eighteen, from Conroe, Texas, was first oboist.

The closest race for first chair was being run in the trumpet section between Barbara Deur from Carroll, Iowa, and Timothy Freriks from Dearborn, Michigan. During the opening week of camp, Barbara had won first chair in both the orchestra and the band. Then in the second week Tim outplayed her on Bloody Friday and got her place in the orchestra. But she held onto first chair in the band. The third week Barbara won her coveted chair back from Tim and was again first in both orchestra and band.

In the fourth week Bloody Friday fell on the thirteenth, which turned out to be an unlucky day for Barbara. She still came out first in band, but Tim challenged her first chair in orchestra again and displaced her.

On the same day, however, the faculty announced the names of the concerto winners, and Barbara was one of them. This was one of the camp's highest honors. Students who won in the concerto auditions were accorded the honor of playing a solo concerto —accompanied by the High School or University Symphony Orchestra. Most concerto winners were also first chair players in their sections, and even though Barbara lost in her see-saw race with Tim this week, she could challenge him next week and win her first chair back, she was sure.

The problem was, however, that in her excitement at hearing the concerto news Barbara made a flying leap off the Interlochen Bowl stage, hit a low beam above a door, and made a three point landing on her head!

The result was a mild concussion and doctor's orders for five days of rest. No more playing the trumpet for five days, and five days knocked out of a week's practice time was fatal to a first chair contender. Barbara also lost her first chair in band, but even with the concussion she pluckily held onto second chair in both groups.

Just before she boarded the plane for Washington, she said, "I guess most of us would settle for any chair to get to play at the White House."

3

There was magic in the air at Interlochen on that sunny Sunday morning. The big Michigan white and Norway pines, still glistening with the early dew, had a fresh, tangy, earth-and-woods scent. And through the trees trilled the song of an early-morning yellow warbler. Beyond the sloping green of the main campgrounds lay Lake Wahbekanetta, a shining wonder of blue and pink morning mists sparkling in the sunrise.

Nowhere in the world could nature create a more perfect setting or a more glorious morning to begin a day like this. It was a morning that smiled in benediction, as if created especially and only for Interlochen.

Sleepy-eyed boys and girls tumbled out of their beds. The great moment was at hand.

Minerva Turner, the camp dietitian, had been up since dawn to make sure that the campers started their trip to Washington on full stomachs. The youngsters, however, were too excited to eat. Counselors hovered over them to see that they didn't spill peaches or scrambled eggs down their shirt fronts.

Knickers buttoned below the knees?

Socks pulled up straight and neat?

Everyone wearing camp badges?

The camp buses were waiting to take them to the airport. The trucks, with all their instruments and luggage, had already left.

Teachers, counselors, secretaries, office workers—nearly the entire camp staff—were up to help herd Dr. Joe's flock of boy and girl musicians through the breakfast line and to the airport.

Yes, their great moment had come and they were ready for it. Their corduroys were freshly laundered, their shirts clean and well pressed. They were scrubbed, brushed, and neatly groomed. Their cheeks were a little pinker than usual, their eyes brighter, their faces aglow with the shiny freshness of youth—and with excitement.

"Eat your oatmeal," said Mrs. Turner. "Second helpings for everyone today. And you'd better eat all you want now. You may not get second helpings at the White House."

There were many besides Dr. Joe who felt a special poignancy that morning as his "kids," as he often called them, trooped into the waiting camp buses. For they were not only Joe Maddy's kids; they belonged to everyone who had shared their dream. No one who ever loved a child could question, at a time like this, what it was that made Interlochen live through all its adversities. The answer was written in the faces of these boys and girls whose frighteningly wonderful freshness of youth brushed the earth with its sweetness. They were kids anyone could be proud of, and they had the world by the tail and a song in their hearts as they boarded the planes for their trip of a lifetime. . . .

There was sixteen-year-old Susan Lowenkron from Sayville, New York. She had cornflower blue eyes and long blonde hair pinned in a pony tail. Susan had an extra-special reason for the sparkle in her eyes. She was the only piccolo player in the group. It was she who would stand and play the piccolo solo part in *Stars and Stripes Forever* for President Kennedy.

Susan was carrying with her a copy of Shakespeare's *As You Like It.* Her seat mate, Alan Balter, a seventeen year old clarinet player from Roslyn Heights, New York, was taking along Bertrand Russell's *Mysticism and Logic* to read. Most of the young musicians were normal, intelligent, well adjusted boys and girls who happened to love music but who did not necessarily consider it their sole interest. Fifteen year old Mark Killingsworth, for example, brought along a paper to study written by his father, a college professor, on *The Modernization of West Coast Longshore Work Rules.*

Among those left behind at the airport was a small pretty woman, wearing a blue corduroy skirt and red sweater, who stood alone at one side smiling and waving as the blue-knickered campers filed into the planes. She knew most of the students by name. Through the years she more than anyone else had shared the hopes and dreams of Joe Maddy. She rarely missed a concert or a rehearsal, especially if it was one Joe conducted. She usually sat quietly somewhere in the background, listening to the music and knitting. It was almost always a red sweater. Sometimes she would look up to smile approval at one of the young musicians, or at Joe. Her hair was white but her face was still youthful, and it had a special glow as she stood waving at Joe and his kids boarding the planes.

Some said, as they waved back through the windows, "Gee, I wish Mrs. Maddy could come with us."

No one could tell what Mrs. Maddy was thinking, but surely

her heart was remembering a time when she was fifteen, and there was a boy named Joe Maddy, and they played the piccolo together in a family orchestra back in Wellington, Kansas. Probably none of the Interlochen campers ever thought of Mrs. Maddy as having once been Dr. Joe's childhood sweetheart.

Certainly none of them had been told the real reason that Dr. Joe wasn't taking Mrs. Maddy to the White House with him. She had given up her seat in the plane so an extra student could go along. Then, at the last minute, Joe had decided, by gum, to squeeze three players into her relinquished place, instead of one.

When all the passengers were strapped in their seats and the roll was called, there were a hundred and three members of the White House orchestra and fourteen ballet dancers. The youngest of the group was thirteen, the oldest eighteen. Most of them— approximately eighty per cent—had never been on a plane before. Aboard also were four counselors, a doctor, and a large complement of staff assistants, librarians, and stage crew, all of whom doubled as chaperones for the students.

At the last minute an "anonymous donor" had agreed to finance the twelve thousand dollar trip, just as Joe Maddy, of course, always knew someone would. . . .

"Let's don't just sit here, everyone. Let's have an honor recital. . . ."

The students began humming parts of Tschaikowsky's *Symphony No. 4 in F Minor,* Wagner's *Overture to Tannhauser,* Johann Strauss' *Emperor Waltz,* and Hadley's *Herod Overture*— all of which they were to play at the White House concert.

"It's a wonderful gang," said Joe Maddy, bouncing up and down the aisle of the plane. "I'd back these kids against any orchestra anywhere."

Joe was particularly pleased because both Deems Taylor and Hugh Downs had heard the orchestra play on Saturday night at Interlochen the same concert they were to give at the White House, and both had declared that the youngsters "played beautifully." Hugh Downs' own thirteen year old daughter Deirdre was an Interlochen student, but she was not on the Washington trip. She was not a music student but was majoring in drama.

The forward part of the plane's passenger cabin was loaded with equipment—a harp, two tympani, chimes, and a hanging rack of dancers' costumes. The students were rationed as to personal luggage—three to a suitcase. About all they needed, however, were toothbrushes, pajamas, and clean shirts.

Two of the prettiest little passengers on the plane were Dana Long, sixteen, from Toronto and Sharon Snyder, seventeen, from Bloomfield Hills, Michigan. Dana was in her sixth summer at camp. She was enrolled on a camp ballet scholarship, and she also was studying piano, violin, and voice. Sharon was in her seventh summer at Interlochen. She was a dance major but was also studying voice, and she played the harp, flute, piccolo, piano, tympani, and organ. She was attending camp on a Toscanini Ballet scholarship.

Sharon and Dana were both blonde, blue eyed, and the best of friends. And both boarded the plane for Washington with a handful of red roses. There was a story behind those roses. Nearly everyone in camp, of course, knew how Sharon felt about Tommy Harmon, a clarinet player from Angola, Indiana, and everyone knew what had happened to Tommy on that last Bloody Friday when chairs were "frozen" for the Washington trip.

Earlier in the season Sharon was positive that Tommy's chances of going to Washington were much better than hers. Then, for a while, they had dared to hope that they *both* might get to go. At least they were keeping their fingers crossed. Sharon and Tommy had met at Interlochen two summers earlier in the wind section of the orchestra. That was the summer Sharon changed her major from ballet to flute because she dislocated her knee and couldn't dance.

Now she was dancing again and Tommy was still in the orchestra but they could be together sometimes between rehearsals and classes . . . and maybe, just maybe, on the trip to Washington.

Then on that last Bloody Friday during challenges, Tommy lost his chair. Even worse, he lost out on the Washington orchestra by *only one* chair. If there could have been one more clarinet player in the Washington concert orchestra, it would have been Tommy. But the clarinetist next in line challenged him and won his chair.

On the same day, after weeks of competitive tryouts in the dance department, the names of the lucky fourteen ballet dancers for the White House concert were announced, and Sharon's was one of them.

The day before the departure for Washington Tommy tried to buy a corsage to wish Sharon goodbye and good luck. But there was no corsage to be found around camp, and he had no way of getting into town to buy one.

Dana Long's own beau, back in Toronto, however, had meanwhile wired her a going-to-the-White House bouquet which was delivered on Saturday evening. And Tommy worked up enough courage to ask Dana if he could borrow one rose to give to Sharon. So Dana shared her bouquet with him—for Sharon.

As the plane took off for Washington, Sharon buried her nose in the roses and said over and over, "And to think he missed by only one chair, only *one!* If we couldn't both go, I'd much rather have Tommy go. I would even have given up the trip myself if it had meant Tommy could go. But he missed—by **ONE** chair."

Both Sharon and Dana were still clutching their slightly wilted bouquets as they started rehearsal next morning on the White House lawn. . . .

A crisis was nothing new in Joe Maddy's life, though no one would have predicted one on the Washington trip. Everything was well organized and had been for weeks. Joe had seen to that. He had, of course, given a great deal of thought to the White House concert and had selected the program which he felt would be most appropriate. Some of it was difficult for a student orchestra, but a staff of twenty-five music librarians had been charged with the responsibility of marking all fingerings and bowings on the more difficult scores, then packing the music in crates and loading it into a special place in the luggage compartment of Number One plane.

The planes made a stop at Detroit on Sunday morning. The Interlochen group was scheduled for a concert at The University of Michigan's Dearborn Center, at Fairlane Gardens, at three o'clock that afternoon. They would continue on to Washington after the concert. They were first taken on a tour of Greenfield Village and the Henry Ford Museum. Then there was a luncheon in the Student Union Building, and a rehearsal scheduled for two o'clock.

At noon Joe was conferring with Dr. William E. Stirton, vice-president and director of the University's Dearborn Center, when staff member George Worden walked in and said, "Well, the instruments are all in from the airport okay." He paused, then added with forced casualness, as if he didn't know quite how to break the news to Dr. Joe, "But it appears that the music is missing."

Peg Stace, a redhead with sharp eyes and ears, and for many years administrative assistant to Dr. Joe—he called her his right arm—was telephoning. She looked up, shot a quick glance at Dr. Joe, and remained cool.

Joe, tapping his fingers impatiently on the arm of his chair, blinked, and then snapped, "With twenty-five librarians, how can the music be missing?"

George said he knew only that the music was not on the buses that brought the instruments in from the airport, and that it apparently could not be found on either plane, although the librarians and stage crew were making another search.

Joe looked at his watch, waited a moment, and then announced calmly, "It's time for lunch."

It did not take long for the news to leak out. The music for the White House concert was missing!

Many of the students saw Miss Stace quietly leave the cafeteria line for consultation. Many saw staff members beating a path back and forth to the pay telephone booth in the hall. Joe saw it all, too. He said nothing until someone at his table innocently inquired, "Where's Miss Stace? Isn't she eating lunch?"

He looked up from his ham sandwich and potato salad and retorted sharply, "She's probably out consoling the librarians."

His jaws were taut, his face grim. No one cared to question him further. Finally, after what seemed like an eternity to those who began to guess the worst, Peg Stace sauntered in, trying her best to look unworried. In her most tranquil manner she said quietly to Dr. Joe, "Now, don't worry. There's nothing to get

Young Joe Maddy with a group of the Maddy family friends.

The house of Mr. and Mrs. W. H. Maddy in Wellington, Kansas.

The Wellington Boys' Band, with Joe, the smallest member, right front.

Harry and Joe Maddy with a fellow member
of the Minneapolis Symphony Orchestra.

The Rochester High School Band, after it paraded to the home of George Eastman in May, 1919. Mr. Eastman later founded the Eastman School of Music in Rochester.

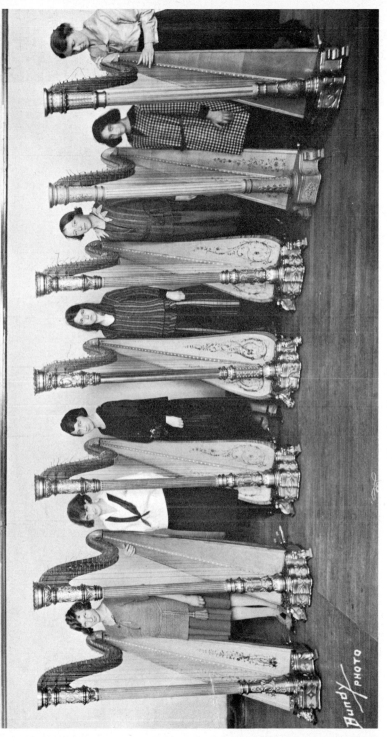

The first public school harp class. Richmond, Indiana, 1923.

Thaddeus P. Giddings, Joe Maddy, John Philip Sousa, and Austin Harding at the National Music Camp.

Thaddeus P. Giddings with a group of students.

Introduction of the Interlochen Orchestra.

President Kennedy greets the Interlochen dancers.

The Interlochen Ballet at the White House.

The Interlochen Bowl with dancers on the roof during one of the yearly closing performances, **Les Preludes.**

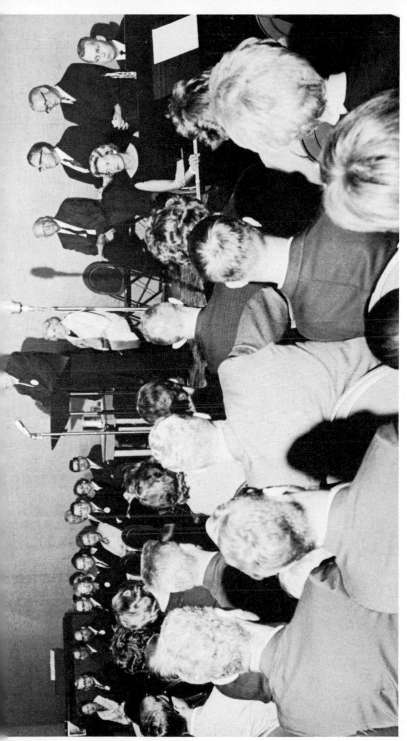

Joe Maddy, with Mrs. Maddy seated behind him, opens the Convocation of the Interlochen Arts Academy.

Joe Maddy of Interlochen.

excited about. Everything is being taken care of." And then, efficiently, point by point, she relayed to him the following items:

1. The music was indeed missing. At least it couldn't be found.
2. The librarians were ready to shoot themselves.
3. They had telephoned camp and were assured positively that the music *had* been placed on plane Number One in three large boxes in the baggage compartment.
4. Airline and camp crews were still searching both planes. The search would continue.
5. Staff members at Interlochen were digging up all the extra parts they could find to send down by special plane.
6. The plane had already been chartered. The pilot was standing by to take off when given the signal.

It was a quarter past one now. The rehearsal was at two. There couldn't be a rehearsal without music. The concert itself was at three. If the music wasn't found, could the chartered plane get the extra parts down to Detroit—and then by bus to Fairlane Gardens in Dearborn—in time?

How much help would the extra parts be in a full concert program? The fingerings and bowings would not be marked. There would not be enough extra parts for complete instrumentation.

It was Sunday. Music stores were not open. There was no place to buy new scores. Someone faintly offered the suggestion that perhaps the Detroit Symphony Orchestra would lend the music for the concert—if the symphony manager could be located, and if the symphony's library had all the numbers on hand, which was doubtful.

One of the pieces on the White House concert program, for example, was an unusual composition called simply *Music for*

Orchestra by a Japanese composer, Yasushi Akutagawa. It was published in the United States by the Interlochen Press and was rarely performed anywhere in this country except at Interlochen. Whether this music was available in other music libraries or in music publishing houses was doubtful.

The concert on the White House lawn was tomorrow morning at ten-thirty.

Perhaps someone would fly to New York, buy all the scores first thing Monday morning—*if* they could be found—and get down to Washington in time for the White House concert? Maybe.

It was clearly a crisis of the first order.

Peg Stace studied Dr. Joe's face as he merely blinked and listened, without comment. Then, trying for optimism, she said, "Well, I'm sure most of the kids know their parts by heart anyway. They could play the concert from memory, couldn't they, Dr. Maddy?"

Up to this moment Joe had not uttered a word. He now uttered one distinctly. It was: "No!"

Then he turned on his heel and went out the door, issuing only one brief command: "I'm going over to Dr. Stirton's office and take a nap. Wake me up when you find the music."

Though he might be a miracle maker and all his kids little geniuses, Joe-Maddy By-Gum had no intentions of asking them to play Tschaikowsky and Akutagawa without their music. He clearly expected someone to turn up the missing crates of music for his White House orchestra, and fast.

The telephone lines between Dearborn, the Detroit airport, and Interlochen continued to buzz. Sheila Reilly found that she had a tape recording of the *Emperor Waltz*. She came up with the idea that perhaps her ballet troupe could dance to the tape recording.

"Big deal," moaned one of the orchestra players. "So we just came along for the ride."

Sheila's tape recording, however, brought forth another last-ditch inspiration. Somewhere, said someone, there was a tape of the entire White House concert. The orchestra had played the numbers at camp, of course. If the tape could be played and amplified in such a way that the orchestra members, but *not* the audience, could hear it, then why couldn't the orchestra members just play along with the tape, by ear? Most of the first chair players knew most of their parts anyway. The others could fake it, and who would know the difference?

Aides were dispatched to find the tape recording. Then it was discovered that the tape didn't have the *Stars and Stripes Forever* on it—but everyone knew this one by heart anyway. However, it was also discovered that the numbers were not taped in the order that they appeared on the programs already printed for both the Dearborn Center and White House concerts. The University of Michigan audience might not mind if the program was switched around a little. At the moment, in lieu of music, it was the best suggestion anyone could come up with, at least for the Dearborn concert. As for the White House program—most of the staff just shuddered and stayed close to the telephones—all but those who were still out at the airport searching the planes.

The young musicians who were to give the concert were far less concerned than the staff over the loss of their White House music. Many insisted that they *could* play their parts from memory if they had to. Others felt that if Dr. Joe expected the music to be found, well then—it would be found.

It was only a few minutes after two o'clock when Peg Stace, who had weathered the brief crisis that seemed to last forever, rapped on Dr. Stirton's office door to awaken Dr. Maddy.

He had slept soundly. He got up refreshed, tranquil, and in good spirits. He didn't need to ask, "Did you find the music?" He had expected it to be found. He knew it would be. And no one would have dared awaken him until it *was* found.

The crates of music had finally been discovered exactly where the Interlochen loaders said they had put them—in the Number One plane's baggage compartment. But they were pushed so far back, behind other luggage, and were so well hidden from sight that even camp workers who knew their jobs depended on finding that music had unearthed it with difficulty.

Joe Maddy's calm certainty that the music would be found was part faith in himself and his Interlochen crew—he knew they *couldn't* fail him—and part faith in something bigger that he knew would help him through any crisis if it involved music. He could go to sleep and sleep soundly while others were frantic with worry, and he could awaken from his nap refreshed and confident that the music was precisely where it was supposed to be.

The music arrived from the airport too late for a rehearsal, but the Dearborn concert started on time.

During intermission a reporter covering the event for a Detroit newspaper left to make a telephone call to her office. She returned visibly shaken, and whispered to an Interlochen aide, "Marilyn Monroe just killed herself. I don't know how much space we'll be able to give you."

The ballet dancers had just waltzed offstage looking like floating pink dreams in their swirling organza costumes. The orchestra players were crowding around congratulating them. The August sun was scalding hot, and the musicians were drenched with perspiration. Their shirt collars were wet and wilting, their corduroys were sticking to them, and their lips were parched.

"I'd love a glass of water," they groaned.

One remarked, "*I'd* settle right now for an ice cube."

At the moment only three things were uppermost in their minds: getting a drink of water, finishing the Dearborn concert, and going on to the White House. The news that was to rock the world had little impact on the young people of Interlochen. Marilyn Monroe's death was far away and unreal to those whose bright and innocent dreams belonged for the moment—and forever—to youth. Few of them even knew that back at Interlochen there was a shy, dark-eyed girl named Jane Miller whose father, playwright Arthur Miller, had once been married to Miss Monroe. Jane was enrolled as a college student at camp, majoring in voice and piano.

Life was here and now and tomorrow for the Interlochen concert group bound for Washington. Competing for space or newspaper headlines was the furthest thing from their minds. All they wanted at the moment was a drink of water.

4

Sharon Snyder pirouetted off the dance platform at the end of rehearsal crying ecstatically, "It's like a dream. I can't get over it. Everywhere I turn I see the White House. It's so BIG."

The young music campers were there at last with their long awaited moment all around them. The green of the south lawn swept off in a vista past flower trimmed, gently flowing fountains to the classic lines of the Jefferson Memorial, glistening creamily a mile away in the humid morning mists.

Everything was all in order for the Interlochen concert, and

Joe could tell at a glance that Miss Baldridge and the White House aides had spared nothing in carrying out his wishes. The big made-to-order acoustical shell was even better than he had anticipated. He inspected the dance platform; it *was* covered with battleship linoleum, the best. At one end of the lawn a red and white candy striped tent had been set up to serve the young guest musicians lemonade and cookies. And to Joe's surprise he learned that the White House had even ordered the noisy jets normally passing overhead to be re-routed during the concert.

The Interlochen group had spent the night in Army barracks and were brought to the White House in Army buses at eight o'clock Monday morning for a rehearsal before their ten-thirty concert. The students swarmed over the White House lawn with their cameras, taking pictures of each other—and of Caroline's playground and swings. Fond of children as most young people their age are, they were still hoping for a glimpse of Caroline and her mother, although they soon learned that the First Lady, who was technically their hostess, was in New York preparing for her vacation in Italy. They were too excited, however, to dwell on this small disappointment. Other than being on perhaps more familiar terms with Bach and Beethoven than some youngsters, the music campers were very much like any other normal, happy teenage boys and girls reveling in the adventure of a lifetime.

The Washington trip had produced a few minor casualties— nothing serious and no more than might be expected in such a large group of healthy young travelers. But Dr. Max L. Durfee, who was the director of health services for Oberlin College during the winter and served as head of the medical services at Interlochen in summers, was kept busy between the rehearsal and

48 ·

concert time administering first aid from his medical kit for those who needed it. Some of his young charges had problems a little out of the ordinary run of medical complaints usually found among adolescents. There was Terel Cox, for instance, who was in a state of terrible distress because, he said, his ears were "plugged up."

"I can't tell whether I'm sharp or flat," he told Dr. Durfee, and this, the doctor knew, was a most embarrassing predicament for a French horn player to find himself in. Terel was a sixteen year old French horn player from Detroit. The trip from Interlochen to Washington was his first plane flight, and there was so much congestion in his ears after the flight that he couldn't hear his own music. The doctor blew out Terel's ears so he could again play in tune.

Barbara Deur, the trumpet player who had banged her head and suffered a mild concussion at camp in the excitement of learning that she was a concerto winner, complained of a splitting headache after the White House rehearsal. "It hurts every time I hit the high notes," she said. Dr. Durfee gave Barbara some pills and prescribed, "Just go easy on the high notes. That will help your head, and President Kennedy probably won't know the difference."

Philip Alexander had cut his finger while sharpening a knife he used for scraping and limbering his oboe reed. The doctor examined and dressed it. One boy had lost the battery in his hearing aid; Dr. Durfee produced a new one for him. A girl lost one of her contact lenses, but it was found in time for the concert.

An August morning in Washington was far different from the cool climate of the Michigan northwoods. The sun was so intense that some of the staff wondered whether Dr. Durfee should give the campers salt tablets to help them withstand the heat. He vetoed the idea. The salt tablets, he said, might induce nausea. He was sure the young players would rather be hot, than become ill and spoil their performance.

Almost equal to the crisis of the missing music in Dearborn was the case of the missing harps at the White House.

There were four harpists in the orchestra, but because of the space and weight logistics involved in transporting students and instruments on the chartered planes, Joe had decided to bring only two of the camp's twenty-two harps—one on each plane— and borrow two more from Lyon and Healy in Detroit for the Dearborn concert, and from the same firm in New York for the Washington concert.

Sam Pratt, in charge of harps for Lyon and Healy in New York, had duly dispatched two of his finest harps to the White House. And Sam himself was there bright and early on Monday morning as overseer of the lend-lease harps.

No one at the White House knew anything about them.

Head usher J. B. West said he had received no orders on harps, and no harps had gone in or out of the White House. Certainly if they had, he ought to know. Instruments that big could hardly slip in unnoticed. White House aides ordered two more harps sent over by the Navy and Marine bands.

For a while it looked as though the Interlochen orchestra might have six harps instead of four. Shortly after the White House ordered the Navy and Marine harps, one of the White House guards stopped Sam Pratt and asked, "Say, aren't you the one I heard asking about harps?" Sam, completely baffled by the mystery of how two seven-foot harps could vanish, said indeed he was the man asking about harps. Did the guard know anything about them?

"Sure," said the guard. "They've been here for days. Follow me." He led Sam through the East Wing of the White House to a room where the harps stood.

"Are these yours?" he asked Sam. They were.

"Well," said the guard, "I don't know how they got here but I guess if they're yours, you can take them. I was wondering what President Kennedy wanted with harps. . . ."

The orchestra was on stage; the dancers, in costume, were behind the shell trying to find a little coolness in the shade of a tree. Children of congressmen and cabinet officers, serving as hosts and hostesses, brought them trays of lemonade and cookies.

The sun was so hot that the dancers finally dipped the toes of their pink ballet shoes in the lemonade to limber them up for their performance.

The audience was gathering. The eighteen hundred guests invited by President and Mrs. Kennedy for the concert included many groups of handicapped, blind, crippled, and orphaned children from various Washington institutions, and a delegation of congressmen. A stir of excitement fanned through the crowd when the loud buzz of helicopters announced the arrival of President Kennedy from his summer home at Hyannisport. The helicopters bringing the presidential party back to the White House —only moments before the concert began—had to land on the ellipse south of the White House grounds because the helicopter pad on the White House south lawn was occupied by the music campers and their audience.

All eyes were on the man in the gray pin-striped suit and red tie who strode out of the White House, flanked by his aides, and up to the orchestra shell to shake hands with the man in the open-neck collar, shirt sleeves, and blue corduroys. Joe Maddy beamed with pride at his orchestra as he told President Kennedy, "There are about fifteen hundred more like these up at Interlochen. This is only one concert group. They put on fifteen concerts at camp yesterday. . . ."

He led his host over to meet Paula Dodez, the girl concert-master, and other first chair players. President Kennedy stepped up front to give an official welcome to the group and an informal greeting to the audience. He called the performers a "most distinguished group from a most distinguished school," and said that "success in the arts comes by hard work and discipline, not because of natural talent."

"There are over thirty-three million Americans who are interested in music, interested in other forms of art," the President said. "That is a tremendous statistic. . . . I was once, when I was younger, one of those statistics." He then disclosed one of the secrets of his past: "I used to play the piano as a boy," he said, "but I gave it up because I played so badly." The President said he couldn't stay for the performance, explaining that he had "other responsibilities." But he promised to leave the door to his office open so he could hear the music.

As he left the orchestra shell, he saw the pretty pink-costumed ballet dancers on the lawn at one side, peeking around the shell to get a good look at him. He stopped and chatted with them. Then he did leave his door open as he had promised, and when the concert was over he sent a message to Dr. Joe asking him to come to his office. He congratulated Joe on his "good work," introduced him to one of his Cultural Relations Committee officers, and then said he would like to meet all the young musicians personally. He asked Dr. Joe to bring the entire group into the Rose Garden at noon, just before lunch, so he could talk to them.

The youngsters were awed as they were escorted into the White House to freshen up. Some were worried about how they had played; others were worried about how they looked. "It even got so hot up there," said Cathy Meints of Hinsdale, Illinois, "that some of the varnish from my cello came off on my blouse."

Many of the players had had trouble keeping their instruments in tune because of the heat. As they explained to the White House correspondents covering the event, "High temperatures like this always make the wind instruments go sharp and the strings go flat."

"I think I was a little flat," said red haired cellist Joel Levin, fourteen, of Highland Park, Illinois. "But I don't believe the President could tell. In fact I'm sure nobody could tell but us."

If the President knew whether the musicians were sharp or flat, he didn't say so. Instead, he told them as they gathered around him in the Rose Garden that they had played "magnificently" and that they were "very good sports" for performing in the Washington heat. He good naturedly answered their questions about his own piano playing, and said he was sorry that Mrs. Kennedy and Caroline hadn't been there for the concert.

The Interlochen group also learned that President Kennedy wasn't the only frustrated musician in the White House. His administrative assistant, Henry Wilson, admitted that he once played "very poor" second oboe—as a student at the National Music Camp at Interlochen. He gave it up, he said, because he couldn't keep up with the other players at the music camp.

The group went on a guided tour of the White House and then were treated to lunch served buffet style in the State Dining

Room. They had spaghetti and meat balls, tossed salad, ice cream, cake, and milk. They took their plates and scattered out in three rooms, the Red Room, the Blue Room, the Green Room. Most of them ate on the floor, picnic style.

Miss Baldridge, who supervised the White House hostessing for the young guests, came into the Red Room and asked, smiling, "Do you realize you're eating on a twelve thousand dollar antique rug?" The campers redoubled their efforts not to spill.

A few minutes later an aide popped in and announced, "The President just said to tell you that all rules about picture taking are off. You can take all the pictures you want. So get out your cameras—the place is yours."

Never before, White House guards said later, had a group of teen-aged youngsters been given the run of the place with such freedom as was granted to the Interlochen students during their tour of the Executive Mansion. The truth was that the White House personnel were as impressed by their young blue-knickered guests as the youngsters were by them. Miss Baldridge later told Dr. Joe, "Everyone from the Army to the White House is talking about how well mannered your children are."

Dr. Joe and all the other teachers and staff back at camp could well afford to be proud of the boys and girls they had groomed so carefully for the trip to Washington. And, as usual, it gave Joe another idea. . . .

They returned to Interlochen on Monday night. The next morning at breakfast Joe gulped his food, tapped his fingers incessantly, and kept looking at his watch every few minutes. It was obvious to everyone that he was hatching a new project. He could hardly wait until it was time for the executive office of the White House to open in Washington. As soon as it did, he got the long distance operator and told her he wanted to talk to President John F. Kennedy—direct.

A voice at the other end said the President was in conference and asked who was calling.

"Maddy," he said. "Joe Maddy."

There was a pause. Then, "Oh, *Dr.* Maddy. From Interlochen? Just a minute."

Soon the President was on the line telling Dr. Maddy how everyone was talking about the concert, and congratulating him again on his "good work."

"The reason I'm calling," Joe said, "is this: I want to take our orchestra on a peace tour to Europe, Moscow, the Iron Curtain countries. Look what we're spending for war. Why can't we spend some of it for peace? These kids would make a fine peace delegation for our country. Would you be interested in helping us?"

"I sure would," said the President.

Within forty-eight hours Joe had confirmation from the White House that "negotiations with the Russians" would be started as soon as possible by the State Department for an invitation to the National High School Symphony Orchestra to make a peace tour to Moscow.

He was disappointed to learn that the trip couldn't be made within the next few months. He was told that often it "took a while" to negotiate with the Russians.

But to Joe, a man whose soaring spirit acknowledged no barriers of time or space or political protocol, this was a small matter. At seventy he started planning his peace trip to Moscow. It might take a while, but he was sure that eventually the project would be fulfilled.

Meanwhile, if Joe had been one to care about details he might have felt satisfaction in the fact that his Washington concert had brought a kind of special recognition. Millions of people who had never heard of Interlochen were enchanted by a news photograph of young ballet dancers on the White House lawn. During a week when the tragedy of Marilyn Monroe filled the nation's headlines, and when newspaper space was at a premium, Interlochen made the front pages of papers from coast to coast. Perhaps because it was one of the prettiest news pictures of the year, or possibly because editors unconsciously felt a symbolic contrast between the tragic death of a glittering movie queen and the hope and happiness of the young student ballet troupe in their shining hour—whatever the reason, the picture caught the fancy of photo editors. Some crowded the Marilyn Monroe story off the front pages to give space to the Interlochen picture. The *New York Times* carried a four column photograph of the dancers on the White House lawn, and in the issue of *Life* devoted chiefly to Miss Monroe's death, the ballet troupe doing the *Emperor Waltz* in their organza costumes and long white gloves received a full page and a half pictorial spread.

No one could tell that their ballet shoes had been dipped in lemonade or that the ninety degree Washington heat had made the orchestral wind instruments go sharp and the strings go flat during their performance. It was a picture that captured the bright splendor of the moment, one that held both the warmth and promise of youth in a world that needed a lilt. If you had tried to explain this to Interlochen's Joe Maddy, he would have said, "Oh? Sure." If he hadn't caught up with the week's headlines, it wasn't from negligence—it was simply that for Joe and his young musicians there was no other world but Interlochen.

Van Cliburn Comes to Interlochen

I

IT WAS early dinner hour in the dining room of the Stone Student Center at Interlochen. There was a subdued and decorous air of excitement as students and guests filed through the cafeteria lines filling their trays with Mrs. Turner's luscious beef pot pies. Outside, parents and visitors had queued up in long lines waiting their turn to get into the student cafeteria. There was a cool damp breeze from the lake and dark clouds were beginning to form overhead.

Dr. Joe and Mrs. Maddy had gone through the line early and were seated at a table with other faculty and staff members. One of them, looking out at the gathering rain clouds, remarked, "Well, I hope it doesn't rain tonight."

"It can't," came a snap retort from the other end of the table.

"It can't what?" asked someone who had come in on the tail end of the chit-chat.

"It can't rain," said Dr. Joe. "It may drizzle or do something but it will stop for the concert."

There was a moment of silence. Everyone felt that if Dr. Joe said it wouldn't rain, it wouldn't, although from the storm clouds outside anyone would normally have laid bets on a downpour.

Dugald Munro, who was a science teacher in winter and a music camp photographer in summer—and also a man who chose his words with deliberate premeditation—spoke up:

"That is correct," he said. "One of the parents asked me a while ago if the concert was going to be rained out. I told her 'No.' Dr. Maddy would see to that." Again there was silence, with a quick amused glance across the table at Dugald. It simply couldn't rain out this concert. It was the Van Cliburn concert with the *Rachmaninoff Third* and it was as important—perhaps even more important to Interlochen than the White House concert.

It was five-thirty in the afternoon. In two and a half hours, rain or shine, an event everyone had looked forward to for weeks was to begin. And it did. Nature must have heard Joe Maddy's ultimatum. Between the dinner hour and the eight o'clock concert, it rained torrents. But then, as Joe walked onto the stage it stopped, as if by magic.

In the audience that night there were rows of faces as far as the eye could see. The concert was held on the open air stage of the Kresge Assembly Hall, a building donated by the Kresge Foundation. The long extension of its roof partially protected outdoor audiences. Most Interlochen concerts are held in outdoor band and orchestra shells or open air concert halls, usually with only a canopy of pine trees protecting the listeners. In the Kresge concert arena that night every inch under and outside the roofed area was packed. And beyond this a standing-room-only crowd stood for an hour under dripping trees, with rainhats and umbrellas. Some spread raincoats and blankets on the wet ground and huddled together in the chilly dampness. There were hundreds who couldn't even see the concert stage.

In the sea of nearly five thousand faces that rainy night one could have heard the drop of a pin. No one left. No one moved. It was almost as though no one breathed, until a tall boyish looking young man in blue corduroys and open-neck shirt took his place at the piano bench. Sound flooded the coolness of the rain-washed air and filled the night. At the end there was dazed silence, as though the crowd could not at once recover from the spell of the music. Then they arose slowly, spontaneously, and broke into thunderous applause.

Instead of continuing his bows, the tall young man quickly turned and grasped the hands of the conductor and the concert-master, and stood modestly directing the applause to the orchestra. Then hesitantly, almost with reluctance, he ambled offstage, his long arms dangling and one hand struggling with an unbuttoned cuff.

This was the young man from Kilgore, Texas, who had been acclaimed by music critics as one of the world's greatest concert pianists. Van Cliburn was one of the most popular and beloved guest artists ever to visit Interlochen. Even concert goers who were not connoisseurs of music knew that Van Cliburn's 1962 performance with the young musicians at Interlochen was one of the most moving experiences they had ever shared. But no one realized that the rapport between Van and the young players in his student accompaniment orchestra was partly the result of a series of minor backstage crises that had almost verged on the catastrophic.

About ten days before the concert, the telephone rang in the music library. The librarian who answered said brightly, "Yes, Dr. Maddy." Then, not so brightly, "Yes, Dr. Maddy." Then, in descending tones that trailed off in a whisper, "Yes, Dr. Maddy, Yes. . . ."

When the librarian recovered he relayed the news weakly, "It's the *Rachmaninoff . . . THIRD!*"

The orchestra was rehearsing the *Rachmaninoff Second,* and there was a great deal of difference.

The *Rachmaninoff Third Piano Concerto* is considered one of the most technically difficult in any professional repertoire, so difficult that only a Van Cliburn would attempt it. Most professional pianists and orchestras steer clear of it, preferring to do the *Second* instead. The high point of the *Third* is a monumental cadenza of fearsome intricacy. Even Rachmaninoff himself found it so hard to keep "in his fingers" that he wrote an alternate cadenza for pianists intrepid enough to tackle the *Third.* Van Cliburn did only the original.

Interlochen already had publicly announced the Van Cliburn program as the *Rachmaninoff Second.*

More important, the students were already at work on their parts. The librarians had marked all the bowings and fingerings. The woodwind players were practicing overtime to learn their solo parts. There had already been full orchestra rehearsal on the *Second.* It was tough but the young musicians loved it.

At rehearsal next morning Dr. George Wilson, camp vice-president, announced, "There's been a mistake. You will be playing the *Rachmaninoff Third* with Van Cliburn instead of the *Second.*"

There was an audible gasp from the woodwind section whose parts were particularly difficult.

The *Second* was difficult enough for a high school student orchestra. Even at Interlochen, where rare and complex masterpieces were frequently performed, the *Third,* with its daring technique and rubato, never had been attempted.

The announcement brought a groan from seventeen year old Suzanne Daehn from Oak Park, Illinois, who was playing second cello. Suzanne had met Van Cliburn in Chicago in March and he told her then that he was playing the *Third* at Interlochen. Suzanne, therefore, decided to do the *Rachmaninoff Second* for her piano concerto auditions at Interlochen. She played the piano and cello equally well. She spent a great deal of her time during the intervening months memorizing the *Second* for her piano concerto audition.

When she arrived at Interlochen, however, and found that the program showed Van Cliburn scheduled to play the *Second,* she dropped her own plans for that work and changed to a cello concerto. She reasoned that she would look pretty silly, by comparison, playing the same number in concertos that Van Cliburn was doing for his concert.

After all her work on the *Second,* Suzanne shelved it and set to work memorizing the *Lalo Cello Concerto in D Minor,* only to learn after all that she could have done the *Rachmaninoff Second* without worrying about measuring up to Van Cliburn.

No one knew whether Dr. Joe had misunderstood Van Cliburn in his discussion of the program during the previous winter, or whether Van simply changed his mind. It was logical to assume that anyone who wanted to do Rachmaninoff naturally meant the *Second*—anyone, that is, but Van Cliburn.

In any event, the misunderstanding was cleared up a few days before the concert in a long distance talk between Dr. Joe and Van Cliburn. Van was doing the *Third.*

Fortunately, the camp did have the *Third* in its library.

Fortunately, too, the Eastman School of Music had the score for Conductor Clyde Roller to look over before flying out to conduct the concert. Joe had invited him as guest conductor—for the *Rachmaninoff Second*.

At faculty-staff meeting that week Dr. Joe mentioned in an off-hand manner that there would be a change in the Cliburn program.

"We're doing the *Third* instead of the *Second*," he said, and went on to the next matter of business on the agenda as calmly as though the *Third* were done every day. His faculty and staff managed to keep their emotions under control, but actually the change was a far greater blow to them than it was to the students. Some considered it a colossal blunder on Joe's part. Others thought he should somehow tactfully have persuaded Van Cliburn to play the *Second*.

And nearly everyone except Dr. Joe and the orchestra players themselves was on edge over the big question: could the young orchestra play the *Rachmaninoff Third* with only two days of rehearsals? Even veteran faculty members admitted they wouldn't care for such a challenge. How could high school musicians learn it well enough to play with Van Cliburn?

Meantime, another problem arose. Joe had ordered a Steinway grand piano shipped up from Chicago for the concert; and Van Cliburn had ordered one from Detroit. Both were ready to be shipped when the duplication was discovered.

Joe canceled the order for the Chicago piano. But for a while it had looked as though there might be a two-piano concerto, and this did not add to anyone's tranquillity. What other complications were waiting?

Van Cliburn arrived with his mother at the Traverse City airport on Sunday night for his concert on Tuesday. He had a rehearsal with the orchestra on Monday morning. That evening he asked one of the music camp staff to drive him in to town to a drug store. He seemed worried. He finally admitted that he *was* worried—about his fingers. He had cut his fingernails the night before, and cut one of them too deep. It looked infected. Van had had trouble with infected fingers before. Also, he had practiced so much on the Rachmaninoff cadenzas that some of his fingers were just plain sore. He telephoned his doctor in Tucson, and the doctor conferred with the druggist in Traverse City. Those who knew about it were keeping their own fingers crossed. Van had a heavy schedule the next day, with rehearsal in the morning, a dress rehearsal in the afternoon, and the concert in the evening. What if his sore and hard-worked hands became simply unable to play? And for a while, though not many knew it, Van himself wasn't sure.

There was something else troubling him, too. On the way back from town he seemed moody. Suddenly he blurted out, "I'm very upset. Can you tell me why Dr. Maddy isn't conducting the orchestra?"

Joe had conducted the orchestra for Van Cliburn the summer before. But having had his turn, he felt that he should let someone else have the honor of conducting a Van Cliburn concert. So he had invited A. Clyde Roller to be guest conductor. There was perhaps a bit of typical Maddy shrewdness in his choice. For Roller was earning a reputation as one of the country's leading symphony conductors. He had led the Amarillo Symphony and only recently had joined the faculty of the Eastman School of Music. He had been on the Interlochen summer faculty for twelve seasons, and Joe was currently trying to attract him to his new year around Interlochen Arts Academy. It was both a generous and an astute move for Joe to invite Roller to conduct the Rachmaninoff concert with Van Cliburn.

But Van had other ideas. He wanted Dr. Joe to conduct the

orchestra. It wasn't that he had anything against Roller as guest conductor. He didn't want *any* guest conductor.

"It's Dr. Maddy's orchestra. He belongs up there," Cliburn insisted. And, as he repeated, he was personally very upset about it. Couldn't something be done?

It was an awkward situation to try to cope with on the eve of a concert.

The whole camp was turning somersaults to please Van Cliburn, but Joe could hardly take back his invitation to Roller, an outstanding artist and a man whom he greatly respected. He finally mollified Van by promising never again to invite a guest conductor but to conduct the orchestra himself at any future Van Cliburn concerts.

Van was also displeased with the piano he had ordered sent up from Detroit. It had poor tone, he said. He was positive the one Dr. Joe had ordered from Chicago would have been better.

But the final ironic twist came in Van's sudden surprise question: "Don't you think we should do the *Second* instead of the *Third?*" He had heard, of course, that the orchestra had been all set to play the *Rachmaninoff Second* before the last minute switch to the *Third.* And he felt responsible for the mix-up. It didn't matter to him which he played. He wanted to do the one the young musicians would enjoy most.

"I thought the *Third* would be a bigger challenge for them," he said. "I thought maybe they would like playing it here since it isn't performed very often. But when you stop to think of it, I guess they would like the *Second* better. It's more romantic. And here . . . with the moon and the outdoors. . . . Yes, I can see why they would like the *Second* better. All right, we'll change. We'll do the *Second.*"

With careful diplomacy he was told that the young performers loved the *Third,* too. The truth was that they would have loved anything Van Cliburn wanted to play, so long as they got to play in his accompanying orchestra. And the truth was that they had been working their heads off to learn the *Third* for him, as they had the *Second.* No one wanted to change again *now!*

But Van wanted to change to please them.

It would have made a fine mix-up for the program department, but the gesture was the kind that made Van Cliburn idolized by all who knew him. There was no pretense in his affinity for these young students. His own mass appeal, his public acclaim, the frenzied adulation that accompanied him everywhere had totally failed to impress him, as his public image impressed others. Van Cliburn's blue-eyed boyish good looks probably contributed to his movie-idol type of popularity. But inwardly he was as far removed from this glamor image as anyone could be. He was extremely sensitive and serious about his work, completely absorbed in it but never satisfied with it, bewildered by his mass popularity but not influenced by it, and unbelievably modest.

He looked younger than his twenty-seven years. He was a gangling six-foot-four, with a soft southern accent, so soft that others sometimes had to strain to hear him. He had a hurried, timid smile that completely dazzled an audience. In fact Van Cliburn often seemed like two different people. There was the artist at the piano, with his huge powerful hands in compelling mastery of the keyboard. And there was the shy, unaffected Van Cliburn making his bow to the audience, with the half-frightened look of someone trying hard to balance properly on a public pedestal when all he wanted to do was play the piano.

He didn't seek publicity. In fact he tried hard to avoid it. He once tore up his contract with a national magazine because he did not like what the writer had written. He refused to write or let others write about certain phases of his professional career, especially those dealing with his concerts in Russia and the Iron Curtain countries. "Those people have been kind to me," he said. "Music has its own language. It can be too easily misinterpreted in the written word."

He was even reluctant to discuss the 1958 international piano competition in Moscow that had catapulted him overnight to fame. Although Van had received both honors and recognition in his own country and had played a concert at Carnegie Hall, he remained comparatively unknown by American standards of popularity until he won the Moscow competition with *Tschaikowsky's B Flat Minor Concerto*. Suddenly he was a hero, a public idol. Khrushchev wanted to hear him. President Eisenhower asked to meet him. In New York he was given the ticker tape parade usually accorded only to national heroes, and he was the only classical musician ever so welcomed in that city. Nevertheless, all of this was a visibly painful subject for him.

"Winning a popularity poll is meaningless," he said. "I'm not a success. I'm only a sensation. There's a big difference."

Someone once asked him, "If this isn't success, what is? What more do you want?"

He was at the piano. He often practiced ten or twelve hours a day. He looked up from the piano, wringing wet with sweat, and said, "I want to play better tomorrow than I did today. . . ."

When Van Cliburn first visited Interlochen in the summer of 1961, it was obvious to everyone that he had a special kinship with the teen-age musicians who shared his love of music.

The camp staff had gone to great trouble to give him the red carpet treatment, only to find that this was not what he wanted. He was installed in a lakeside cottage outfitted with a practice piano, and arrangements were made to have meals served in his room. Nobody had ever been given room service at Interlochen—but this once it was scheduled for Cliburn. And then it turned out he didn't want it. He preferred having his meals with the students in the crowded dining hall.

Stalwart student guards were posted outside his cottage to keep celebrity seekers and autograph hunters away. Van Cliburn invited the guards in, and anyone else who wanted to come. He was never too busy to sign autographs for his admirers or talk to them.

Between rehearsals he roamed the grounds peeking in on classes and practice sessions. He was so fascinated by what he found that after his benefit concert, which grossed more than twelve thousand dollars for the music camp, he pledged a personal donation of three thousand more. He also insisted on paying for his own transportation and other expenses of the concert. This was an uncommon gesture for guest artists of any kind, anywhere.

For his first Interlochen concert Van Cliburn played the *Tschaikowsky B Flat Minor Concerto.* He had only three rehearsals with the orchestra. The orchestra had one week of rehearsals without him.

In their eagerness to please Cliburn, not many of the Interlochen faculty realized, when he returned in 1962, that Van was paying the music camp orchestra and Dr. Joe Maddy the highest tribute by assuming that they could perform the *Rachmaninoff Third* in the first place—and then asking for an eleventh-hour change from the *Third* to the *Second* because he thought the youngsters liked the *Second* better.

Furthermore, he was insistent about it.

How far had the orchestra gone on the *Second?*, he asked. Had the woodwind players learned their parts?

When Van went into his cottage after dinner that evening, probably to spend the rest of the night practicing, no one knew whether he was going to play Rachmaninoff's *Second* or the *Third*—or even if his fingers would have healed sufficiently to let him play at all.

But one thing was certain.

Though some among the faculty would have been close to nervous prostration if they had heard of Van Cliburn's last minute indecision, there wasn't a flicker of a doubt in Van's own mind about the youngsters in the orchestra or their ability to play anything they wished.

After orchestra rehearsal Tuesday morning Van was scheduled for a session of picture taking with Dr. Joe and other camp officials. An area was roped off on the roof of the dance building to insure privacy. As usual, husky stage hands were instructed to keep a throng from assembling and to see that Van got off stage and over to the dance roof on time without a trailing phalanx of students.

The stage hands, however, while they could manage the campers, could do nothing with Cliburn himself. He stood answering the students' questions, congratulating them on the rehearsal, and inviting some to come along for the picture taking. Interlochen campers were strictly disciplined and well mannered. But Van took two of the woodwind players by the hand, led them over to the dance roof, and insisted that the photographers make pictures of the three together.

These students were first flutist Nancy Howe from Iowa City, Iowa, and first oboe player Philip Alexander from Conroe, Texas. Both had difficult wind passages which joined the piano in its cadenzas. Van's personal interest in them may have had something to do with the polished performance they gave at the concert that night.

No professional orchestra could have had a greater impact on the audience, nor on the guest artist at the piano. Van Cliburn appeared to be not even aware of his audience. When his hands were not on the piano he turned full face toward the orchestra in a panorama of intense emotion. Sometimes he seemed to be pulling for them and with them, urging them on. Sometimes he beamed approvingly. Whatever his mood, he wore the dignity of unforced masculinity not afraid of sentiment.

Music critics have said of Van Cliburn that while many pianists can excite an audience by a flashing performance, it is not Van's dazzling technique—although he has this, too—but his genuinely rare musicianship, his honesty, and his natural affinity for the very soul of great music which has made him one of the finest pianists in the world. Nowhere was this better demonstrated than on the concert stage at Interlochen where his mere presence helped pull the blue-knickered high school musicians up a veritable Mount Everest of accomplishment. When Van played, all eyes in the orchestra were on him in youthful hero worship. But it was the way Van returned their tribute which made the young musicians play their hearts out for him. The entire audience felt the contagion. One jaded non-concert-goer said later, "I don't know Rachmaninoff from chop suey. My wife roped me into this.

All I can say is, it was a thrilling thing to watch. And believe me, when you can still be thrilled by something at my age, it must be something. . . ."

After the concert a reporter from *Newsweek,* notebook in hand, dashed into the camp's news bureau and asked, "Say, who runs this place?"

"Dr. Maddy," someone said.

"Joe Maddy, by *gum!*" someone else corrected.

"No, I mean who *really* runs it," the reporter insisted. "And tell me—this kid in the corduroy pants at the piano, does he play anything besides the *Tschaikowsky Third?*"

Those Maddy Boys . . .

I

BACK in Wellington, Kansas, around the turn of the century, there were times when it seemed doubtful that William Henry Maddy's son Joe would ever amount to anything. Certainly no one could have been outwardly a less likely candidate for "culture," although Joe was exposed to more of it in his early boyhood than most children of pioneer families. His parents were schoolteachers, and were leaders in the cultural life of the community. His mother was a musician and an artist; she did more to further an appreciation of the arts in the frontier town of Wellington than anyone else, and the Maddy home became known for miles around as a gathering place for anyone interested in the arts.

But it took quite a while for this to penetrate young Joe. He was too busy with other pursuits more to his liking. He acquired all the proud boyhood habits of the era: he could roll cigarettes with one hand while riding horseback; he learned to shoot and swear and chew tobacco and raid watermelon patches. It was all part of a boy's normal growing up in those days, but Joe's parents, proud and sensitive people with gentle ways and refined manners, sometimes despaired that *their* son should turn out to be the town's roughneck.

Oh, perhaps he wasn't *really* any rowdier than the other boys; he only seemed so to them.

Joe had a violin before he was five years old, but he also had a habit of hiding the violin behind the family's claw-legged tin bathtub and sneaking off with his brother Harry to find what he regarded as livelier occupation. Joe was small for his age, and Harry was a year and a half older than he. These facts combined to make Joe perhaps a little more obstreperous than his parents thought he should be. Everything Harry did, Joe had to do, too, and sometimes more. In the rough frontier town of Wellington everyone knew Joe and Harry as Those Maddy Boys—not really *bad* boys, just always up to some mischief, and with such nice refined parents, too. . . . When Joe and Harry ran out of the usual boyhood pranks, they invented new ones.

One summer, for example, Joe and Harry and two other boys went on a camping trip for two weeks, with thirty-five cents capital between them. With the money they bought oatmeal and sugar. Everything else they foraged—fish from the rivers, berries and sweet corn from the sun-warmed fields, and an occasional pail of milk from a farmer's cowbarn. They got along very well. What they wanted most, however, was watermelon, for it was watermelon season and how could a camping trip be a success without a nice big ripe melon fresh from the patch?

The boys knew a farmer named Esherman who, according to town gossip, once had raided another farmer's patch for not only one but a whole load of watermelons which he then took into town and sold. Farmer Esherman now had a patch of his own. The boys took a straw vote and agreed that justice was long overdue. They rounded up an old wagon, a pony, and a riding horse. They didn't have a team. The pony and riding horse had never been in harness before, but the boys hitched them to the lumber wagon and started off one evening for Farmer Esherman's watermelon patch.

An eye for an eye, a tooth for a tooth, they decided. So, following Farmer Esherman's example, they helped themselves to not one but a whole wagon load of watermelons. They loaded the melons in gunny-sacks, tied them, and gingerly heaved them into the lumber wagon. With a full creaking load they turned around and started back for camp. Everything had been well planned and the adventure seemed to be going well. Even the horses were performing adequately.

Then the unexpected happened. In turning they hit a rut in the road. The wheels stuck. The horses balked. And Farmer Esherman came out with a shotgun and ordered them to halt. For emphasis he fired a shot in the air. The horses lurched and the wagon started off at top speed, with the outraged farmer close behind, spraying it with bullets.

It was a wild rough ride, with the boys trying to duck both the gunshot and the bouncing melons. They rumbled by a country schoolhouse packed with excited people who happened to be taking part that night in an important episode in Kansas history —the first primary elections held in the state. The schoolhouse was jammed with citizens waiting for the early returns, and when the wagon whizzed by with Farmer Esherman in righteous pursuit, the election night crowd vented its tensions by joining the chase.

Somehow in the wild scramble the boys got back to camp. Joe escaped without a scratch but Harry had a split eyelid and a couple of pellets in his hand, and one of their companions had been peppered by gunshot in his back.

Luckily at daybreak they located another camper nearby who had a medical kit. He was a dentist. It also turned out that he was the son of the Governor of Oklahoma. He was familiar with the spirit of the territory and the uncontrollable urge of young boys during watermelon season. Without asking too many embarrassing questions he smilingly took the boys in, cared for their wounds, and removed the gunshot.

Everyone in Wellington, of course, knew there had been a shooting, but no one ever learned the full story. Nor did anyone ever know that Joe and Harry returned to haunt Farmer Esherman for years afterward. They always came during quail hunting season and they probably scared the farmer half out of his wits, which was just what they meant to do. They would hide out in the plum trees, across the creek from Esherman's land, and wait for him to start plowing his fields. Then, with their Civil War Springfield rifles, they would take pot-shots—not at him but at the field he was plowing. Nothing pleased them more than to watch Farmer Esherman retreat, in a geyser of dust, to his cyclone cellar, probably to brood—they hoped—over his ill-tempered past. Didn't he know he might have killed somebody? And for nothing more serious than stealing watermelons? Well, the Maddy boys felt it their duty to remind him with their annual quail-season "shoots" and at the same time they could, literally, kill two birds with one stone, for they always came home with quail.

Joe and Harry, in fact, were expert shots. They learned about guns at an early age from an older boy who was hired to take care of them one summer while their mother worked to earn money to buy her family a new piano. The young man, a doctor's son, was instructed to supervise the boys while they practiced on their violins for at least one hour a day, and also to teach them to swim. The young man, however, had other ideas about what to teach Joe and Harry. He initiated them into chewing tobacco, smoking, and drinking the local brew—"snake medicine"—

which he filched from his father's supply; he gave them diligent practice in the various ways of handling rifles, shotguns, and pistols; and his version of swimming lessons was to escort the boys to a muddy pond known as Rock Island Creek, toss them into water over their heads, and shout, "Swim or drown!"

Joe Maddy was learning many of the ways of the rough world he was growing up in, but at the same time he was developing qualities that were to stand him in excellent stead throughout his life. He was a born rebel and he learned the stubbornness that goes with rebellion. He could take tough treatment, and he became adept at picking his way through crises.

One night, for example, while he was fetching in the cows, he started to climb through a fence when his twenty-two caliber rifle accidentally went off, sending a bullet through his leg. Bleeding profusely but unwilling to cause disturbance at home, he limped to a nearby farmhouse and got the neighbor to drive him to the doctor. On his return he told his mother that it hadn't amounted to much—he had just been grazed a little, he said, while "fooling around" with his gun. He missed eight weeks of school, but was hobbling around on crutches by the end of the term.

Although younger and much smaller than Harry, physically Joe was the stronger and tougher of the two. His brother, in fact, was a fragile boy, subject to more than his share of childhood illnesses. He had pneumonia five times before he was ten years old. Perhaps because of Harry's frailty, as well as the normal attachment a small boy has for a big brother, Joe followed Harry like a shadow. Wherever Harry went, Joe went too. Whatever Harry had, Joe had to have too, and whatever Harry did, Joe would do as well—with all the dash and daring he could summon.

Neither in his boyhood nor in his adult life could anyone ever tell Joe Maddy that he *couldn't* do something. His "by gum!" spirit was solidly carved out of the rough-and-tumble experiences of childhood. There was, for instance, the year Harry got his first bicycle. Naturally, Joe had to have one too, although his parents felt that he was not really old enough. As soon as Joe learned to ride his bicycle, he took it to the top of a smooth hill that sloped steeply toward the tracks of the Rock Island Railroad. Joe no sooner reached the summit than a train whistled around the bend. It was the 4:16 Kansas City Flyer to Fort Worth, the newest and fastest train on all the windswept prairie.

One of the boys said to Joe, "I bet you can't beat her to the crossing."

The reply was inevitable: "I bet I can!"

Joe was almost to the tracks when a horse and buggy got in his way and he had to swerve around them. He struck a rough spot in the road. The wheels got mixed up, and Joe landed with the bicycle on top of him and the train only a hair's breadth away. He rolled off the track, not forgetting to pull his precious bike with him, and lay on the quivering ground as the Flyer thundered past. The minute the last car cleared the tracks, the horse and buggy that had almost been Joe's undoing came alongside, and Joe, to his dismay, recognized the driver.

It was the town marshal!

Gruff and glowering, he threatened to take Joe to jail. In the mind of a small boy back in Wellington in those days, harsh words from the town marshal were ten times more fearsome than an oncoming train. The marshal was only scolding, of course. He had no intentions of taking the boy to jail. But he thoroughly terrified Joe. For weeks afterward he had sudden attacks of trembling, and his mother, unaware of his experience but seeing that the boy was ill, kept him out of school for the rest of the semester.

Missing school never bothered Joe. The plain truth was that Joe didn't like school, a fact which distressed his parents more and more. They wanted so much for their sons! But they were often at their wits end to know what to do with them. Joe's unruliness, they felt, was having a bad influence on Harry who in spite of his poor health sometimes showed signs of aesthetic leanings—when his rambunctious little brother wasn't around.

Sometimes his mother would shake her head sadly and ask Billy Maddy, "Whatever *is* going to happen to Joe?" And Mr. Maddy would comfort her by saying, "Don't you worry about him. He's just a boy still. He'll turn out all right."

2

Joe was not the first Maddy to make his mark in the world as a high spirited non-conformist. His great great great grandfather James Maddy, humorously known in the Maddy clan as James the First, earned somewhat dubious fame by trying to swim the Shenandoah River with a log chain around his neck. He did it on a bet, and he lost both the bet and his life. James, who was born in Herefordshire, England, was called the First because he was the first Maddy to emigrate to this country, where he served in the army of Virginia under George Washington. He and his wife, Ann Morris Maddy, were strong individualists with the same imperturbable approach to personal goals that later developed in Joe Maddy.

There was a time many years later when Joe Maddy was to recall vividly the family legend of the first Maddy's death. Joe was fishing in Florida from a small motor boat far offshore, when a squall hit and threw him into the sea. The boat floated out of reach and out of sight. "This is it," he thought. "They've always said I was going to sink the camp. If I drown that is certainly what will happen; the camp will go to the bottom with me." Through his mind flashed a picture of that earliest Maddy trying to make it to shore with the log chain around his neck. Somehow the memory seemed frightfully symbolic and Joe was prepared— almost—to give up hope when suddenly out of the sea and out of nowhere appeared the empty little boat, pilotless but its motor still running. It sputtered and chugged straight toward him and then, as though guided by unseen hands, it slowed and circled and came close enough for Joe to climb in. For Joe it was the ulti- mate proof—his music camp couldn't go under; it was unsink- able. From then on whenever anyone dared to mention to him that he was going to "sink the camp," he would tell this story and end it by snapping, "Why did that boat come back for me?"

But his great-great-great grandfather James the First didn't have Joe's luck. His widow, Ann Morris Maddy, was a spunky woman who took her brood of ten children and moved to land on Indian Creek in what later became Monroe County, West Virginia. In settling her husband's estate, it was necessary for her to make frequent trips through the mountains to her original home and she always went on horseback and alone. On one of these trips, after transacting her business, she started home with a considerable amount of money which she hid in a belt under her clothing. On the way she stopped at a mountain settler's house and was invited to spend the night. The settler guessed that she had money. The next morning he gallantly offered to show her a closer way home through the mountains than the regular trail. She accepted the offer. He led her to a lonely place over a ravine. Then turning to her he said he knew she had money and that unless she gave it to him he would throw her over the cliff.

She descended from her horse as if accepting her fate and asked him to turn his back, explaining with feigned modesty that the money was hidden in the top of her stocking. He obligingly turned away, whereupon she made a dash, threw him off balance, hurled him over the cliff, and resumed her journey.

With the blood of such intrepid ancestry running in his veins, it was small wonder that Joe Maddy grew up not knowing how to give in to an obstacle. There was no record of any Maddy ever being subdued by anything less than a log chain around his neck!

Joe's father, William Henry Maddy, was also a man of strong will and definite goals. Many of them he never reached, but he consistently refused to give up. He was the first of the Maddys to show any interest in music. He came to Kansas in 1870 with a shotgun under one arm and a fiddle under the other. He wasn't really a violinist. In his youth he had played the hoedown square dance fiddle but apparently not too well, and he gave it up when he married. His children never heard him play hoedown.

When he first came to Kansas, William Henry Maddy staked out a claim just west of Wellington and planted a cornfield. He lost it in the "grasshopper scourge," as it was called at the time. Undaunted, he planted a peach orchard. He had a fine peach crop, but so did everyone else, and there was no market for his crop. He started a peach drying business but discovered that there was no market for dried peaches either.

It was about this time that people in Wellington were beginning to take notice of a pretty young teacher named Mary Elizabeth Harrington who had just become superintendent of schools. William Henry Maddy was among those who took notice, and he promptly decided that he, too, would like to be a teacher. He applied to the new superintendent for a job and got it. The next year he married her.

From his father's side of the family Joe inherited the fighting instinct that he was to rely upon a great deal in his adult life, and from his artistic mother he inherited a natural affinity for music in spite of his early rebellion against it.

The Harrington family had moved to Kansas from Illinois and settled on a claim southwest of Wellington on the old Chisholm cattle trail leading from Texas to the end of the rail line in Wichita. Mary Elizabeth Harrington had been an outstanding art and music student in school; and as a teacher, artist, musician, and poet it was no wonder that after her marriage to Mr. Maddy she became a leader among the frontier families. She wrote and published two small books of poetry. She led the school and church choirs, sang and played the piano, and gave art lessons in her home. The front parlor of the Maddy home always smelled of paints. She charged a small fee for her lessons and never lacked for pupils.

Many took lessons from her not so much to learn to paint as to start a painting and then have her finish it for them—so they could boast of owning one of her works.

She also did porcelain painting and her intricately decorated table china was much in demand. One of young Joe's first jobs was firing his mother's kerosene kiln. She was still working with paints until the time of her death in 1939. Her last painting was for the Methodist church in Wellington when she was eighty-three.

The Maddy children were born in a little story-and-a-half

house that backed up against the Rock Island track at the north end of town. There was a picket fence around the house, hopefully put there by the Maddys to keep their boys from playing too dangerously close to the trains. Needless to say, the fence did not keep in Harry and Joe; their mother was always having to bring them back off the tracks onto safer ground. Finally, when Joe was six, the family moved to a big twelve room house on North Washington street near the center of town, a location somewhat safer for the boys, and more in keeping with the atmosphere of security and accomplishment that Mr. and Mrs. Maddy hoped would one day penetrate, at least in some small degree, the rough little world in which their young sons were adventuring.

The Maddy home was the first one in Wellington to have plastered walls. It also had an old square piano, a reed organ, and William Maddy's old hoedown fiddle. It was only natural that such a home would become a center for music in the little town. It was several years, however, before Joe and Harry developed any real interest of their own in music.

William Maddy's marriage to the pretty county school superintendent was a turning point in his own professional career. He was much more successful at teaching than at farming. For several years he served as secretary of the school board. Although less talented in the arts than his wife, he encouraged and supported her activities. He also became active in civic affairs, and from time to time was elected to various public offices—county clerk, registrar of deeds, and county treasurer. Later he became cashier of the Farmers' State Bank, a position he held until his death in 1918 at the age of sixty-five. He also was on the bank's board of directors.

But he never completely gave up farming. In those days all

families raised enough produce and livestock to provide for their own needs. As soon as young Joe was old enough, it was his duty to bed down the horses at night, feed and water them during the day, and wash the buggies when they were muddy. The Maddys had a very fine driving horse and two buggies, including a very elegant one with fringe on the top. They also had two cows, and it was Joe's job to clean out the stalls, feed, water, and bed down the cows, and take them to pasture and back. On one of his trips to the pasture he figured out a way to make a little money. He decided that as long as he had to escort his own cows, he might as well take along a couple for the neighbors. He earned fifty cents a month for walking the extra cows.

He also developed into what was possibly the first one-boy dairy in Kansas. After milking the cows, he would peddle the milk to the neighbors from a three- or four-gallon milk can which he wheeled about on a little cart. He learned to dip out the milk in quart measures into pans which the neighbors supplied for this purpose, and his father gave him a percentage of the money he collected. His various business enterprises also included a paper route: he earned a dollar and a half a week delivering the *Wellington Journal*. And he added another twenty-five cents each Saturday by carrying buckets of coal up to a doctor's second floor office.

Harry could not undertake heavy work because of frailty and frequent illness, and sometimes this created a rather awkward family situation. Joe, for instance, would save the money he had earned until he had enough to buy something he wanted. His first purchase was a pony. After he got it, Harry wanted one too. Since he did not have the money, his parents bought one for him. Joe saved more money and bought a big western style saddle with bearskin saddlebags. Harry wanted one too, so his parents got that for him too. Joe saved his money and bought his own buggy; his parents bought one for Harry. In spite of this apparent favoritism, however, the boys got along well together and had a warm affection for one another. Joe simply took it for granted, as did all the Maddy kin, that Harry required special treatment because of his poor health. And the favoritism worked both ways. For if Harry got something first, Joe always made sure that he got the same thing.

This, in fact, was how Joe Maddy got his first violin. Harry had been given a violin at the age of six, and although Joe was only four and a half, he nevertheless demanded a violin just like Harry's. It wasn't that he particularly wanted the instrument, for he didn't like its looks nor the sounds it made, but he had to have it because Harry had one. His parents yielded to his demands.

Little did Joe's father suspect when he placed a violin in Joe's hands that he was wrecking his own dreams for his son's future. Buoyed by his own modest success in the business life of the community, William Maddy began early to think about fitting professions for both his boys. Harry would be a banker; Joe a lawyer. He gave them violins only to stimulate in them an appreciation of music—and because their mother was eager to have them start on some form of training in music as soon as they were old enough. Music, their father agreed, would be a good antidote to the rough frontier ways of Wellington, and for the next few years he had no reason to suspect that the instruments would do even this much for the boys.

At that stage of their lives violins were just about the last thing in the world that either Joe or Harry really wanted. They weren't interested in music; they wouldn't practice. Their progress was far less than rapid, so far less, in fact, that it was not only disappointing but embarrassing to their talented mother. Even their violin teacher, Theodore Huuse, was ready to give up. He was getting nowhere with the Maddy boys until finally, in desperation, he developed the idea of trying them on simple violin duets. In later years this would not have been considered an earthshaking idea, but then, in the early nineteen hundreds, instrumental group music instruction was virtually unknown. Students were taught separately. No one had ever thought of teaching two or more youngsters together.

To Joe's surprise when he started playing violin duets with Harry, he found that music wasn't work, it was fun. And the course of Joe Maddy's life was set. It was Joe Maddy who in later years was to develop the basic methods of teaching instrumental group music, teaching methods that were to become a standard part of the American school curriculum, and these methods had their roots back in Kansas, when "those Maddy boys," who didn't like music or school or practicing the violin, started playing duets together.

3

Violin duets did not immediately change the Maddy boys from rowdies to earnest music students. They still had some growing up to do. However, when their violin teacher Theodore Huuse organized the Wellington Boys' Band in 1900, Joe and Harry were among the first to join. School bands and orchestras were unheard of in those days but "boys' bands" had begun mushrooming throughout the Midwest. The Wellington Boys' Band was one of the first in Kansas. For fifty cents a month a boy could select an instrument that appealed to him, join the band, and, theoretically, receive enough instruction to learn to play. The violin, of course, was not a band instrument so Joe started on the piccolo, one that cost two dollars and fifty cents, while Harry chose the cornet.

The band started off with great enthusiasm. Sixty boys signed up. At the end of three months all but twenty had dropped out. Among those left were Joe and Harry.

The first dollar the boys ever earned from their music was for playing in a Fourth of July celebration in Jefferson, Oklahoma— but they never personally collected. The twenty piece band had been promised twenty dollars—a dollar for each player—and expenses for the engagement. They took an early morning train down to Jefferson, were treated to a sandwich at noon, and got back to Wellington about midnight. But the twenty dollars they had been promised went instead into a uniform fund and the boys got none of it.

The band, however, blossomed out in bright new gold and green uniforms. They learned to play six tunes rather well, and soon became one of the most popular "kid" bands, as they were called then, in the Midwest. They were in great demand at political rallies, particularly during the McKinley election campaign, and usually traveled about the countryside in carry-alls, vehicles similar to trucks but drawn by a team of horses. It took about two hours to travel ten miles, but the boys enjoyed the trips, the horseplay and the horn-tooting—and also the election cigars the politicians passed out to them. The cigars usually made them sick, but that was part of the fun.

Joe was the youngest and smallest boy in the band, and his piccolo was the smallest instrument. It was only natural that he was teased by the older and bigger boys whose favorite trick was to sneak up behind him and bounce the piccolo out of his mouth. He was debating whether to change to another instrument when he had an experience that helped him make up his mind.

On this occasion the band had to play an engagement about a mile outside of town, and, as was customary, the boys marched back, carrying their instruments. It was a long walk, especially for the young bass drummer, whose burden was heavier than most. Because Joe's little piccolo would fit into his pocket, he was assigned the chore of carrying the front end of the bass drum. He decided then and there that the piccolo, though small, was not the instrument for a small boy. He put an end to lugging the drummer's gear by switching to the clarinet.

It is difficult to trace any movement to its absolute source because beginnings often seem so insignificant at the time. But Joe Maddy's first experience with a summer music camp dates all the way back to 1900 when Theodore Huuse took his boy musicians for a week's camping trip in a scanty grove called Drury. It was near a muddy creek about a day's buggy ride, twenty miles, from Wellington. The following summer Huuse took them again on a music camping trip in the same spot for two weeks. They did manage to have daily rehearsals and to put on a concert in the neighboring village of South Haven, but Mr. Huuse eventually decided it wasn't worth it. Harry and Joe Maddy were the ringleaders in what appeared to be a concentrated effort to drive the band director out of his mind. They spent most of their time doing a lot of fishing, a lot of swimming, a lot of horseplay, and very little practicing. And they delighted in tormenting Mr. Huuse by putting turtles and snakes in his bed. Because of the

Maddy boys' disruptive influence on the others, Huuse ordered them to go home. They refused. Musically the Wellington music camp was a flop, largely because of Harry and Joe Maddy. Huuse had no recourse but to disband the group. Eventually he also gave up the boys' band.

When, twenty-eight years later, a University of Michigan professor named Joe Maddy started a music camp in northern Michigan that was to become recognized as the largest and most noted in the world, how was anyone to know that this same Joe Maddy had contributed to the downfall of what possibly was really the first music camp in America? And if any of his own boy and girl musicians had been even half as ornery as "those Maddy boys" in Wellington, Kansas, he would have shipped them home immediately. . . .

By the time Joe was twelve years old, in spite of his unruliness, he was good enough to play clarinet with the grown-ups in the Wellington Town Band and under the sharp eye of that impressive assembly of adults, his behavior also began to improve. He soon learned that he couldn't be as capricious with the men—in numbers—as he had been with Mr. Huuse.

The Maddy boys' disciplinary problems, however, were not the only factor in Huuse's decision to give up the boys' band. Huuse was principally a violin teacher, and his real interest was in orchestral and chamber music. From the time he started Joe and Harry on violin duets he had recognized their talent, and in spite of his frustrations, he continued to encourage it.

He finally suggested to their parents that they take up viola and cello to make a family string quartet which he felt might inspire the boys to be more serious about their music and—he secretly hoped—have a calming effect on their behavior. The idea worked. Mrs. Maddy bought a viola. Mr. Maddy bought a cello, and though William Maddy had the least training in music of anyone in his family, he developed a great affection for his instrument, practiced faithfully, and continued studying and playing as long as he lived. Because he started late, he never became really proficient, but his enthusiasm probably had much to do with molding his sons' careers.

Mrs. Maddy, the real music enthusiast of the family, did not do as well on the viola as she had on the piano. But to everyone's surprise, Joe promptly became enchanted with the tones of the viola, and his mother was delighted to turn it over to him. He eagerly and quickly learned to read the viola clef, and for the first time it began to look as if both Joe and Harry were beginning to settle down and practice in earnest. At that time there were not more than half a dozen violas in the State of Kansas, so young Joe Maddy was immediately in demand wherever a viola player was needed.

The first orchestra in Wellington, and one of the first in the territory, developed in the Maddy home with the family quartet as its nucleus: Mrs. Maddy at the piano; Mr. Maddy playing the cello; Harry, the violin; and Joe, the viola. Anyone else with an instrument was welcome to join them, and Sunday afternoon orchestra practice at the Maddy home soon became a tradition in Wellington. They didn't consider themselves a formal organization; their little orchestra didn't even have a name. Anybody could come. If a player was sick or out of town, or if he moved from Wellington, there was always someone else to take his place.

Word of the little orchestra soon spread to other communities, and before long out-of-town families were dropping in on Sundays for practice at the Maddy home. The constantly changing personnel didn't make any difference because the orchestra never gave a concert anyway; they played just for the fun of it, and because Mr. and Mrs. Maddy had the belief, which they infectiously imparted to others, that music was good for people and gave them something they could receive in no other way.

Some days there would be only eight or ten at orchestra practice. More often there would be twenty or more. But no matter how few or how many, Theodore Huuse always came over to conduct. He would always lead off at the start with his violin, and then beat time with his foot on one of Mrs. Maddy's pie-pans on the floor. This was a necessary part of all rehearsals, because no one—least of all Conductor Huuse himself—could keep time to the waving of his violin bow. The rhythmic beat had to be clearly and noisily defined.

Mr. Huuse may not have been the world's greatest conductor but frontier Wellington was getting its first dose of "culture" and some of it finally was beginning to rub off in earnest on Joe Maddy!

4

Along with the Maddy boys' increasing interest in music came an unexpected and disappointing development in the Maddy household—their increasing disinterest in school. It was quite easy now to find excuses to shirk their lessons. Joe and Harry were in great demand and appeared anywhere they were asked to play—in bands, orchestras, ensemble groups, quartets, duets, and as soloists.

Their parents, although pleased by the boys' development in the field of music, were chagrined that they should show such a complete disregard for a formal education. It was only natural to think that children whose parents were teachers, whose mother had been county superintendent of schools and whose father was secretary of the school board, should understand the importance of school. And even though a college education was rare in those days, it was something Mr. and Mrs. Maddy expected and especially wanted for their sons.

They were to be sorely disappointed. Joe managed to skim through grade school, graduating half a year behind the rest of his class. He dropped out of high school after only one semester. Harry had dropped out the year before.

It wasn't that the boys couldn't do well enough in school when they put their minds to it, for they could. Once, for instance, when Joe was in the fifth grade, his teacher told the students they could go home as soon as they listed the names of all the bones in the human body. Joe swiftly memorized the names, wrote them down, and was the first out of the room—not because of any intense interest in anatomy but because it was a sunny day and he was anxious to get down to the creek and go swimming.

In high school Joe did well in algebra but, again, not because he liked it. The teacher was new and from Yale, and Joe and a couple of other students soon discovered he was keeping just about a day's assignment in advance of his class. The boys took mischievous delight in getting ahead of him. They studied their textbooks two or three assignments past where they were supposed to be and came up with their own questions which he couldn't answer but they could. In the process, they learned a lot of algebra.

Joe divided his interest between music and love for nature and the outdoors. From early childhood he delighted in hunting, fishing, and trapping; and, ironically, two of his early music teachers inadvertently nearly led him away from the fine arts and into the field of natural science. There was a period in Joe's young life when he wasn't sure whether he wanted to be a musician, an astronomer, or a taxidermist.

Theodore Huuse, who had once been a civil engineer, had accumulated considerable knowledge of the earth and skies from working outdoors. His special interest was astronomy. Once when he was at the Maddy home instructing the boys, the violin lessons ran late and Mrs. Maddy invited him to stay for dinner and overnight. He slept upstairs on the screened porch with Joe and Harry. The warm summer sky was filled with stars, and Huuse began pointing out planets and constellations and reciting the corresponding legends from mythology. Joe kept Huuse awake half the night with questions. The next day, with some of the earnings he had saved from his odd jobs, he bought a book on astronomy and virtually memorized it.

It was about this same time that Joe's father decided to raise chickens. He bought an incubator and a brooder and went into the chicken business. It became Joe's job to take care of the chickens, gather the eggs, and clean out the chickenhouses. When Joe discovered that the neighborhood cats were breaking into the brooder at night and feasting on newborn chicks, he decided to take care of the cats and combine the chore with his newly developed enthusiasm for astronomy. At night he would lie atop the chickenhouse, his rifle beside him. He bought all the books he could find on astronomy, eagerly devouring every word, so that at night on top of the chickenhouse, between firing at cats, he

could study the skies. Among the happiest memories of Joe
Maddy's boyhood were these hours when he lay solemnly awake
all night long, guarding the chickens and watching the stars.

Another teacher who greatly influenced Joe's early years was
Charles Johnson, who taught science in the Wellington school
and who was also assistant director of the Boys' Band. Johnson
played the alto horn and many times had to direct the band rehearsals when Theodore Huuse was not available. He was a great
hunter and fisherman and an avid taxidermist. He gave instruction in taxidermy to any student who wanted to learn to mount
animals, and Joe became one of his favorite proteges.

Joe's proudest taxidermy feat was the mounting of an iguana,
known in the territory as the "Chinese dragon." The monster, a
member of a circus troupe appearing in Wellington, died during
the engagement and its body was dumped in a weed patch, where
it remained for several days before Mr. Johnson and Joe learned
about it and decided they would mount it—a rather formidable
task, considering its size and the length of time since its demise.

They hauled the five-foot long lizard to the basement of the
school, sprinkled formaldehyde all around, constructed a body
the same shape, then carefully removed the reptile's discolored
skin, cured it, and applied it to their mount. Never having seen
a live iguana, and not knowing from the dead lizard what color
it should be, they could only guess from pictures how it should
look. The finished product, a gruesome greenish creature with
big prickly spines on its back understandably attracted a great
deal of attention.

One of the main features of the Sumner County High School
was Mr. Johnson's museum, a large room built especially to
house and display the birds and animals that he and his students

mounted. For many years the "Chinese dragon," mounted by Charles E. Johnson and Joe Maddy, was the pride of the museum.

In later years, when the school building was torn down, most of the mounts were moved to the basement of the First National Bank in Wellington, and this showroom eventually became known as the Maddy Museum because so many of the mounts had been done by Joe. The Maddy Museum became a center of civic pride. The town didn't yet have a public library but at least it could boast a museum, one of the first in Kansas.

The Maddy Museum, with Joe's birds and animals and his famous "Chinese dragon," was the delight of Wellington citizens long after Joe had established himself in other, quite different pursuits. In fact the museum continued in existence until only a few years ago, when the decrepit old bank building was torn down and replaced by a new one.

In his youthful adventure with taxidermy Joe again bought as many books as he could find and afford, including the prodigious four-volume set of *Lydecker's Natural History*. And again, as with his astronomy books, he eagerly devoured every word. He became an expert on birds and was aghast to discover in Lydecker's authoritative descriptions an omission which to a boy brought up in Kansas amounted to a monumental oversight. In all four volumes there wasn't a single mention of one of the most common birds around Wellington—the meadowlark. Joe lost faith in men who presumed to be authorities. At seventy he was still calling Lydecker a scoundrel for overlooking the meadowlark.

Young Joe's enthusiasm for taxidermy waned only after he learned from an unhappy experience that it was not compatible with music. Once when he was preparing to mount a deer head he somehow made a mistake in his chemical mounting mixture.

One by one, over a period of several weeks, all his fingernails dropped off. And during most of this time he was out of commission as a musician. It was his final fling as a taxidermist.

In spite of Joe's extra-curricular interests in astronomy and taxidermy, he knew pretty well by the time he entered high school that he wanted to study music—if for no other reason than that Harry had decided on music. In those days music was not included in the public school curriculum. Then, as in the years since, those who wanted an early start in serious training had to get it by private instruction outside of school hours or in specialized private music schools.

The nearest place to Wellington where Harry and Joe could go for the training they wanted was the Wichita College of Music, thirty miles away. When the boys entered high school they asked the school principal for two half-days a week in which to go to Wichita and study music. This was out of the question, they were told. School was school, eight hours a day, and no youngster could skip any of it just to take music lessons. The boys offered to make up their school work during evenings or on week-ends, but the principal was adamant. In his mind, as in the minds of many school administrators, music was a frill, and even the fact that the boys' father was then serving as secretary of the school board and that both parents were civic leaders made no difference. Joe and Harry could not be permitted to miss school to study music. The result was inevitable. Harry quit school in the ninth grade to go to Wichita. Joe followed the next year, after completing only one semester of his first year in high school.

It was a bewildering and bittersweet blow to their parents, who had so painstakingly opened the door for them but who never had dreamed that their sons would give up high school for

94 ·

music. They regarded the arts as a means of enrichment, but certainly not a substitute for education. They sensed too that careers in music would be precarious, offering little hope for the security they dreamed of for their sons.

But the Maddy boys went off to Wichita with the blessings of their gentle parents, who could only quietly pray that somehow everything would turn out all right.

The Pettit Girls

I

IN MACON, Missouri, around the turn of the century, Mrs. Agnes Pettit, a music teacher, and her three daughters were attracting almost as much attention by their musical attainments as the Maddy family was in Wellington, Kansas.

Mrs. Pettit played the piano and string bass. She had organized and directed the Episcopal church choir, and generally held a role similar to Mrs. Maddy's in Wellington as a patron of the arts. Two of Mrs. Pettit's daughters, Ailene and Gladys, were twins. Ailene played the violin; Gladys played the piano and sang. Fay, the youngest and prettiest of the Pettit girls, had been given her first piccolo at about the same time as little Joe Maddy was learning to play his. Fay also played the flute, and she gave readings, recitations, and impressions. Ailene was the best musician of the three, but Fay had the liveliest personality. Her impersonations had that true gift of typical American humor—wit without malice, fun with no desire to hurt. She delighted her audiences.

As soon as Ailene and Gladys were old enough, their mother sent them to live with their grandparents in Wichita so they could take private lessons from the instructors at the Wichita College of Music. During vacations Mrs. Pettit and Fay would visit them.

It was Harry Maddy who met the Pettit girls first. Joe was

still in school in Wellington. Harry and Aileen had the same violin teacher in Wichita, Theodore Lindberg, who was head of the music college. Harry and Aileen soon began finding all kinds of excuses to practice violin duets together. Then once during a week-end at home Harry casually mentioned the Pettit family to his father. Mrs. Pettit was a fine music teacher, he said. He hinted that possibly his father could engage Mrs. Pettit to teach in Wellington.

At about the same time Ailene Pettit was writing her mother in Macon, Missouri, that Harry Maddy's father was on the school board in Wellington, Kansas.

"Wouldn't it be nice," she asked, "if you could get a teaching position in Wellington so we could all be closer together?"

Mrs. Pettit applied for the position and got it.

Everyone knew by now that there was more than violin duets between Ailene and Harry. "But just wait till you see Ailene's little sister," Harry told Joe.

Joe was still taking cues from Harry. If Harry's girl was a Pettit girl, naturally there had to be a Pettit girl for Joe too.

Joe Maddy and Fay Pettit met in the early spring of 1907. She was thirteen, and he was fifteen. When Mrs. Pettit and the girls moved to Wellington, the Maddys invited them to stay in their home until they found a house to rent. And of course, came Sunday and the Pettits joined the Maddys' afternoon of orchestra practice. Between them they could play enough instruments to form their own orchestra even if no one else came.

The two families became very close. They organized an orchestra in the Christian church, with Mrs. Pettit directing. Harry and Ailene played violin, and Joe switched from viola to clarinet so he could sit next to Fay, playing flute. He didn't consider her nearly as proficient on either the flute or the piccolo as he was. Every time they played the *Lustpiel Overture,* he had to help her with her flute part. Fay was the youngest of the group and her musical training was the sketchiest. She had taken only six piccolo lessons—back in Macon—from a clothing merchant who was in the town band. She had had no flute lessons. Joe had to admit that Harry was right about Fay as the *girl* for him—but as a *musician,* well. . . . He had to spend hours with her, helping her practice. For one thing she couldn't even yet play the piccolo part of *Stars and Stripes Forever* and teaching her the part was a role that young Joe enjoyed very much.

With Joe's help Fay learned to play piccolo well enough to join the Wellington Girls' Band when it was organized a few months later. It was the first all-girl band in the country. Joe had been the youngest and smallest member of the Wellington Boys' Band. Fay was the youngest and prettiest in the girls' band.

During that first summer together the Maddy and Pettit families also organized their own music camp. It was held at Drury, in the same pleasant countryside where a few years earlier the obstreperous antics of Joe and Harry Maddy had broken up the music camp of the Wellington Boys' Band. The Maddy-Pettit music camp had fewer musicians than the boys' band; it was confined to the two families. But it was launched on a far grander scale, with a full size old carnival tent to house both families and all their musical instruments, including even the Maddys' old upright piano.

It took two covered wagons and a little one-horse spring wagon to transport all the equipment—the spacious old tent, the hammocks, the supplies, the piano and other musical instruments, not to mention the Maddys and Pettits with their broods—out to their prairie campsite for two weeks of music and outdoor living.

The Maddy-Pettit music camp turned out to be somewhat more successful than the boys' band camp—possibly because of the Pettit girls. At least Harry and Joe deported themselves in more gentlemanly manner than on previous camping trips. They were attentive during rehearsals, and between sessions they sat around in the old-fashioned hammocks doing nothing more disrupting to camp life than holding hands with Ailene and Fay—which turned out to be not disrupting at all.

All the Maddy and Pettit children helped with the chores. Harry and Ailene and Joe and Fay took turns driving the spring wagon to Caldwell, seven miles away, to buy groceries. It always turned into an all-day trip. Ordinarily it shouldn't have been but with two budding family romances it usually was.

The days were happy and long and sparkling, and filled with music. There was something about discovering music together with Ailene and Fay that seemed to bring a new steadiness to the Maddy boys. It may have been just that Joe and Harry were growing up; or it may have been the deepening that comes sometimes to young boys and girls at their first encounter with love. But the fact was that they were experiencing for the first time the sense of adventure and discovery in music and the inherent balance of freedom and discipline which music inspires. No one could ever really discipline Joe Maddy, in the ordinary sense. Years later when he shocked the music world by establishing his own co-educational summer music camp, there were many who warned him that it would be impossible to discipline boys and girls together at a summer camp. Joe Maddy knew better. He knew the trust he could place in young boys and girls who loved music together. He knew it because of those days back in Kansas, when a little two-family music camp at a place called Drury gave life a new meaning, when music filled the days and nights with enchantment. The spirit of Dr. Joe Maddy's Interlochen had its beginnings in the simplicity and happiness of that summer camping venture of the Maddy and Pettit families in Wellington in the early nineteen hundreds.

The *Wellington Daily News* began to carry items in its news and society columns about the musical activities of both the Maddy and Pettit families. Their concerts usually consisted of light music that was typical of the period. One program printed in the *Daily News* of September tenth, nineteen seven, included the following:

Hungarian Lustspiel and *Light Cavalry* overtures by the orchestra; *Military Fantasie,* violin solo by Joe Maddy; *Give Me Thine Eyes,* soprano solo by Gladys Pettit; *Romance,* violin solo by Ailene Pettit; *Annie Lauri,* vocal trio, Gladys, Ailene and Mrs. Agnes Pettit; *Home, Sweet Home,* violin duet, Harry and Joe Maddy; *Spring's Awakening,* contralto solo, Mrs. Pettit; *Speckle Sheik* and *A Confidence,* readings by Fay Pettit; *Hungarian Dance,* violin solo by Harry Maddy.

And the following year, one of the major events of the social season in Wellington was an affair headlined as "Mrs. Maddy's Musicale," which rated a great deal of space in community newspapers for miles around.

In glowing words the reports described Mrs. Maddy as an excellent entertainer and "one of the foremost patrons of the arts" and her musicale as "one of the most prominent and highly successful society events which has taken place in Wellington for a long time." A hundred and twenty-five invitations had been issued. Punch was offered to the guests during intermission, and at the conclusion of the program, strawberries, ice cream and cake were served, "after which some time was spent in social conversation." And in addition to local talent, including of course a violin duet by Harry and Joe Maddy, Mrs. Maddy's musicale presented several guest artists from the Wichita College of Music.

By now Joe had followed Harry to Wichita. There the Maddy boys and the Pettit twins were beginning to receive recognition at the same time their mothers were gaining prominence as "foremost patrons of the arts" throughout the entire Wichita-Wellington area. The two towns were close enough so that the Pettit and Maddy children could get home for week-ends. Their parents often attended concerts in Wichita, and their musicales in Wellington began to feature more and more visiting artists from Wichita, thus bringing added distinction to Wellington.

2

Fay was the last of the two-family musical clan to study at Wichita, and by the time she got there, Joe and Harry had moved on to Minneapolis and her sisters were out on the Chautauqua circuit. In the Pettit family, it was Fay who had to follow in the footsteps of two older sisters, just as Joe followed Harry.

In Wichita in the local world of music, Ailene Pettit had gained almost as prominent a reputation as Harry Maddy. She and Harry were already engaged, and Joe and Fay were planning to be engaged soon. Maybe next summer when he came home from Minneapolis? It was a long way between Wichita and Minneapolis, and a big jump between the Wellington Girls' Band and the Minneapolis Symphony Orchestra, where Joe and Harry now were. But they would all be back home in Wellington next summer and things would work out. Meantime, Fay could hardly wait for her turn to go to the Wichita College of Music. She wanted to study flute. She was determined to be as good a musician as her sisters—and Joe Maddy.

Fay was underestimating her talents. Managers of Chautauqua and Lyceum circuits had heard about the Pettit girls and their music. Gladys and Ailene already had been engaged to go on the road, with separate companies. And about the time Fay was getting all set to go to Wichita to study, she was invited, sight unseen, to join the Redpath Lyceum and Chautauqua Company in Chicago as a flute and piccolo player and reader for a company known as The Anitas, organized by Harry Harrison. She was sent to Winona Lake, Indiana, where she was to receive training with the company before going on the road.

When Fay arrived in Chicago with her old five dollar piccolo and her old Myer system flute she was told, "You can't play on those things in my company."

"Well, they're all I have," Fay said, "so I'll just have to go back home. Anyway, I'd rather go to the Wichita College of Music."

Harrison liked her spunk and her personality. He was also sure the fiery little blond girl had potentially profitable musical talent. He called the Wurlitzer Company and made arrangements for Fay to buy a Boehm system flute and piccolo, costing about two hundred and twenty-five dollars and pay for them at the rate of ten dollars a week out of her thirty-five dollar weekly salary from his company.

Fay was an immediate hit with her readings. At the end of the season Horner decided that the three Pettit girls should be performing together instead of in separate companies, so he formed a group called the "Military Girls" with Fay, Gladys, and Ailene Pettit as featured entertainers.

That winter, after her first stint with a road company, Fay finally did get to the Wichita College of Music, as a flute student. Theodore Lindberg and his wife who had founded the school, had an affinity for young people, especially those who showed promise, and they took a liking to Fay as they had to the older Pettit students.

All the musical brood had had to work for their board and room, and for money to pay for their music lessons. But when they ran out of money, the Lindbergs continued to sponsor them until they were in funds again. The Lindbergs knew that Fay was still making payments on her flute and piccolo. They permitted her to live in their school dormitory rent free.

"Music is more important than money," they told Fay. "You can pay us back someday if you're working and can afford it. But don't worry about it now."

It wasn't long, though, before Fay was earning enough to pay back every penny she owed the Lindbergs.

While in school she earned her board by playing in a trio at a place then called the English Inn. Both the trio and the dinner music were Fay's idea. The English Inn had the finest cooks in all of Wichita. Fay decided if she had to work for her meals, she might as well try for the best food in town. She convinced the Inn's proprietor that his business would improve if he had music during the dinner hour. Then she recruited a piano student and a cellist to form a trio with her flute. They were an immediate success. Business did improve. The girls earned only their meals but they ate well. By the end of the school year, when Fay joined her sisters in the Chautauqua circuit's "Military Girls," the English Inn had both satisfied Fay's appetite and improved her abilities with the flute and piccolo.

The "Military Girls" were a versatile group. They appeared in one act as a fife and drum corps in military drills; in another called *Just Off the Ranch,* they wore the costume of the plains and sang ballads of frontier life. In another act they were featured in a six piece orchestra. The Redpath advance promotion described the "Military Girls" as: "Six refined, attractive girls who know the Lyceum perfectly well, and are thoroughly trained and tuned to it. . . . There is one reader in the company, and most of the girls are individual soloists."

But it was the three Pettit girls who got star billing—Fay as reader and flutist, Gladys as soprano and pianist, and Ailene as violinist. Little Fay was the pet of the troupe. Small, graceful, blond, and sparkling with spirit and fun, she brought down the house with her readings.

Meanwhile, during the same years that Fay Pettit was out captivating audiences all over the Midwest as a star of the Chautauqua circuit, young Joe Maddy was struggling to get a firm foothold in the world of serious music as the youngest member of the Minneapolis Symphony Orchestra.

Summers when Joe and Harry came home to Wellington, the Pettit girls were out on the road. Home ties were strong; their families were closely united. Mrs. Pettit was as proud of the Maddy boys as she was of her own girls, and Mr. and Mrs. Maddy looked on Fay and Ailene and Gladys as part of their family. When any of them came home there were family concerts, musicales, quartets, quintets, and just the sheer delight of playing music together. Nevertheless, the Maddy boys and the Pettit girls were growing up and away from one another. Music had once drawn them together. Now it was leading them in opposite directions.

Had the world of symphony music changed Joe and Harry? Or had the "Military Girls" changed Ailene and Fay?

In the years just before World War I, the "Military Girls" became a top entertainment attraction. Its program combined the nostalgia of early Americana with the fervor of patriotism then sweeping the country. One of their perennial hits was a song by Carrie Jacobs Bond, *The Captain of the Broomstick Cavalry*. It went in part:

> Say, how would you like to be a soldier?
> A soldier in a uniform of blue,
> With a cap and cape so bright,
> Buttons shined like stars at night,
> And a pocket full of bullets,
> Goodness me!
>
> Mamma says I really am her soldier,
> And the bravest soldier that she ever knew,
> From the foe I'll never run,
> You will find me with my gun,
> I'm the Captain of the Broomstick Cavalry. . . .

In this number, as in most of them, little Fay was always the center of attention, with her expressive blue eyes, her bouncing curls, her vivacious personality.

During one of their tours the "Military Girls" made a stopover in Minneapolis. The Pettit sisters looked up Joe and Harry

and they all went tobogganing together. The romance between
Harry and Ailene was turning into no more than a friendly
brother and sister affection. With Joe and Fay, however, there
was something that lingered from the enchantment of first love.
Something—but it was not quite the same—like playing in the
same key but with a chord missing. In some ways Fay had more
than caught up with Joe. Maybe she wasn't as good a musician.
But she was earning more money. She was better known. Indeed,
she was almost famous. She was traveling, seeing the world,
having fun. She was gay and popular and radiantly beautiful—
much too beautiful, Joe thought, to be won by any mere viola
player who was at the foot of his section.

Even to get into a major symphony orchestra at his age was an
achievement, but Joe was not satisfied. Fay noticed that he seemed
quiet, reserved, and intense. And there was a strange new look
in his eyes, a look that seemed to flick on and off between a
burning restlessness and some far-away dream.

He was now twenty-one and too earnest about music to appreciate the Broomstick Cavalry, even with Fay as the lead. She was
nineteen, too young to understand what had changed Joe—how
could he be *that* serious about music? He would probably wind
up being a music teacher or a college professor. How dull. . . .

It was the old, old story of young people growing apart without being able to comprehend one another. To both it brought
heartache and years of painful remembering as they went their
own separate ways, both of them proud, stubborn, high-spirited,
rebellious. But they both knew, as they had always known since
that first summer at Drury, that they belonged together. . . .

Later, in the swift enchanted summers of Interlochen there
were many who marveled at the stamina and devotion of a pretty

blue-eyed little woman who seemed always to be there, close by, if Joe Maddy needed her. With her red yarn and knitting needles, no one would guess that she was once the vivacious little blond star of the Lyceum circuit while Joe Maddy in silent anguish played last chair viola in the Minneapolis Symphony Orchestra. The years, the young heartaches, the little misunderstandings could never dim the luster of dreams they once shared. It seemed as natural as the wing-beat of a prairie meadowlark that Fay Pettit and Joe Maddy would one day pick up the thread of a first love spun from music and song and a one-horse spring wagon in Kansas.

For Music—The Long Lean Years...

JOE MADDY had followed his brother Harry to the Wichita College of Music. It was perhaps a mark of the quality of both the Maddy boys as musicians that although neither had finished even a ninth grade academic course, the college president, Theodore Lindberg, accepted them as special students. As musicians they were already far more advanced than the school's college-age students.

For some time Theodore Lindberg had been anxious to have a faculty string quartet but he didn't have enough faculty. There was one violin teacher, Mr. Lindberg himself, and one cello teacher. Mrs. Lindberg had attempted to play the viola but she couldn't quite master the instrument. Lindberg decided to have his faculty quartet anyway, with the Maddy brothers as its other two members. Next to Lindberg, Harry was the outstanding violinist in Wichita. And Joe was the only other person besides Mrs. Lindberg who even owned a viola.

Viola players are sometimes regarded as mere second-rate violinists who couldn't make the grade; and the viola probably never would win any popularity contest among musical instruments. But Joe Maddy had inherited from his mother an affection for the viola, and he kept it as his major instrument later, not only because he liked it better than the violin, but because its scarcity created a demand. It was a wise choice, for the viola opened the doors he couldn't have reached with violin, clarinet, or piccolo.

Lindberg's faculty quartet was the best group of musicians Joe had played in so far. Joe wasn't yet sixteen, but the quartet gave frequent concerts in Wichita and nearby towns and was recognized as one of the finest in the state.

One day Wendell Heighton, manager of the Minneapolis Symphony Orchestra, came to see the head of the music school about booking the Minneapolis Symphony in Wichita. Heighton walked in during a faculty quartet rehearsal. He was astonished to find two young boys playing a difficult piece with the two top faculty directors—and doing very well.

Lindberg introduced Joe and Harry. Heighton complimented them and asked, "Why don't you boys come to Minneapolis and try out for the symphony?"

"How much will it cost us?" asked Joe.

Heighton laughed and assured them that if they could pass the tests and were accepted, the orchestra would pay them. They could actually earn their living playing in the orchestra. To the boys, this idea was overwhelming.

The Maddy boys had never heard a symphony orchestra. They knew nothing about it. A full symphony in those days was a rarity. Harry and Joe couldn't even imagine how one might sound. The radio, the microphone, even the phonograph had not yet put in their appearance. The only phonograph record Joe and Harry had ever heard was one made by John Philip Sousa with a seven-piece band playing into a megaphone.

A symphony orchestra?

Professor Lindberg explained to the boys that the Minneapolis

Symphony was even bigger than the Wichita Philharmonic, which rehearsed once a week. The Minneapolis Orchestra rehearsed three hours a day, every day.

The Maddy boys were appalled. Where could they find enough music to practice three hours a day? Their knowledge of orchestral works extended no further than *William Tell* and a few other overtures. But when the Minneapolis Symphony Orchestra appeared in Wichita a few months later, the die was cast for the Maddy boys. For the first time Joe and Harry heard Tschaikowsky's *Nutcracker Suite* and other music that sounded different from anything they had ever heard before. It was a new world. They could hardly wait to get to Minneapolis and try out for this magic wonderland where such music was played regularly.

Harry got into the orchestra first. Much to Joe's disappointment—and surprise—there were no vacancies in the viola section, but he was promised the first one that came along. Meanwhile, he passed his examination for membership in the musicians' union* where he was accepted with the understanding that Wendell Heighton from the Minneapolis Symphony would be his sponsor, because Joe was not yet of age.

Joe immediately started viola lessons with the first violist in the symphony. He practiced ten hours a day, and the orchestra's conductor, Emil Oberhoffer, permitted him to listen to all rehearsals.

The Minneapolis symphony season of 1909 marked an epoch in the history of that six year old orchestra, one of America's first complete symphonies—and in the lives of young Harry and Joe Maddy, who were exposed for the first time to the music of Bee-

* American Federation of Musicians.

thoven, Berlioz, and Brahms, and to such distinguished guest soloists as Ernestine Schumann-Heink, Mischa Elman, and Fritz Kreisler—names that were to illuminate for all time the pages of musical history.

While waiting for a seat in the symphony, Joe Maddy lost no time in further broadening his enchanted horizons. He was invited to play viola with the University of Minnesota Orchestra, which rehearsed once a week. It was a non-paying job, but excellent experience. He also played in theaters, hotels, park bands, dance bands, and chamber music ensembles.

All the money Joe earned he invested in more music lessons. While Harry concentrated only on violin, Joe was learning every instrument he could get his fingers on—bassoon, French horn, oboe, English horn. He gained most proficiency as a violinist, violist, and clarinetist. He played clarinet in bands and some orchestras, viola in string quartets and orchestra, and violin usually as a soloist.

And when the vacancy came in the symphony he was ready. For his try-out, Conductor Oberhoffer gave him one of the most exacting tests for viola, an intricate passage from the third movement of Tschaikowsky's *Fifth.* Joe had thought he would be grilled on the viola clef, and he had purposely put himself through a rigorous round of preparation, including the prodigious task of hand-copying a whole book of forty études for violin, transposing them from violin to viola, and writing the names of all the notes under each bar. When he finished he knew the viola clef very well. And when Oberhoffer tossed him the test from Tschaikowsky's *Fifth,* he played it without a halt.

Joe was seventeen when he got into the Minneapolis Symphony Orchestra. He received a magnificent salary of ten dollars a week, which amounted to apprenticeship pay. But the next year his salary was more than doubled—twenty-eight dollars, big money in those days. And he still had time for other paying jobs now and then.

Joe was not the most accomplished violist in the orchestra, but he could out-play some of the others in his section. Conductor Oberhoffer frequently required each player to perform difficult passages alone to keep them alert and to show what each could do. Joe practiced diligently in hopes of receiving recognition or promotion, and time and again he demonstrated that he could play better than the other viola players, but he was kept in the last half of the section because he was the youngest member of the orchestra. It was this discrimination that later led Joe Maddy to throw all positions open to all members of his orchestras at Interlochen, so that anybody, regardless of age, was allowed to challenge in weekly competitions for the next higher ranking chair.

In Minneapolis most of the symphony members were German and spoke only German. Young Joe began studying German, thinking this might help his status. He became quite proficient in the language but still no promotion: he stayed in the back of the section. This, perhaps more than anything else, also implanted in Joe his ambition to be a conductor so he could make his own rules. Up to then he had been busy just learning to be a musician. At his age, wanting to be a conductor was like reaching for the moon.

But Joe Maddy's blood was at the boiling point, and inwardly he made a resolute vow: "Someday I'm going to be a conductor and have my own orchestra. I'll hold tryouts regularly and promote players who deserve promotion according to their ability— not according to age or length of service." Only a few years were to pass before Joe would have his first chance to make good his self-imposed pledge, thereby beginning a revolution of a segment of American orchestral tradition that had its roots in foreign imports in the first place. Joe was still to pioneer his system of competitive tryouts for promotions based on ability which later·became standard practice in high school and college orchestras, as well as in many professional groups.

After four years in the Minneapolis Symphony without promotion, Joe tried out for the post of Assistant Concertmaster in the St. Paul Symphony—and got it. Although he would be with a smaller orchestra, the position in St. Paul offered a great deal more prestige than that of sixth-chair violist in Minneapolis, and a considerably higher salary too.

Joe resigned from the Minneapolis Symphony to go to St. Paul. But about the middle of summer it was announced that the St. Paul Orchestra was to be disbanded and would not function at all during the coming season. The war in Europe had begun, the country was readying its industrial might to help the Allies, and orchestras were not part of the mood of the times.

Joe was finally offered a job in Illinois at Peoria's Orpheum Theater. He accepted. He was not in a position to choose, and the post promised to be a steady one. There was also the fact that playing clarinet in a vaudeville house would be valuable experience. The Orpheum Theater Orchestra in Peoria was known as one of the finest.

The work was a challenge, especially for a clarinetist, since about half the music had to be transposed, and Joe had to improvise quickly and often. More important to Joe, it would pay for food and rent while he waited for pupils for the private lessons he was offering. He hung out his shingle—and he waited. Maybe he wasn't a good teacher; maybe Peorians just weren't interested. In any case, young Joe's first venture in teaching could not be called a success. On the other hand he became so proficient at his Orpheum Theater job that it soon lost its challenge for him.

He was in Peoria only three months. Just when he was beginning to get most discouraged, two offers came, unexpectedly, and both on the same day. One was for the position of director and violinist of a small theater orchestra in his home town of Wellington. The other was an offer from John Philip Sousa to become solo clarinetist with his famous band. It was not an easy decision to make. The Sousa offer meant a big reputation as a clarinetist. But the Wellington job would give him a chance to try his hand at conducting.

He went home to Wellington—and for the first few weeks he wished he hadn't. After his first rehearsal he was positive that he was a complete failure as a conductor. From earliest childhood Joe had followed Harry like a shadow. He wondered whether he had been so conditioned that he could never be a leader— whether he was doomed forever to be a follower.

It took all the courage Joe Maddy could muster to stand up before the ten players for his first public appearance as conductor in the small-town theater orchestra in Wellington. He would have given anything to be back in the easy security of his job as a clarinetist in Peoria's Orpheum Theater. Most of his orchestra members were much older than he, fellow townspeople and old friends of his family. The theater owner had once played string bass in the Maddys' informal Sunday ensembles. He finally brought his string bass over and played in the theater orchestra to give Joe moral support.

The players, perhaps sensing Joe's mood, began calling him

"Professor," and somehow the title helped him gain confidence. Gradually Joe got into his stride as a full-fledged orchestra conductor—and leader.

There was no such thing in those days as formal instruction in how to become a conductor. Joe had no way of obtaining instruction on how to set a tempo or lead an orchestra. He had to devise his own system, and he did. There was no drummer in the group so he rigged up a bass drum with a beater and cymbal, which he worked with his feet while playing the violin. He soon got so he could lead the orchestra with his violin, play the melody and all the cues with whatever instruments were missing, and put in all the cymbal crashes and bangs to coincide perfectly with the silent motion picture, precisely at the moment such sound effects were needed. It was quite an achievement!

After two or three months he was thoroughly at home, and even though it was only on a small-town scale, the experience was invaluable. It changed Joe Maddy, Harry's little brother, from a follower to a leader. Harry meanwhile escaped the restlessness that haunted his younger brother. He had none of Joe's physical indestructibility, nor was he obsessed with the spirit of challenge and wild endeavor as Joe was. He was happy in his niche as a violinist with the Minneapolis Symphony Orchestra, and he was content to remain there all his life until his retirement a few years ago.

2

Joe's parents were becoming steadily more prominent in Wellington. They were proud of Joe and anxious to help him in every possible way. They suggested that he organize a community orchestra, chorus, and band for a music festival in the spring.

Joe Maddy's music festival in May of 1915 was an epoch making event on the Kansas prairie. He led a chorus, band, and orchestra totaling two hundred performers through the *Messiah,* the *William Tell Overture,* and Schubert's *Unfinished Symphony.* It was the first time a Wellington orchestra had ever played a complete symphony, the first time a Wellington chorus had performed the *Messiah.* Joe had hired guest soloists from the Wichita College of Music to assure the success of the festival, and his brother Harry came home from Minneapolis to play in the orchestra.

Joe was too frightened and self-conscious when he mounted the podium even to raise a baton. Instead, he led his performers with his violin bow. Nevertheless, the event attracted attention throughout the state and put both Wellington and Joe Maddy in the limelight.

The head of the music department at the Kansas State Teachers' College at Emporia wrote to Joe congratulating him on the development of musical activity in that part of the state.

The newspapers praised him "for giving Wellington an opportunity to hear good music. . . ."

Joe was able to leave his theater job and start a small music school on the wave of favorable attention. He called it the Wellington Conservatory of Music. It had three teachers, including himself. He directed a concert orchestra composed of the best talent in Wellington and introduced his home town to some of the fine music which had so deeply moved him when he had played with the Minneapolis Symphony. Joe's orchestra had the enthusiastic backing of the townspeople, who by now regarded their distinguished young citizen and his violin as far superior to any out-of-town talent that might come their way.

In promoting one of Joe's concerts, a benefit for the Belgian Relief Fund, the *Wellington Daily News,* in a story headlined, "Wellington's Popular Orchestra Will Aid Valiant Relief," pointed out editorially, "This concert should not be missed by any person. Each season we go out and sometimes pay exorbitant prices to hear some long haired man play the fiddle or some man or woman from a cheap vaudeville circuit try to play something or sing something.

"Right here, let us say that this concert will be as good as any and better than many, of the number we have heard on the circuits. Professor Joe Maddy who is leader of the orchestra was formerly with the Minneapolis Symphony Orchestra. He will have in his instrumentation some of the leading talent of Wellington. And we have some good musicians. . . . Mr. Maddy has arranged a very high class program for this concert. . . . So let's all go and show the home folk that we appreciate not only their music but their . . . spirit in helping a starved nation."

The Belgian Relief Fund was richer by nearly a hundred dollars from the concert. It was a sum in those days that would buy a great deal of food. And young "Professor" Maddy had made another discovery: it gave him a special kind of pleasure to use music to help people and to spread a message. This was a discovery that would last and increase all the years of his life. Music became a mission, an obsession with Joe—and no one knew better than he how much more there was yet to learn about it.

Joe's success in Wellington led to a position as Director of the Wichita Falls College of Music and Art in Wichita Falls, Texas.

To Joe it seemed a big name and a big school, for it offered him a guarantee of eleven hundred dollars for eleven months' work as school director, and as teacher of violin, viola, cello, string bass, and wind instruments. To his disappointment, however, he found that Wichita Falls had far less cultivated tastes than his own native Wellington. There was very little interest in music, and the College of Music and Art turned out to be a small and not very successful private school, owned by a woman who taught "voice culture."

But Joe soon noted that the Wichita Falls High School was just across the street from the little music "college" and had choral music but no instrumental accompaniment. There was little or no instrumental music in any high school in those days. The only high school orchestra Joe had heard or knew about was a small beginning orchestra in Minneapolis.

He offered to start an orchestra at the Wichita Falls High School, if he could be permitted to use the auditorium stage when it was not filled by other activities. Joe furnished the music, the music stands, and his service, and he finally established a small orchestra among the students. It was an exciting development for everyone in town, including Joe. It never occurred to him that schools would someday pay teachers for directing orchestras.

He also started a children's band in the small town of Burkburnet, about thirty miles from Wichita Falls. Burkburnet later became famous throughout Texas for its rich oil wells. It was just a small town then, however, with all the inevitable financial problems. Its children's band held rehearsals in a defunct hotel. Joe came from Wichita Falls once a week for rehearsals and to teach his pupils. He gave them lessons in the little hotel's abandoned dining room.

This was his first experience with group instruction for all instruments, and it taught him a great deal. He had to write all the music for the students because suitable beginning instrumental music was at that period totally unavailable. One of the most important things he learned in his entire teaching career came while teaching the Burkburnet band members clarinet and saxophone.

He would show them how to place their fingers on the instruments. Then he would quiz them—how many fingers to place down for the notes in a certain tune.

They would say, "Oh, yes, three." Or "two." Or, "two sharp" —not C sharp, or G sharp.

From this Joe began to mark their fingerings on a note by simply putting three if there were three fingers down, two if there were two; and if any of the tones was sharped, he simply put a sharp after the finger number—for example, "3 #." There was nothing more logical, but apparently no one had ever yet thought of it for beginning instrumentalists.

In Wichita Falls Joe had to duplicate what he had done in Wellington. He organized a symphony orchestra. The instrumentation was so weak that he had to substitute baritone saxophones for cellos, but as always he was undaunted. He called it the Wichita Falls Symphony Orchestra and began giving concerts. He also organized a chorus and band and started to prepare a music festival similar to the one he had put on in Wellington.

The Wichita Falls Festival could not be nearly as elaborate, however. Joe had only a thirty piece orchestra and seventy voices in the choir. But Wichita Falls hailed its Music Festival as "sensational" and heaped praise on Joe Maddy, the "star of the program," for giving the city "a taste of good music." In true

Texas spirit the local citizenry, whether they knew good music or not, made much of the fact that with its Festival, Wichita Falls now had the distinction of being "the first city in the State to give Handel's great production, the *Messiah,* and carry it through successfully."

Joe's experience in Wichita Falls, especially with his high school pupils and younger classes in group instrumental instruction, helped both to crystallize his professional ambition and to show him how to overcome his difficulties in achieving it. He knew by now that he loved to teach, and that introducing young people to music was fully as important to him as performing himself. He wanted first of all to have a large, good high school orchestra that would be a credit to him and to all who took part in it. And he wanted to develop and test in this orchestra some of the ideas that had come to him from his own orchestral experience.

He wanted, for example, a group that could test his idea of competitive tryouts for promotions, the plan that had been haunting him ever since his own discouragement in the Minneapolis Symphony. He wanted more than choral music in schools. He wanted school children to have instruments, to play in school bands and orchestras. He wanted to develop a system of class teaching of all instruments, which would be more economical for the students than private lessons, and would at the same time provide them with the incentive and background to perform in bands and orchestras. At the time there were no instrumental music *classes* anywhere that Joe knew of, except one called the "violin method" for violin students which was being tried on an experimental basis in Boston.

There was one big drawback to Joe's ambition. He was not officially qualified—either musically or academically.

Fortunately, he was aware only of his deficiencies in music. If he had known that his own lack of academic education was about to catch up with him, he probably never would have conceived the notion that music in the schools could be his life's work.

As a performer, he had mastered the violin, viola, and clarinet well enough to be assured of always finding work. And with the Minneapolis Symphony he had learned enough about other instruments perhaps to manage to teach them. But that was not what he wanted. It was not his nature to settle for half measures. He determined to learn more, for example, about the oboe and bassoon, two of the most difficult instruments. And he needed to know more about theory, composition, and conducting.

Joe gave up his post in Texas and moved to Chicago for the purpose of preparing himself for teaching in such a way that he would be able to launch a band and orchestra program in America's school systems. It simply did not occur to him that with less than a ninth grade education this was—as they might have said back in Wellington—"quite a hunk of mountain" he had picked to climb.

There was one thing about Joe Maddy that always intrigued those who knew him over the years: part of his genius stemmed from never knowing when he was licked.

Joe Meets the Jazz Age

I

JOE was startled when he got to Chicago to find that he and the jazz age had arrived in the city almost simultaneously.

He had expected to earn his living while studying by playing violin, viola, or clarinet in some good orchestra. But it turned out that no one was interested in the violin, viola, or clarinet; no one wanted concert, symphony, or chamber music. The country was now in the middle of the greatest war in history. As part of its mood, the entire population appeared to have gone mad over jazz music.

Dance bands were frantic for saxophone players, who were in short supply, while Joe's stomach went empty and his shoes wore thinner as he searched for concert work. He had never heard jazz before he came to Chicago, and when he did hear it he didn't like it.

Monday was the big day at the headquarters of the Chicago Musicians' Union. There all musicians seeking employment and the contractors seeking musicians would assemble weekly, and someone would call out the names of players needed for jobs available that week.

One day at union headquarters Joe met a friend from Minneapolis who introduced him to a high union official who inquired if he could play saxophone. In desperation, Joe said, "Yes," thinking that on the basis of his clarinet experience he could probably learn enough in a week or so to hold down a job. He assumed he would have that much time before starting work.

The union official turned him over to a contractor who asked, "What kind of sax do you play?"

"Tenor," Joe's friend replied for him.

"Can you transpose?" asked the contractor.

"Oh, yes," Joe replied vaguely, conscious of his thinning shoes and empty stomach.

"Can you fake?"

Joe wasn't sure what the word meant, but he said, "Yes."

"Can you play cello parts?"

"Yes." Of this at least Joe was fairly certain.

"Okay," said the contractor. "Meet me this evening at five-thirty at the Northwestern Station. We play at Highland Park tonight."

Joe didn't even have a saxophone. He barely had time to rush over to Lyon and Healy, take a tenor sax out on approval—wrapped in newspapers because they had no cases in stock—then dash to his northside YMCA room to change into a rented tuxedo.

Joe had taught saxophone, after a fashion, but he had never played it. On his job that night, when the cello parts in bass clef were passed to him, he was in despair. Nevertheless, by guesswork and ear, he began picking out a few notes that seemed to suit the melody. When he was off key he just bluffed along softly so no one could hear.

Somehow by the end of the dinner hour he had learned a few things about improvising, and when the dance music started, with the same pieces played over and over again, he was able to play in tune without looking at the score. With each new tune he did a little more improvising by ear, secretly pleased with his progress as a professional saxophonist. But when the dance ended at two in the morning, he quickly folded his music, picked up his instrument, and left, assuming that at the very least he would be thrown out of the Chicago union for incompetence.

On the train home the dance band director came over and asked Joe if he would like to work for him regularly. Joe was astonished. Then on reflection he decided that this was really no compliment to him. The band must simply be no good—so inept that the director didn't know a shoddy performance when he heard one.

But on Monday, booking day at union headquarters, Joe walked in and heard his name being called out again and again. Everyone wanted him. He was dumbfounded. Over the weekend he had acquired a reputation as one of the best saxophone players in Chicago.

Well, Joe thought grimly, at least he would be eating again until something better came along. He was soon booked into the Edgewater Beach hotel, one of the most desirable engagements in the city.

One offshoot of the jazz era was that many fine clarinet players had been thrown out of work. The saxophone had replaced the clarinet. And although clarinetists could have learned the saxophone without too much difficulty, most of them didn't want to. The saxophone was looked on as a low-brow instrument unfit for any but musical illiterates; and most clarinet players would rather shovel snow than touch a saxophone. At the same time jazz directors wanted nothing to do with the clarinet. That instrument, they felt, was too high-brow for popular appeal and not suitable for jazz music.

Joe felt sorry for the unemployed clarinetists who, he knew, could have done as well as he did on the saxophone, or better. And besides, as a serious musician and a clarinetist he did not think too highly of the saxophone either, though he was earning his living—and a good one—with it. One evening as he left for his Edgewater Beach dance job, he put his clarinet in his tenor sax case, and when the band leader wasn't looking he pulled it out and let loose with a cacophony of screeches and squawks. The director was enraged. He probably would have fired Joe on the spot but for one thing—the dancers went wild over it. They demanded more. And more.

Jazz clarinet became the rage. And Joe Maddy, who wanted to teach school children Tschaikowsky, suddenly found himself the most popular jazz artist in Chicago!

Joe now had his choice of the highest paying dance jobs, and he got extra pay for doubling on two instruments. And thanks to him, out-of-work clarinetists were back in business again with jazz bands. Word spread rapidly that the way to get "in" around Chicago was to know this fellow Joe Maddy.

One morning boarding the "L" train with his tenor saxophone Joe bumped into a man carrying what he recognized as an alto saxophone case. They introduced themselves. The man's name was Isham Jones. He had just arrived in Chicago from Saginaw, Michigan, and was looking for a job. Joe found him a place in the same band he worked in, and thus began one of the best known early jazz sax teams, Jones and Maddy. Joe discovered that the alto sax could do things his tenor sax couldn't do, though he became quite an expert with the glissando. The two complemented each other, and at the height of the jazz era the Jones and Maddy sax duo was in great demand.

Some years later when Joe was teaching in Los Angeles, Isham Jones and his band came to town. Isham offered Joe a place in the band with a substantial salary, plus a share in his record royalties. It would have been a lucrative opportunity but by then Joe was on his way with his real vocation—as a teacher. And Isham Jones was well embarked toward becoming one of the great figures in American jazz.

In Chicago Joe's pockets now were jingling, his shoes were new and his stomach comfortable, but he hated his work. He could feel no pride in being known as one of the country's best jazz artists. His one consolation was in the fact that jazz was beginning to pay off in something more important than dollars. His original purpose in coming to Chicago had been to study serious music. And serious musicians were finally beginning to take notice of him. Harry Diamond, Chicago's best violin teacher at the time, was giving him violin lessons in exchange for Joe's services as a teacher of wind instruments at the Metropolitan Conservatory of Music.

And at the Columbia School of Music, Ludwig Becker gave Joe lessons in violin in exchange for lessons in instrumentation from Joe. No one would take money from Joe; in fact some offered him jobs. He organized six string quartets, one meeting each day of the week; and for almost two years he spent his time in Chicago playing serious music during the day and jazz music at night. For several months he played clarinet, saxophone, and even banjo!—at the Terrace Garden of the Morrison Hotel, which featured ice skating and a floor show.

He had tried to enlist in the Army and had been turned down. And he was becoming more and more discouraged with the monotony of making a living in the world of jazz. Somehow he must get back into teaching. But how?

In the spring of 1918 the Minneapolis Symphony Orchestra came to Chicago to play at the North Shore Music Festival in Evanston. And with it came Wendell Heighton, the same manager who had sponsored Joe in the Minneapolis Symphony. The symphony now had only ninety regular members, and Heighton turned over to Joe the job of hiring thirty-five extra players for the Evanston engagement. One requirement was that all should be former members of the orchestra now living in Chicago. Joe of course assigned himself to viola, and during the entire festival he was seen about frequently in company with members of the Minneapolis Symphony, including the manager.

This raised his status considerably with educators and those in the music field who had regarded him as only a jazz musician. Joe had long been registered with a teachers' agency in Chicago, but had been turned down time after time because he lacked a college education. One evening after the symphony concert the head of the teachers' agency approached him and asked if he would be interested in a position in Rochester, New York, as a "Supervisor of Instrumental Music." The post was the first of its kind in the country. It had only recently been created and was not yet filled.

The agent told Joe that Rochester wanted a man who could

teach *all* orchestral instruments and lead two high school orchestras—if there was such a person. Joe assured him there was, and
promptly applied. The teachers' agency highly recommended
him, not on the basis of his reputation as a versatile performer of
jazz, but as a member of the Minneapolis Symphony Orchestra—
which had actually played in Evanston only one week. Nevertheless Joe got the job. He was to begin work in the fall.

With the summer before him, he accepted an engagement to
play in Kansas City's Electric Park with a vaudeville show, in
which Orpheum Circuit performers were learning and preparing
their acts for the next season. It was work that not only paid well
but held a new challenge, for Joe was hired not only as a player
but also as an arranger.

Electric Park was the summer proving ground for vaudeville
artists, a place where acts were reworked and tested on local
audiences. It was Joe's task to do all musical arrangements and
orchestrations. Often he made two or three orchestrations a day,
to be played the same night. Sometimes an actor would merely
sing or whistle a tune for Joe to write down and have ready for
the orchestra by evening. Sometimes the piano player would jot
down a melody for the actors, and Joe would work out harmony
and orchestration.

Although Joe's enforced career in jazz was giving him an understanding and appreciation of the jazz form, one thing he never
learned to bear with any ease was the monotony of limited melody, recurring over and over. At Electric Park he deliberately
created variations and counter melodies to relieve the numbing
reiteration characteristic of the period. One day he was handed a
simple little tune which, when it was played that night with Joe's
orchestration, took the town and then the country by storm. It

was first called *The Trombone Jazz*. It became one of the most popular of all jazz band dance tunes under another name— *Wabash Blues*.

Joe was becoming an expert at improvisation, a talent that was to prove of great help to him in orchestration later, despite his distaste for jazz. Besides doing the arrangements for the Electric Park vaudeville acts, Joe also played violin, viola, clarinet, saxophone and banjo with the orchestra. The musicians' union in Kansas City required that he be paid full union scale for each instrument, plus extra pay for arranging. Joe was making big money.

And he was spending every spare moment studying and practicing the bassoon and oboe, and writing out exercises for teaching all instruments in preparation for his school job in Rochester in the fall.

2

On Saturday mornings in the autumn of 1918 a group of ragged youngsters could be seen making the rounds of pawnshops in Rochester. Their feet were wrapped in burlap; they were too poor to afford shoes. But their eyes were bright with excitement as the "professor" who was herding them bargained with the pawnbroker inside. Sometimes their eyes filled with tears as the "professor," after talking the price down to five dollars, gently placed in their hands a battered violin and urged them on to the next pawnshop.

In the development of music in Rochester, a city that was to become recognized as one of America's great musical centers, it was a significant role that was played by that Saturday morning

Pied Piper who stripped all the pawnshops of every violin that sold for less than twenty-five dollars in order to give lessons free to slum children who couldn't afford even shoes.

When Joe Maddy accepted the job as Rochester's Supervisor of Instrumental Music, the first such position created in any American school system, he was told that the Board of Education would buy fifteen thousand dollars worth of instruments for use in the classes he was to organize. He was disappointed to find that actually the fifteen thousand dollars did not exist; the Board of Education had been counting on private donations to provide the money, and the donations had failed to materialize.

A few children had their own instruments, but these were limited to violins, drums, trumpets, and saxophones. Hundreds of children from the city's poorest families were begging to get into the free music classes, but they had no instruments. Most of them wanted violins.

When Joe arrived in Rochester he found two small high school orchestras numbering about twenty players each. They rehearsed one evening a week after school, and without school credit. There were no bands and no instrument classes. He took a poll to find out how many pupils were interested in forming bands and orchestras, and how many had instruments of their own. Then in a few weeks every boy and girl in Rochester who wanted a musical instrument had one.

Joe had no difficulty organizing his classes, though his largest ones were in violin and drum. In his violin classes it seemed logical enough to him to add an occasional viola, cello or bass, and teach all the instruments in one group. It was far more practical and economical than trying to establish separate classes for each instrument, though no one had attempted it before. Joe's chief problem was the lack of any published music for such classroom instruction. He had to write his own.

He spent evenings and week-ends in the office of the Board of Education, laboriously turning the mimeographing machine to make copies of material for his classes. Note by note, he wrote out each part, marking the bowings and fingerings for all instruments. He would spend the week teaching, conducting, and drilling the students on their lessons, then start over with new material for the following week. He had not, of course, counted on having to prepare his own teaching material. It was an exhausting, time consuming task. Nevertheless, though he didn't realize it at the time, the experience was laying the groundwork for his first important published work, the *Universal Teacher,** which is still widely used as a basic textbook in beginning music classes, and is generally recognized as the first practical system for teaching instrumental music in numerically acceptable school classes.

Joe Maddy's disappointment in Rochester's Board of Education for not having a music instrument fund was minor compared to the shock to school officials when they learned, shortly after he arrived, that their new Supervisor of Music did not have a high school diploma. He had not been asked about this when he applied. The requirement was that he be able to play and teach all instruments. He had demonstrated satisfactorily that he could do this, and it probably had never occurred to anyone that "Professor" Maddy had any but the most complete formal schooling. The Board found itself with a serious dilemma. The State of New York required at least a high school diploma for granting a teaching certificate. And no one could be permitted to teach without one.

In consternation the Board debated what to do with their prob-

* Published 1922.

lem "Professor" and finally sent him to see Dr. Rush Rhees, then the President of the University of Rochester. They had a pleasant half-hour visit. When Dr. Rhees indicated that the interview was at an end, Joe asked, "When do I take my examination?"

"You've just had it," said Dr. Rhees.

On the basis of the interview, Joe received a life certificate to teach music in New York State without a high school diploma.

Meanwhile Joe was making as good an impression on Rochester's professional musicians as he had on school officials. Less than a week after he arrived, the director of the Municipal Band invited him to join the band for a week's performance at a community festival. Joe agreed and asked which instrument the director wanted him to play.

"Didn't I hear a bassoon just before you came to the phone?" the director asked.

"Yes," said Joe hesitantly.

"Bring your bassoon," said the band director.

The bassoon was the last instrument Joe would have chosen to play in public. He knew less about it than any instrument, and in fact he had been trying to figure out how to reach some of the high notes when he was called to the telephone. At least he did know more about the bassoon than he knew about the saxophone when he found himself in a similar predicament in Chicago. But the bassoon was an infinitely more difficult instrument.

The band music for the horse show, which was part of the festival, was written mostly in flat keys, and flat keys are difficult for an inexperienced bassoonist. Joe struggled along, hoping his mistakes would not be too noticeable in an eighty piece band.

About the middle of the evening the conductor announced that some of the musicians were to go inside and play for an indoor ballet; the others were to remain outdoors in the band. He called the names of about a dozen players for the indoor performance. As he heard the word "Maddy," Joe felt a short moment of apprehension. He couldn't hide his mistakes in a small group of players. But luck was with him. The music for the ballet turned out to be Mozart and other classical numbers—all in sharps, and easy on the bassoon. Joe came through in fine shape, thus enhancing his reputation with Rochester's professional musicians.

Meanwhile, Joe had his ever recurrent problem—money. The harder he looked for talented youngsters among the poor of the town, the more of them he found. And none could afford to buy their own instruments. Somehow the funds going into the ready hands of Rochester's pawnbrokers and second hand dealers had to be supplemented. Joe signed up with Rochester's musicians' union, and as soon as the word spread that he could play jazz, he was busy almost every night.

In those days a normal evening's remuneration for playing a dance was four or five dollars. Joe sometimes came away with forty dollars on a single night, playing several engagements the same evening. Sometimes he played in one place after another all night long. As long as he could stay awake, he didn't feel he should turn down an offer. His school salary was two thousand dollars for the year, and he was always at the bottom of his pocket. He didn't mind playing jazz at night. By day he was doing what he wanted to do—teaching music to school children.

Joe was also gaining a steadily wider respect as a musician. He was invited to join the Rochester Symphony Orchestra, the forerunner of the Rochester Philharmonic. The orchestra rehearsed once a week. For public concerts, professional musicians had to be imported from New York City to supplement the instrumentation. Joe filled in wherever needed, depending on the number of musicians and the kind of instruments supplied from New York. Sometimes he played oboe, sometimes string bass, sometimes bassoon or English horn. He became almost as highly regarded as an oboist and English horn player in Rochester as he had been known as a jazz player in Chicago.

His experience with the oboe, however, had ironic repercussions. Joe's reputation as a teacher initiating a new and significant experiment with group instruction in grade and high schools was beginning to attract attention throughout the country. But as might be expected when a young newcomer rises so quickly to prominence with a radically new approach, not all the attention was complimentary. Joe was startled one day to find himself the target of an attack charging that he was contributing to insanity by teaching children to play the oboe.

"Everyone knows that playing the oboe drives people crazy," the reports went.

Apparently it was all right if Joe wanted to drive himself crazy by playing the oboe, but he shouldn't inflict the oboe on children.

Joe went right on playing the oboe, even more than ever, to disprove the argument, but the absurd charge made inroads nevertheless. Parents began to worry. Children who had started to play the oboe gave it up. Soon Joe couldn't get a single pupil in Rochester who would touch the oboe.

His beginning violin classes, however, were flourishing and by January, Joe considered the progress of the children so remarkable that he mustered the courage to invite George Eastman, head of the Kodak company, to visit the school.

Eastman was an admirer of music but not a musician. He ad-

mitted that he scarcely knew *The Star Spangled Banner* from
Yankee Doodle and had to be told which one to stand up for. But
he was interested in all the arts as a mark of America's increasing
maturity. In his own home Eastman had a fine organ, and he also
employed a string quartet to play during the dinner hour when
he had guests. His first violinist, in fact, was taking oboe lessons
from Joe Maddy in exchange for violin lessons. Obviously that
was one musician who did not share the superstition that the
oboe led to insanity!

Eastman came to visit one of Joe's classes. He was frankly
amazed, and he said so.

This gave Joe more courage. For the first time he did something which was deeply antipathetic to his nature but which he
was to repeat many times during his life; he boldly composed a
letter to George Eastman asking for fifteen thousand dollars for
musical instruments. It was Joe Maddy's first experience at begging for money so children could have music. He promised East
man that he would produce a hundred piece band by Memorial
Day if he could have the instruments by March first. Eastman
sent the money, and Joe produced an even bigger band than he
had promised, a hundred and fifty enthusiastic young players, all
in brand new uniforms—Joe had talked a Rochester clothing
manufacturer into donating them.

The Memorial Day parade led by Joe Maddy's new student
band was a big event in Rochester that year. George Eastman was
impressed, and he invited Joe to bring the whole group to his
home in the evening for an oyster stew party.

The band marched to the Eastman mansion in the early darkness. Joe rigged up a long baton with a flashlight attached to one end and led the parade waving the light back and forth so the players could see to keep time. He soon sensed an off-beat tempo and was chagrined to find his excited young players keeping time not with his torchlight baton but with the bass drum, which is customary with marching bands. Joe's musicianship didn't yet include much experience with marching bands. He didn't know about drum majors then.

More important to him at the time was the fact that he had made a good impression on George Eastman, who became more and more interested in Joe Maddy and in music in general. Eastman decided to have a thorough survey made of the city's potential as a music center. Will Earhart, a man who was gaining prominence as Director of Music in the Pittsburgh schools, was invited to Rochester to make a survey of the city's possibilities. And it was Joe Maddy whom Eastman chose to guide Earhart on his tour.

Earhart took a liking to his young guide, and together they discussed the possibilities for the community. They began to envision what seemed to them both at the time a hope too high to achieve—a great music school and symphony orchestra, permanently endowed, in the city of Rochester.

Earhart sent his report to George Eastman. And it was this report, with its recommendations and outlines for the future, that influenced Eastman to underwrite one of America's greatest early ventures in the field of music, the famous Eastman School of Music and the Rochester Philharmonic Orchestra.

Joe Maddy, the young musical upstart and "crazy" oboist, took no credit for the project. By the time it got under way he was happily off to other important projects. His immediate personal goal was to create more opportunities for more school children to play in bands and orchestras.

Though Joe developed school music in Rochester until by the end of his first year he had four assistants, his experiences with the school system were not always smooth.

The Superintendent of Schools once told him that although he was a fine musician and teacher, he lacked administrative and organizational ability. Instead of sulking over the criticism, Joe turned it to advantage. He made up his mind to overcome this weakness. Seven years later, after a demonstration of his National High School Orchestra for a convention of school superintendents in Dallas, the Rochester superintendent came up to shake hands with him and said, "I take back what I said to you several years ago." Joe considered that one of his greatest compliments. He also continued his efforts in self improvement until he became as well known for his organizational ability as his musicianship. Rochester was a milestone in Joe's stubborn progress toward his dream.

In his own mind, however, Joe later decided that he had made one of the most glaring errors of his career in Rochester, and he spent the rest of his life regretting it. His mistake, he felt, was that he did not establish in-school classes with school credit when the instruments given through Mr. Eastman's generosity became available for Rochester school children. In later years Joe had no hesitation in admitting, "I just didn't have sense enough to think about it at the time." The fact was that the idea apparently had never occurred to anyone, for at that time there were no music classes offered for credit in any American public schools. With Mr. Eastman's interest and support, Joe had a golden opportunity to suggest and establish schooltime classes with credit.

The School Board would have met any condition Eastman might have chosen to name. All Joe would have had to do would have been to tell Eastman what to ask for, but it simply did not occur to him. Joe's self blame was perhaps exaggerated. It was true that he didn't think of it, but then neither did anyone else at the time.

The unfortunate result, however, was that many years passed before music classes with formal credit became common in America's schools. Joe finally established the music-for-credit system in Richmond, whence it spread slowly into the public schools of the nation. However, he was never able to stop thinking about the thousands of children who were deprived of music in those early years simply because, as he put it, he was too dumb to know it could be done. After that, his eye for possible opportunity became sharper than ever.

In Rochester, Joe was involved in another incident that made a lasting impression on him.

During his program of developing music in the schools, the Seashore Musical Aptitude Tests were in vogue, as they still are in some educational systems. Joe knew nothing about the tests, and with only a ninth grade education, he did not feel that he was in a position to question them. School officials felt there should be some testing procedure to serve as a basis for lending school-owned instruments, so Joe accepted the Seashore tests as a matter of course.

Then one day a ten year old Italian boy named Vincent Capasso came to him and asked to play the French horn. Joe duly put him through the usual musical aptitude test, and the child failed. According to the test, Vincent had absolutely no sense of pitch differences, the most important qualification for attempting the French horn.

Joe tried as gently as possible to turn Vincent away from the horn to another instrument. The boy, however, was insistent. He wanted to learn the French horn, nothing else. His seriousness impressed Joe. Moreover, French horns were going begging. Most youngsters preferred other kinds of instruments. The French horn was difficult to learn. Joe finally gave in and let the boy have the horn, expecting to see him bring it back within a few weeks. Instead, Vincent kept it, and to Joe's great surprise did quite well—in spite of the Seashore tests.

When Joe left Rochester, he lost track of little Vincent Capasso —until about twenty years later. Then one evening, during a brief stop-over in Cincinnati, he attended a concert by the Cincinnati Symphony Orchestra. During intermission he went backstage to say "Hello" to some of the players he knew. He was immediately pounced on by a fine looking young man whose face he could not place.

"Hi, there, Professor!" he said. "Remember me? I'm Vincent Capasso."

He was playing first horn in the Cincinnati Symphony Orchestra.

Joe filed a cryptic mental memo to himself on the inanity of musical aptitude tests. Later he was to devise his own methods of exploring talent in younger children. At Interlochen, the newcomers simply try their skills at any and as many instruments as they wish until they decide which one they want to learn to play.

Richmond, Indiana

I

WILL EARHART, the Pittsburgh music educator who made the Rochester survey for George Eastman, had learned to respect young Joe Maddy. He felt that in the two years Joe spent in Rochester he had done more for music than most men could have done in ten.

During one of Earhart's visits to Rochester he invited Joe to sit down with him in the park and "talk a bit."

He told him about the little town in Indiana where he had spent the happiest years of his life building up a music program that had since deteriorated for lack of leadership. Earhart had left Richmond for a more substantial post in Pittsburgh, but he still had a warm attachment to Richmond. He recognized in Joe Maddy a special affection for music and for young people, and an unusual knack for bringing the two together, which he frankly told Joe was better suited to a smaller community such as Richmond than a city like Rochester.

"You have the ability to bring to music something inspired, imaginative, creative," he said. "And you're the only man I've ever met who could bring back what we had started to build up in Richmond—the symphony orchestra, the choral society, the school music program." In the ten years since he had been gone, he added, the music program in Richmond had sunk to a low ebb. It needed re-awakening.

Joe was pleased at the compliment from such an important man as Earhart. But he was hesitant. The job entailed supervising all music, choral as well as instrumental.

"I don't know the first thing about vocal music," he said.

"You can learn," said Earhart. "If you go to Richmond and make a success of the instrumental program, they will wait for you to learn how to manage the vocal part. I'll guarantee that."

Earhart also told Joe that he could start finding out about methods of teaching vocal music and almost surely discover enough to begin at his new post—especially if he would take a short course from a man named T. P. Giddings, who was scheduled to teach at Chautauqua the following summer.

Earhart was so insistent and so positive that Joe's future lay in going to Richmond that Joe finally agreed to a meeting with the Richmond Superintendent of Schools. The upshot was that he accepted the position at a salary of twenty-five hundred dollars a year, five hundred less than the sum to which he had been raised in Rochester. The understanding with the Richmond Superintendent was that he could have two years to learn to teach vocal music.

He followed Earhart's suggestion and spent the summer at the Chautauqua Summer School of Music. When he applied for admission, he was pleasantly surprised to find that his reputation had preceded him. The director of the school offered Joe free tuition if he would teach a class in "instrumental methods." Terminology was entirely new to Joe. He had been teaching youngsters to play musical instruments by whatever methods seemed most natural to him, and not being versed in the official pedagoies of the time, he knew nothing about what might be meant by "methods." But he would attempt to teach anything rather than pay tuition.

In only four weeks at the Chautauqua summer school he learned enough about music education to wonder how he ever had acquired a reputation as a successful teacher in Rochester—and to quail at the thought of the new position in Richmond. His teacher was Thaddeus P. Giddings, who, with his black goatee, his brittle humor, and his stern, unrelenting principles of both moral and musical discipline, was to become one of America's most beloved and respected music educators. After two days in Giddings' classes, Joe Maddy was almost ready to abandon any ideas of his own that he had formed about teaching.

Giddings, meanwhile, was becoming an enthusiastic admirer of Joe Maddy. In Chautauqua all members of the music department stayed at the same boarding house, and in the evening after dinner they would sit on the front porch to smoke and talk shop. Once in a brash burst of teacher-worship and youthful boldness Joe told his teacher that he would like to write a course for teaching instrumental music and maybe—said Joe hopefully—Mr. Giddings could help him?

Giddings replied that while he understood choral teaching he did not know enough about musical instruments. But the next evening during their usual chat on the front porch Giddings said, "I've changed my mind about that course of yours. I believe my lack of knowledge in the field would enable you to plan an instrument method that any fool could learn by."

Thus began an alliance and personal friendship that lasted until Giddings' death in 1954, and left a decisive impact on America's musical development. The instruction books Maddy and

Giddings wrote together revolutionized instrumental teaching and played a major part in the development of school symphony orchestras. More American children have learned to play by their *Universal Teacher* than by all other methods combined.

2

Joe Maddy arrived in Richmond in the fall of 1920, after only four weeks of instruction from T. P. Giddings in vocal teaching methods. Nevertheless, by the end of his first month he had reorganized the Richmond Symphony Orchestra and Festival Chorus, and planned the programs for the year. He organized instrumental classes and took over the American Legion Band. At the end of two months—instead of two years—the school superintendent said to him, "I won't worry any more about your ability to handle vocal music. Go to it."

Joe had the usual problems with parents and school board, however. One of his first moves was to banish all school pianists from his orchestras—except in the few orchestral pieces that required piano. He told the pianists they could stay in the orchestra only if they would get out the old string basses, packed away in a storeroom since Will Earhart left, and learn to play them. The parents of the pianists were not pleased. School officials complained that the new music supervisor was "moving too fast." But the youngsters themselves went to work with a will, and by the end of his first year Joe had ten string bass players. This was not bad for a small Indiana town.

Joe went exploring in the school's basement and store room, found oboes, bassoons, French horns, and string basses that had not been touched since the days of Will Earhart. He dusted them off, repaired those that needed repairing, and gave most of them to saxophone, cornet, or piano players in junior high school with the promise that if they worked hard enough they might soon be able to play with the high school orchestra. With his knack for inspiring enthusiasm he soon had boys and girls enthusiastically tooting away in practice sessions. The Richmond High School Orchestra would have no shortage of candidates.

Joe also organized classes in string and wind instruments for all ten of the system's elementary schools, during school hours. On Saturdays he taught classes for pupils who came in from the country. When his schedule was too crowded, he sent his best high school players to take over his grade school classes. They did a fine job. Some of these older students organized orchestras, in addition to their instrument classes, and put on contests each spring. One high school student developed an orchestra of more than fifty in a grade school of a hundred and fifty pupils.

Most of Joe's high school music leaders later became school music supervisors; some became professional musicians.

In the spring of nineteen twenty-one Joe went to a Music Supervisors' National Conference in St. Joseph, Missouri, where he heard a high school orchestra from Parsons, Kansas, that sounded far superior to his own—or any he had ever heard. He made inquiries and learned that the orchestra rehearsed every day for an hour during school, and that all members received the same credit for orchestra as they did for English or mathematics. This was the idea that had never occurred to Joe, either in Rochester or Richmond. It was a brand new plan still in the experimental stages in Parsons.

Joe went home to Richmond determined that his own orchestra should become a part of the regular school curriculum. He convinced the school superintendent, but unfortunately the man resigned soon afterward and Joe had to deal with the new incumbent the following year. School officials agreed in theory with the idea of holding orchestra rehearsals during school hours and giving credit, but at the same time teachers advised their students against taking orchestra, saying that if they did, they would not be able to graduate with adequate credits for college entrance.

As a result, Joe's orchestra began to dwindle. Students were reluctant to risk their chances of going to college and began to fall away from orchestra rehearsals held during school hours. At the same time Joe refused to backtrack and call after-school rehearsals. Instead he devised a new plan for luring students into the orchestra. If the orchestra from Parsons, Kansas, could travel a hundred miles for a music conference performance in St. Joseph, Missouri, why couldn't his own Richmond orchestra travel four hundred and fifty miles to play for the same conference in Nashville, Tennessee, next spring? This was long before the days of national band and orchestra contests, which Joe later inspired. Parsons had been probably the first school system to send its young musicians out of town for conventions. Joe liked the idea, and characteristically he decided to improve upon it. He knew a long trip would attract many new players, so he wrote to Frank Beach, then President of the Music Supervisors' National Conference, and suggested that Beach invite the Richmond orchestra to the Nashville meeting.

The invitation came, much to the surprise of Richmond school officials, and from then on nothing could hold down the enthusiasm of Richmond's high school students. Practically all of them wanted to get into the orchestra.

The sudden keen competition gave Joe a chance to experiment

with setting right the injustice he had felt ever since he had played last-chair viola in the Minneapolis Symphony. He would now put into practice his "try-outs" for seats. He first approached the string section: he wrote out a bowing exercise which could be played in unison by all stringed instruments and handed a copy to each string player on Friday, with the announcement that try-outs would be held on Monday and that seats would be determined by the ability of each student to play the exercise.

There was a lot of practicing that week-end. And there was wholesale shifting of seats as a result of Monday's tryouts. Joe saw limitless possibilities in the system. He would hold the try-outs every week and inspire the youngsters to keep on competing, thus motivating them to practice and improve their abilities continually. Surely he had discovered the ideal way to teach technical skills in music.

Joe was not prepared for what happened. Within thirty minutes after the close of the first tryouts, telephone wires were crackling. Parents and private music teachers were indignant. Joe Maddy had forced children to over-exert themselves. Boys and girls were being "demoted" in his orchestra. School authorities ordered Joe to "stop this nonsense" immediately.

Joe persuaded them to allow him to hold one more session of tryouts the following Monday, with parents and teachers invited to be present. He agreed to abide by their majority decision on whether the system should be abandoned.

The whole town was stirred by the controversy. The concert-mistress, who had lost her place in the first tryouts, stayed home from school all week and practiced nine hours a day on the assignment for the following Monday.

The atmosphere was tense that Monday morning as the auditorium filled with silent and somber parents and teachers. Probably never before nor since has an orchestra performed for a more interested audience.

On the great day Joe made only one change in his initial procedure. Instead of judging each player's ability himself, he called on members of the orchestra to make the decisions by a show-of-hands. The young player who won first chair earned the honor not on the basis of the teacher's verdict, but by popular vote of his own fellow competitors.

The young musicians took seriously their job of judging one another's ability, and never had they played better or with more enthusiasm. The concertmistress won back her place; she later became a professional violinist in Chicago. Many of the players got back the seats they had lost the previous week. More important, their improved musicianship, their pride and enthusiasm were communicated to the audience, and when, at the end of the session, Joe called for a vote from students, parents, teachers, and school officials on whether the weekly tryouts should be continued, not a single person voted no.

This was the first such tryout ever held. It soon became established procedure in school bands and orchestras, as well as in many professional music groups. And it was an important victory for Joe. He found unprecedented cooperation and enthusiasm growing among his students. He had never known youngsters to work so hard. Many volunteered to take up such instruments as oboe, bassoon, and string bass.

If there was ever any shortage of volunteers, Joe went out and found them. One of these recruits was a boy named Perry Botkin. Perry had a loud voice and a habit of using it in the hallways outside the auditorium while the orchestra was rehearsing. One day, goaded past endurance, Joe dashed out, grabbed Perry by the arm, and hustled him off toward the principal's office. On the way, however, he noted that his captive was a husky youth with good strong biceps. Suddenly he said, "Perry, you ought to try making your noise on a bass fiddle instead of hanging around outside the rehearsal room."

Perry perked up. Playing bass fiddle, he figured, would be easier than going to the principal's office.

Joe turned around, took him back to the auditorium, and gave him a bass fiddle. Perry learned to play, and was soon performing with gusto. Some twenty years later, in Los Angeles on a business trip, Joe received a telephone call from Perry Botkin, who reintroduced himself, "Remember me? I was the most unpromising pupil you ever had in high school back in Richmond." Perry had made progress. He was string bass player, guitar soloist, and orchestra manager for Bing Crosby—and all because he had once preferred the string bass to a dressing down from his school principal.

Three weeks before the trip to Nashville, Joe had a complete symphony orchestra in his Richmond high school—with one exception: he didn't yet have a tuba player. No one wanted to play the tuba. But another boy named Johnny Fansher was making a nuisance of himself by hanging around during rehearsals. Joe had tried to interest him in playing, but in vain. Johnny was left-handed and he used this for an excuse for not learning an instrument.

He was a big strong boy, however, with plenty of energy and good lungs—just the kind Joe needed as a tuba player. Joe finally asked him how he would like to go to Nashville with the group. Johnny leaped with joy. "To handle baggage?" he asked.

"No. To play the tuba."

Johnny's jaw dropped. But Joe led him to the tuba, showed him the tuba part in the *Rienzi Overture,* and told him if he would learn to play just those few notes, he could go to Nashville. Johnny was so excited by the thought of the trip that he applied himself diligently to the tuba. If Mr. Maddy thought he could do it—well, maybe he could. Both Joe and Johnny eventually turned out to be quite right: Johnny grew up to be a top-notch professional tuba and string bass player.

The Richmond orchestra had to raise its own funds, twenty-eight hundred dollars, to finance the trip to Nashville. The father of one of the players was in the record business. He suggested that the orchestra make a recording and sell it to the townspeople. He charged twenty cents each for making the records, and the students sold them for a dollar.

The new superintendent, however, had meanwhile developed a feeling that Joe was "trying to turn the school into a conservatory of music." He got wind of the record-selling project and issued an order prohibiting house-to-house canvassing. By that time, however, the young musicians already had sold twenty-eight hundred dollars worth of records, sight unseen, in less than a week.

The sixty-five piece Richmond High School Symphony Orchestra created a stir among the music educators at the Nashville conference. It was the first complete high school symphony orchestra, and its repertoire included standard symphonic works: Tschaikowsky's *Fifth Symphony,* the *Rienzi Overture, Valse*

Triste, and *Dance of the Hours.* Their performance overshadowed that of the Parsons orchestra the previous year, and the result of the Nashville demonstration was that high schools throughout the nation began working toward a new goal: a real symphony orchestra among their own students.

At the end of the performance, Will Earhart from Pittsburgh shook Joe Maddy's hand and said, "I told you so!"

The Richmond High School Orchestra soon grew into two orchestras—A and B. The A orchestra numbered one hundred players; the B orchestra, seventy-five. Joe also had two sixty piece junior high school orchestras, ten in the elementary schools, and numerous beginning classes.

He went on to develop a music major course, in which high school students spent two or three hours a day. His standards were higher than those generally required of college graduates. Although most school officials could not adjust to Joe's vision for music's role in the schools, they felt powerless to do anything about it in the face of his popularity with students and townspeople.

Despite all Joe's ingenuity, there was for a while one instrument conspicuously missing from the Richmond school orchestra —a harp. In fact, there was not a harp nor a harpist for miles around. The closest harp was in Indianapolis, and no one in Richmond was willing to spend a thousand dollars to purchase the instrument, and then have to go to Indianapolis or Cincinnati to learn how to play it. But Joe wanted a harp in his orchestra.

The students themselves became determined to have a harp in their orchestra. They started a harp fund and raised four hundred dollars by selling season tickets to six concerts. Joe then wrote to instrument companies to see if anyone would supply a harp for that price. One company was sufficiently moved to offer a seven-hundred-and-fifty-dollar harp for the money the students had raised. But there was still no one to play it.

It didn't take Joe long to fix this. He put on a concert deliberately calculated to promote the harp. He invited Pasquale Montani, a fine harpist from Indianapolis, as guest artist. Montani played a harp concerto with orchestral accompaniment; and the entire program was planned to feature the glamorous golden instrument. The music included Debussy's *Afternoon of a Faun* and Rimsky-Korsakov's *Capriccio Espagnole*.

At the end of the concert the Richmond audience knew what a harp was like and what it could add to the orchestra. Furthermore, Joe had made a special point of inviting all piano students and their parents to the concert. He had been forced to banish them from his orchestras, but here was their chance to get out of the overcrowded field of piano by playing one of the most beautiful and fascinating of all instruments, the harp.

After the performance Joe announced that anyone interested could stay and talk with Mr. Montani. He also explained that the school now owned a harp, and any harp students could practice on it for no charge except a share in the cost of strings. Then came the best part—Mr. Montani himself, the distinguished guest artist they had all just heard, had agreed, Joe said, to come to Richmond once a week to give lessons!

Ten students signed up that very night.

This surprised even Joe. And more came in during the next few days. In a short time Joe had sixteen eager harp students— with only one harp. It was soon scheduled eleven hours a day, including Sundays, for practice. He finally persuaded Lyon and

Healy, on his personal guarantee against damage, to lend him ten more instruments for the school.

The students learned quickly, and in the spring Joe decided to take his orchestra with its rare and proud ensemble of ten harpists to another music convention in Cincinnati.

A week before the trip he was called out of bed at three o'clock in the morning. An excited voice asked over the phone, "Are the harps safe?"

"What do you mean, are the harps safe?"

"Don't you know the high school's on fire?" the voice shouted.

Joe rushed over to the school. His heart sank as he saw the smoke, the burning building, and flames leaping from the wing which housed the musical instruments—including the ten harps for which he was personally responsible. They were not insured.

For blocks around the sky was red with flames. Joe stood in helpless horror. Then in the red glow his gaze fell on something that would be etched in his memory forever—harp silhouettes against the crimson sky. No, it couldn't be! He ran toward them. There on a corner, a block from the schoolhouse were the eleven beautiful harps; and string basses, cellos, drums, music stands, and incredibly high stacks of music—all safe and sound, and surrounded by disheveled, red-eyed, solemn-faced boys and girls from his orchestra. They had risked their lives to break through the police guard, and had reached every single instrument and music score in the building.

Not only that, but some of the students had already made arrangements to use the privately owned Coliseum in Richmond as temporary rehearsal space. This was three-thirty in the morning. When the school superintendent a few hours later asked permission to use the Coliseum for classrooms, he was told that it had already been promised to the orchestra.

While the rest of the school remained closed, the Richmond High School Orchestra held rehearsals not one but six hours a day for a full week before their trip to Cincinnati. The first Coliseum rehearsal began at 8:30 the morning after the fire—with every member present. But there was some delay while the librarians sorted the music, and the impatient youngsters started playing Tschaikowsky's *Sixth Symphony* from memory. To Joe's amazement, they played through the entire work—without their music!

The Richmond harp ensemble in Cincinnati started another new movement—harp classes in schools.

The orchestra also astonished music educators by its abilities in sight reading. Some skeptics had been saying that Joe probably rehearsed his young people all year for one or two programs. They didn't believe high school students were capable of reading such difficult music at sight. Joe invited one of the scoffers, a music director from New York City, to bring any piece he chose, to be read at sight by his Richmond orchestra during the Cincinnati convention. He listed the works the orchestra already knew, to make sure they would get something new and unfamiliar.

The selection was the *Meistersinger Prelude* by Wagner, with horns in D, trumpets in F, alto clef trombone, and other similar complexities. The orchestra members read it at sight as fluently as if they had been mature professionals.

The Cincinnati Conference forthwith put its official seal of approval on Joe Maddy's position in the front ranks of music educators.

Ironically, almost as soon as Joe returned to Richmond, he again encountered the problem of his own lack of formal schooling.

It was some time before anyone in Richmond had bothered to check up on his academic qualifications. He was attracting nation-wide attention among music educators by his new methods and his teaching programs.

He had finally succeeded in establishing schooltime music classes with school credit. He had also started a Vocational Music Course for high school students who were planning to become music teachers or supervisors—a course in which instrumental players could get school credit for home practice, supplemented by examination before a jury of local music teachers appointed by the music supervisor or superintendent. In addition to establishing these programs, he had also joined the faculty of Richmond's Earlham College. He was teaching other teachers how to teach music; and his students were automatically granted teaching certificates when they completed his course.

As once before in Rochester, it had occurred to no one to suppose that a man who was making such outstanding contributions to music education was in fact not properly educated. Richmond's school officials were horrified to discover that their nationally prominent young teacher had not even finished the ninth grade. To Joe himself, the matter simply did not seem important. After all, a man knew what he knew, and anyone with common sense understood that pieces of paper formally presented at the end of a course of study were just trimmings. What counted was what was in the man's head, not what might or might not be on his certificates.

Richmond's school officials, however, lacked Joe's insouciance. Joe was not academically qualified to teach in Indiana and something would have to be done. Eager to keep the man whose innovations had attracted the attention of educators all over the nation, school officials anxiously began thumbing through all the state's formal teaching regulations for a possible loophole.

They finally found one: a high school diploma was required of everyone on the school payroll except two persons—the superintendent and the janitor. There was some debate over which classification to put Joe in, and for a while it appeared that he might have to be listed officially as a janitor—a prospect which disturbed him far less than it did everyone else. While members of the School Board wrestled with the problem and their consciences, Joe, of course, went right on teaching music.

Under pressure from parents, students, and townspeople, all of whom were solidly behind Joe, the Board of Education finally made a concession and granted him the official title of "assistant superintendent." The reprieve, however, was short-lived. Every area of education was turning more and more to formality, with ever deepening respect for what Joe thought of as "pieces of paper." Indiana State laws were even then being revised to require superintendents to have high school diplomas, and Joe suddenly found that he had four months in which to get "educated"—or he would be dismissed from his job.

The State licensing agency finally agreed to accept Joe's education in music, his teaching experience, and his Chautauqua summer course as the equivalent of the two-year *college* course required of music teachers, but officials were adamant about the necessity of his having a high school diploma. Somehow he would have to get one.

Joe wrote to Wellington and asked that the few high school credits he did have be sent to him. Back came the doleful news: All the records for that year had been destroyed in a Kansas cyclone.

There was no alternative but to cram four years of high school into four months of study. Between orchestra rehearsals and instrument classes, Joe buckled down to mathematics, algebra, civics, and English literature. He then passed the required examinations and was duly presented a high school diploma. He had just turned thirty. At long last Joe Maddy was Educated!

Grand Old Man of Music

I

T HERE were others in the world of education who shared Joe's attitude toward those "pieces of paper." By the third day after Thaddeus P. Giddings met Joe Maddy in the summer of nineteen twenty at Chautauqua, he was certain that he was dealing with a young man of extraordinary brilliance and he had not hesitated to say so.

Giddings did not trust diplomas and seldom relied on them for judging a man's quality. He regarded the graded school system as a late invention of the devil and never hesitated to tell anyone on the slightest provocation that he himself would have preferred working in a starch factory to sitting in the school classrooms of his day. In later life, at the height of his illustrious reputation, Giddings would delight in shocking reverent interviewers who inquired where he had studied. His aloof reply: "I never studied."

Under duress, he would explain matter-of-factly, "I had a very thorough education; when I was eleven years old I had thirty piano lessons." And to persistent questioners who went on to ask about his higher degrees, he would add, "I was one of the smartest men who ever went through the University of Minnesota. It took me only eight months to get a request never to return."

Nevertheless, Giddings had become Supervisor of Music in Minneapolis, taught at the University of Minnesota for fourteen years, as well as several summers at the University of Southern California, and was regarded with awe by the thousands of teachers who studied under him. He was recognized everywhere with reverence and affection as one of America's greatest pedagogues.

In the nation's still infant and inadequate system of education in the nineteenth century and the early years of the twentieth, there was a built-in safety valve. Although the United States had few universities and almost no secondary schools that could measure up to Europe's best, and the modern innovation of scholarship programs for help to brilliant minds was then almost nonexistent, gifted men and women could by dint of heroic efforts study "on their own," and in a time when teaching was in many areas abysmally incompetent, avoid the formal process altogether. This was the safety valve through which Giddings, like Joe himself, had passed. In Joe's period it was being closed off—with effects on minds born to genius that would be forever debatable. However, at the same time American schools were also being radically improved—an improvement in which both Giddings and Maddy were to play prominent roles.

Thaddeus Giddings was born in Anoka, Minnesota. When he was ten, he decided he wanted to play the piano. His first teacher was a young woman who had charge of the organ in his Sunday School. When he asked her which songs she had picked out from the hymn book to sing next Sunday, she replied, "I never pick them out ahead of time." So Thaddy, as he was known in childhood, took the hymn book home and memorized all two hundred and forty songs.

He later admitted that it was not the music so much as the

chance to show off that drove him to toil, but most children would have been incapable of the feat. It was an early mark of his unusual attainments, as was the delight he took in pleasing the audience when he made his debut at the church organ at the age of twelve. His young teacher said dryly, "You played very nicely, Thaddy, but it was obvious who enjoyed your playing most."

Young Giddings grew up in the typically casual country-school era, in which teachers were scarce, most lessons were learned by rote and were dull, and family chores were often regarded as more important. Thaddy's mother was ill and needed him at home, but she always saw to it that he kept ahead of their country school teachers by memorizing whatever textbook was in hand when each new incumbent arrived. On those occasions when Thaddy attended school there was always a debate among the other children. "No, Thaddy belongs in *our* class." No one was ever quite sure *where* Thaddy belonged.

Thaddy could both sing and play the organ. And he enjoyed teaching music to the other school children much better than he liked the notion of continuing with more classroom instruction. So while his classmates went to school, Thaddy went out as a country school teacher himself. His first position earned him twenty dollars a month. He had sixteen pupils in his one-room school. Teachers in those days usually "boarded around" with families who could take them in for the term. Giddings boarded with all sixteen of his pupils, spending a week in the home of each. At the end of the year he was earning thirty-five dollars a month, and the respect and affection of his pupils.

Most important of all, he was discovering that lessons need

never be dull; that they can be voyages of discovery, full of enchantment and meaning.

Thus up in Anoka, Minnesota, a great teacher had been developed, and when he began teaching the earnest younger man from Wellington, Kansas, it was the beginning of one of the brightest chapters in America's progress toward modern methods of music education.

During the four years Joe taught in Richmond, he spent his summers studying and working with Giddings. In the summer of 1921, Joe again was asked to teach instrumental class methods at Chautauqua, and resumed with Giddings their plans to collaborate on the instruction book that was to be called the *Universal Teacher*.

The following year Giddings was offered a summer position at the University of Southern California and refused to go unless the University would take Joe too. It did, and then proceeded to advertise both teachers so widely that their classes were overwhelmingly filled.

Joe was startled to find himself confronted with a class of eighty eager music teachers, most of them much older than he. They wanted to learn how to teach string classes, but few knew even how to play stringed instruments. Joe also discovered that he also had sixty in a class for methods in beginning teaching of wind instruments. How he was expected to teach that many teachers all at one time he had no idea. But the school had accepted the enrollments, scheduled the courses, and Joe must get along as best he could.

Giddings tried to calm him. "There's nothing to it," he said. "You just teach the entire group at once. Go ahead. You can do it."

It was one of Joe's most challenging summers—and the most

exasperating. For Giddings was known as one of the strictest pedagogues who ever walked through a school door. And he was not about to let his young protege get by with anything he regarded as less than inspired teaching. He had probably planned deliberately to have his own classes scheduled at different hours from Joe's. In any event he sat in on every one of Joe's two sessions each day, watching and taking notes, point by point, on every flaw.

Each afternoon after classes, Giddings would produce his notebook of criticisms and go over them with Joe. The discussions usually lasted approximately two hours. And they were brutal.

"Why did you stop the class to tell them that? Couldn't you find a way to tell them without interruption?

"You must realize that they are learning *only* when they are playing. Keep them playing—and keep your mouth shut. Don't talk."

There was no printed material in those days for such classes as Joe's. He wrote out the lessons in advance, then put them on the blackboard. He started by copying all parts for each instrument.

"That's not necessary," Giddings snapped. "Write the tune on the board only once, and make your students transpose for their parts."

To Joe's amazement, it worked, and the students learned a great deal in the process.

In order to eliminate Joe's talking during class periods, Giddings rigged up a tapper or slap-stick, so Joe could guide his classes by code. One tap meant: Stop and hold whatever tone you are playing—until further orders. Two taps meant: Start playing the next note. Three taps meant: Stop playing.

Giddings rearranged the seating in Joe's classes, putting the best students in the back of the room, the poorest in front. Those who most needed individual instruction would thus be nearer the teacher, while those in back could go on playing and learning without wasting time waiting for the rest to catch up. Giddings' foremost criterion of good teaching was one that could be applied to any type of instruction. It was: Every student must be purposefully occupied every minute of every class period.

He often said: "Most education we've had in this country so far is trash. Teachers have always been trying to find some easy way to teach students. There isn't any. Just get them interested in hard work and you've got the problem solved. . . ."

As Joe's classes progressed, he found himself in the ironic position of teaching teachers how to teach a class while he himself was still studying teaching from Giddings. The late afternoon seminars with his older mentor became more and more critical, more severe, and mentally and physically exhausting. Giddings berated him for each false move, every wasted second. A man with less stamina than Joe would have given up the project. Giddings, however, knew his pupil well. Joe could "take it" and still go on. Joe couldn't know then that Giddings was the man who would one day stand by him when his friends turned against him; or that in his later years the Grand Old Man of Music would remain steadfastly always in the background while the world smiled on Joe. In the mellow years shortly before his death in 1954, Giddings once said, "I feel if my people shine, I'll shine better."

But back in California that summer, Joe wasn't able to feel he was shining very well. Only once, toward the end of the season, Giddings ripped a blank piece of paper from his notebook, handed it to Joe, and said, "See? Today I have no criticism. You gave a perfect lesson."

That was one of the happiest days of Joe's life.

The music instruction books which Maddy and Giddings wrote together, *Universal Teacher, Instrumental Technique,* and the *Willis Graded School Orchestra Series,* later became standard equipment in most American school music libraries and for many years played an important part in the development of high school symphony orchestras. And these works grew almost entirely from those nightmarish—for Joe—student and teacher inquisitions of the early 1920's. Joe had been commissioned by the Willis Music Company to write the *Willis Graded School Orchestra Series,* but the idea grew with the collaboration of Giddings. The *Universal Teacher* went begging for a publisher for the reason that it was based entirely on familiar, uncopyrighted songs and publishers demanded material which they could protect by copyright.

In desperation Joe went to Mr. Carl D. Greenleaf, president of C. G. Conn, Ltd., manufacturers of band instruments in Elkhart, Indiana. Mr. Greenleaf believed in Joe and accepted his belief that the *Universal Teacher* would make it easier to teach students to play band instruments and would therefore promote the sale of instruments.

As a result the *Universal Teacher,* a set of twenty instruction books, selling for 75¢ each, was first published by the Conn Company which was organized to sell band instruments costing $75.00 or more each.

Conn was soon swamped with orders for the 75¢ books and gladly sold out to the Willis Music Company within the year. Willis had acknowledged the error in judgment and the Conn

Company was happy to let an experienced publisher promote the sale of band instruments.

Meanwhile Joe was becoming involved in other activities on a national scale. He began to take part in the state and national band and orchestra contest movement, and he headed a committee which prescribed contest rules, selected the music scores, and awarded the prizes.

Ironically, his own Richmond High School Orchestra was denied the privilege of entering the first Indiana State Music Contest at Indianapolis in the spring of 1924—for the reason that it was too far ahead of the other orchestras competing.

Joe did send his junior high school choir to the contest, however, and it won first place, outshining even the older high school groups. It also won the frank admiration of Madame Schumann-Heink who was a guest soloist and one of the judges.

In the summer of 1924, while Joe was again in Los Angeles with Giddings, he was invited to be guest conductor for one of the works to be played by the Los Angeles Philharmonic Orchestra in the Hollywood Bowl. Joe was flattered by the invitation—perhaps doubly so because only forty-eight hours earlier he had received another tempting offer. He was asked to come to Ann Arbor as supervisor of music in the public schools and to serve as head of the public school music department of the University of Michigan School of Music.

Ann Arbor and the University of Michigan could give him more prestige in school music, and now suddenly he was also being selected to conduct a big professional symphony orchestra. To be sure, it was for only one short piece, but that was enough to set any young man on fire with sudden self esteem.

Giddings warned him, "You should stick to teaching. The schools need you more than the professionals."

As usual, Giddings was right. The professionals, in fact, didn't need him at all, Joe decided. When he arrived for rehearsal with the Los Angeles Philharmonic, he found that the regular conductor, Alfred Hertz, would allow him only twelve minutes to rehearse his number, the *Fingal's Cave Overture*—which takes exactly twelve minutes to play!

Furthermore, the members of the orchestra, some of whom were old friends and former members of the Minneapolis Symphony conveyed a distinct impression that they were both annoyed and bored by having to play through an entire overture that they knew perfectly well, just to please this young upstart. To Joe, accustomed to the alertness and enthusiasm of young school children, these older musicians now seemed callous and commercial. They were playing for money instead of for love of music.

And he knew one thing for certain: as a conductor he felt far more excitement in drawing great music out of school children than in leading these hard-shelled professionals. If even for a moment he had harbored any secret wish to become a professional symphony conductor, as Giddings perhaps had feared, this experience would have killed it. Giddings was right—Joe belonged to teaching.

2

It wasn't easy for Joe to leave Richmond and the youngsters who had once risked their lives to rescue their instruments when the school burned down. In his heart he hoped there would come a time when he could remember his Indiana students with even bigger and better opportunities, though he didn't know exactly how. There did come a time, however, and it wasn't far in the future.

Ann Arbor was fertile territory for Joe Maddy. The only instrumental music in the entire high school system was a mandolin club! Joe faced much the same problems that he had found in the schools of Rochester and Richmond—lack of funds, lack of instruments, lack of cooperation from school officials. Moreover, he was expected to produce a music program as fine as the one he had developed in Indiana, but with far less natural resources. In Richmond, Joe's friend and predecessor, Earhart, had already done a great deal before Joe arrived, and also had left behind a supply of appropriate instruments that needed only dusting, repairing, and playing. Joe's duties at Ann Arbor consisted of half-time as teacher of vocal, instrumental and theoretical music at Ann Arbor High School, as a teacher of instrumental music in two junior high schools, and as supervisor of vocal and instrumental music in Ann Arbor's elementary schools. The other half of his time was devoted to teaching vocal and instrumental methods and other music education courses at the University School of Music.

In Ann Arbor Joe again bumped into the problem of school credits. The University of Michigan did not then accept music credits toward entrance, and high school teachers generally advised their students not to take music. Or they were apt to order the students to drop music when they made poor grades in any other subjects. Joe thus lost three out of four horn players the first month, and more candidates for other instruments each succeeding month. Their teachers ordered them to drop band and orchestra in order to spend more time on their Latin and mathematics. The notion that music might turn out to be the student's natural career did not appear to apply to the problem.

Nevertheless, Joe managed to develop a band and orchestra that received honorable mention at the State contest in Mt. Pleasant the following spring. He also organized a marching band for football games, and induced the Ann Arbor Rotary Club to donate two thousand dollars for its uniforms.

In his early years in Ann Arbor he made several innovations which neither he nor anyone else—so far as is known—had ever tried before. One was a conducting class in the University's School of Music. On this level, his students were more advanced musicians than those in high school. They were potential music educators and conductors, and Joe decided they should have some training in conducting.

Joe himself had had only one lesson in conducting, and that was from Albert Coates of the Rochester Philharmonic Orchestra and former Conductor of the London Symphony. Joe remembered that one lesson well, however. Coates had simply pointed to a symphony score, Tschaikowsky's *Sixth,* and said, "The way to conduct is to learn your score. Then *lead,* don't follow." That was all.

Joe started his class in conducting by having the members of his orchestra sign up for it. By this procedure he got both his conducting class and an orchestra for it to conduct. All students brought their instruments to the conducting class and took turns leading the group. All players were instructed not to play unless the student-player-conductor was actually *leading*. As players, they were used to following along with the group; and, as Joe himself had once learned, the transition from following to leading was not easy. Nevertheless, within a year Joe had a number of fine student conductors among his orchestra members, as well as fine orchestra players in his conducting class. Many later became conductors of university bands and orchestras. And every member of that class achieved success as a music educator.

Until Joe started his class in conducting, there was a widely held theory that conductors were born, not made. Joe's belief was that conductors could be trained—if they had a natural ability for leadership and if they knew the music. Conducting classes which later sprang up in schools began teaching students to conduct by following phonograph records—the worst possible way, in Joe's opinion. The best conductors, he always told his students, were first of all performers, players who knew the scores thoroughly.

Toscanini, for example, one day had stepped up from the cello section and conducted an opera when the regular conductor became indisposed. It was the first time he ever conducted—at least in public—and he went through the opera without faltering, though he had played only the cello part.

Joe started giving music lessons by radio from Ann Arbor. Nineteen hundred thirty-one was a time long before educational programs on radio and television came into vogue. The University's Director of Broadcasting had first asked Joe to give lessons in music appreciation. In the wake of Walter Damrosch, ever larger audiences were taking up a fad for music appreciation by radio. Joe asked if he could give music *lessons* instead. The Director was startled, but he apparently decided that if Joe wanted to risk his reputation by a public failure on the air, that was his privilege. If the program became embarrassing for the University, it could be eliminated.

The program, however, was no failure but a success that far exceeded Joe's hopes. In three years he had radio classes in band instruments, string instruments and songs in more than a thousand towns in Michigan. After his first lesson he started traveling to visit his audiences and see how his invisible students were coming along. In one area he found the wife of a local doctor in charge of the group, in another a janitor. Throughout Michigan, families were going through their attics and basements, getting out old and neglected instruments, and learning to play them in Joe Maddy's radio classes.

He would announce to his radio pupils on Monday, "I'll visit the following classes on Thursday: Standish at 8:30; Sterling at 9:30; Au Gres at 10:45; Omer at 11:45; Twining at 1:30; Turner at 2:30 and East Tawas at 3:30." His pupils were always watching at the schoolhouse windows for their radio teacher. The purpose of the visits was to check their playing, their instruments for repairs and his own teaching procedures, including the timing of each item. He altered his teaching plans in accordance with the results he was getting with his unseen pupils.

Joe's radio pupils were always welcome to go to Ann Arbor and take their lesson "live" in a room adjoining the broadcasting studio. Joe could watch them and thereby time his lessons. Sometimes as many as one hundred students came to the studio. At every broadcast he would select one or two of his visiting radio pupils to play a tune, or try to. Brief interviews were held and were always unusual. For example, one radio class, at Au Gres, traded chickens for a piano so they could have an orchestra in their two-room school. The City of Midland, Michigan, dismissed its music supervisor for economical reasons when the depression was at its height, and substituted Joe's radio lessons. By midwinter the interest in music—he was teaching folk songs—was so great that they reinstated the music supervisor.

By 1936 Joe was presenting five educational radio programs every week; four from the University of Michigan over Station WJR (Detroit) and one from Chicago over Station WMAQ (NBC). For four years he presented weekly radio lessons over NBC's coast-to-coast network, to an invisible class estimated at more than 225,000—scattered from New Zealand to Persia.

Instruction books with many pictures were distributed by NBC, and a union band of Chicago musicians demonstrated tunes and procedures in the radio studio. James C. Petrillo, president of the Chicago Federation of Musicians, objected to the radio music lessons because they were training musicians to compete with "his boys." No radio pupil was permitted to play over the air and no visitor was allowed in the studio under any circumstances. Petrillo finally induced NBC to include a ten-minute program of elementary chorus singing in the middle of each radio band lesson—"for entertainment" he said.

In 1937 an experiment was carried out in Columbus, Ohio, to test the effectiveness of radio music lessons. In a school for underprivileged children two comparable classes of ten each were formed to begin learning to play band instruments. Instruments were furnished by the school.

One class was taught in person by a regularly employed instrumental class teacher. The other class received instruction only by radio—in Joe's NBC Band Lessons—30 minutes once a week. At the end of 16 weeks members of the National Institute for

Education by Radio (which meets in Columbus annually) visited the classes and tested the comparative results.

The radio class has learned four times as many tunes; played better in tune; were highly enthusiastic over their music—and had increased from ten to fifteen in numbers. The personally-taught class had dwindled to seven; played fewer pieces with less enthusiasm and not so well in tune. Joe received an official Honorable Mention from the Institute for his effective demonstration.

Joe used many of the methods which he and Giddings had evolved for their instruction books. But all Joe's pioneering in music lessons by radio would before long have to be dropped. His pending struggle with Petrillo, the so-called Czar of Music, was about to end that.

3

From Ann Arbor Joe had been rapidly broadening his horizons. He was becoming even more active in school band and orchestra contests. In the early 1920's there were many more school orchestras than school bands, so the manufacturers of band instruments decided to do something about it. They approached C. M. Tremaine, who had founded the National Bureau for the Advancement of Music, an association whose goal was to promote music in general in the United States on funds provided by a tax of fifty cents on every piano made and sold in the country.

Would Mr. Tremaine undertake to promote school bands? He said he would if the manufacturers would finance the project under the control of music educators and without any commercial influence.

So the Committee on Instrumental Affairs of the Music Supervisors' National Conference came into existence in 1923 Joe accepted membership on the condition that orchestras as well as bands be included in the promotion. Before two years had passed Joe had become chairman of the committee, and he was full of ideas about how to remodel the military band into what he termed a "symphonic" band capable of performing symphonic music. The usual band music of that era was limited to military music and marches. By expanding the clarinet section to include alto and bass clarinets and substituting symphonic instruments such as the French horn and bassoon, Joe could plan for a band of sixty or more players able to play transcribed versions of the world's greatest symphonic works. Because he could play all band instruments, Joe also knew that the clarinet was the only wind instrument that could endure the extended passages assigned to violins and other stringed instruments.

The idea appealed to music educators, but nothing happened —until Joe got the idea of including instrumentation in the contest ratings of the state and national school band contests, which were conducted under the supervision of his Committee on Instrumental Affairs. He then formulated a list of instruments that he believed would enable a band to perform orchestral music and announced that competing bands would receive additional credit points for instrumentation based on the list.

Joe used the state and national school band and orchestra contests, which he managed as chairman of the Committee on Instrumental Affairs, to promote his ideas designed to convert the military band into a musical organization capable of rendering orchestral transcriptions of symphonic music in a satisfactory manner.

John Philip Sousa, Arthur Pryor and the directors of the

United States Army, Navy and Marine bands had developed bands which included many instruments usually found only in symphony orchestras. These bands had to have their own transcriptions which were made by their personnel. School bands, town bands and all other bands used published editions designed for the traditional military band of fourteen to twenty players; designed for marching and other military uses.

Joe could see no future for bands with such limited instrumentation. He envisioned great symphonic bands of a hundred or more players, with carefully balanced sections of clarinets, flutes and all other wind instruments—even with harps and string basses for special effects. He believed that, by emphasizing instrumentation in contest ratings he might gradually convert school band directors to his "symphonic" band instrumentation.

When Joe advocated two or more alto clarinets in a high school band there arose a storm of protest because no American band except Sousa's had ever boasted an alto clarinet and such instruments were not manufactured in America. Furthermore, Sousa stated that, since his alto clarinet player had died, there was no one to teach students to play that instrument—so there could never be any alto clarinetists in American school bands. But Sousa had never heard of the *Universal Teacher*. Alto clarinets were imported and school children learned to play them. Now alto clarinets are regularly included in the soprano, alto, bass and contra-bass clarinet choir of every top rating high school symphonic band.

Joe's symphonic band plan encountered obstacles at every turn. First, there was no published music for such a band. He met this problem by arranging orchestral pieces himself and including them in the national band contest lists. Secondly, school authorities criticized him and his committee for demanding purchase of instruments not then considered standard for bands—and therefore useless in sales promotion for the band instrument manufacturers.

Moreover, the band instrument manufacturers, who were financing the contests as promotion, attacked Joe and his committee because the expanded instrumentation often listed foreign-made instruments, while trumpets and saxophones, which accounted for most of the profits for the manufacturers, were strictly limited. In addition, school band directors were apt to know nothing about teaching instruments that had never been part of any band they knew. Therefore, they had to learn to play and teach those instruments. They complained that they were being bludgeoned into turning their bands into orchestra—by that fanatic, Joe Maddy.

In desperation, Joe formed an Advisory Committee of professional band leaders, including Sousa, Goldman, Pryor, and the directors of the United States Marine, Army, and Navy bands, who agreed with him that his instrumentation would make possible far better performances than were possible with the limited instrumentation of that era's standard military band, for which nearly all band music was then published. Unfortunately, the publishers of band music agreed unanimously that they would *not* put out any music for symphonic band. They demanded unequivocally that the Committee develop school bands to fit their investment in already published works. They felt that widespread adoption of the symphonic band would make obsolete every band publication in the United States, and thereby force publishers into expensive new areas based on the Committee's required instrumentation.

Joe and his committee stood their ground. They were thinking in terms of human beings, young musicians and their needs, and they would not surrender for the sake of expediency or commercial pressure. It may have been at this time that Joe rediscovered in himself the quality that had been so much a part of his early youth—an intransigent stubbornness. Sure he was right, he would not give way. From the moldable pupil of Thaddeus Giddings were emerging the first signs of the man who through his later years would often be called an "ornery cuss"—though usually less in anger than in resigned admiration.

At the time, however, Joe was simply a maturing music educator plunging into the heat of his first really major controversy. His sense of justice was flaming, and he rejected every thought of retreat. Finally new music publishers saw their chance: they offered to publish music for symphonic band if the committee would include *their* publications on the annual contest lists for the state and national contests. This gave the committee an opportunity to guide these publishers in providing suitable transcriptions of orchestral works, and to reward composers who wrote suitable music. Stubbornness had its reward. Within a year or two all publishers capitulated, as did the manufacturers, school authorities, and school band directors.

The symphonic band, as envisioned by Joe Maddy back in 1924, has now been adopted, with minor variations, as standard for the nation and the civilized world. And the association between Maddy and Tremaine that began with the formation of the Committee on Instrumental Affairs developed into a friendship based on shared ideals similar to those shared by Maddy and Giddings—ideals which resulted in the founding and developing of the National Music Camp at Interlochen. For it was the Maddy-Giddings-Tremaine triumvirate which was to shape Interlochen from an embryonic dream into its present actuality. True, it was Joe's dream, but he was always first to admit that without the trust placed in him by Giddings and Tremaine it could never have reached fulfillment. Throughout the years at Interlochen, Tremaine and Giddings usually remained quietly in the background, observing young Joe with sympathy and benevolence. Whenever Joe's growing determination led him into trouble, they gently—or sometimes perhaps not so gently—reproved him, but they were always there when he needed them. Tremaine served as treasurer of the music camp and financial advisor until his retirement in 1960.

Joe's involvement in the band-versus-orchestra controversy in the early twenties led to another commercial problem—this time with the piano makers. Until the advent of the radio, a piano in the living room was an indication of culture, as well as an attractive piece of furniture. More children took piano lessons than instruction in any other branch of music. Every small town furniture store sold pianos. Then came the introduction of the automatic "player piano," with high-powered promotion emphasizing the slogan, "Why learn to play when you can buy a piano that plays itself?"

The sale of player pianos and rolls reached its highest point about the same time that the school band and orchestra movement was getting under way, and when radio broadcasting was still in its infancy. When the sales of all pianos, including player pianos, began to drop off, the manufacturers looked about for the reason and decided it must be school bands. They failed to realize that they themselves had discouraged piano study by introducing the player piano. No manufacturer dreamed that people would tire of listening to the mechanical notes of the new product; but tire they did, especially when radio began to bring the finest performers into their homes.

By 1928 the piano companies decided to do something about the competition they believed was coming from the band movement. The blame lay, they contended, with Tremaine's National Bureau for the Advancement of Music, which had been supported almost entirely from funds supplied by themselves. They virtually accused Tremaine of using the prestige and facilities of the Bureau which the manufacturers had financed, to destroy the piano business.

Joe Maddy, as a member of the Board of Directors of the National Bureau, was present at the meetings where the accusation was discussed. The directors decided that something should be done to restore the popularity of the piano, and a committee of music educators was named to plan a campaign. This Piano Class Committee was a sub-committee of the Committee on Instrumental Affairs, of which Joe was General Chairman. It was his assignment to get the five authors of rival published piano class methods to agree on certain statements that could be printed and distributed to revive the lagging interest in piano. The result was a booklet entitled *Public School Piano Classes,* which was published and circulated by the National Bureau.

Within a few months after the booklet was released, more than five thousand schools sent in requests for information. The project seemed assured of success, and thousands of school piano classes might have been started if the piano manufacturers had had patience. Instead, they decided to withdraw their support from the National Bureau, and the piano was left to its own devices to achieve a return to popularity.

Nevertheless, in spite of these ripples of contention between factions in the music world, instrument manufacturers, publishers, school supervisors and directors, music was beginning to be firmly established in America's educational system. In the spring of 1925 Joe was asked whether he could organize a National High School Symphony Orchestra, composed of outstanding high school musicians from all over the United States, to play for the Music Educators' National Conference in Detroit the following year.

The idea of a national, or all-American high school orchestra was new. Joe had been instrumental in organizing all-state high school orchestra in Indiana and Michigan and other states were following his organizational pattern in similar projects.

The idea challenged Joe. No such national organization had ever been attempted. The student musicians would have to pay for their own transportation to Detroit, but they would be housed for four days with private families, and would have four days of rehearsals for the convention concert. Joe placed announcements in music journals that winter and drew four hundred young applicants. He had been expecting difficulty in recruiting enough competitors to form an adequate hundred and fifty piece orchestra, for he had sent out announcements that he would hold tryouts to select the best players, a provision that he expected would automatically discourage many who might otherwise have applied.

Joe then asked Ossip Gabrilowitsch, the famed conductor of the Detroit Symphony Orchestra, to conduct his National High School Symphony Orchestra at the convention. Gabrilowitsch at first refused. He informed young Maddy that all good oboe, bassoon, horn, cello, and bass players were imported from Europe. There might be enough fairly competent young violinists in the country but certainly there could not be enough good musicians in *high schools* who played the more unusual and essential orchestral instruments!

Joe knew that even Richmond, Indiana, alone could provide good players for all instruments needed. He assured Mr. Gabrilowitsch of this fact, and the famed conductor finally agreed reluctantly to undertake two of the works on the program, on condition that he could hear the group before he rehearsed it and that he could then decide if they had the capacity to perform to his satisfaction.

As it turned out, so many states and towns wanted to be represented in this first National High School Orchestra that Joe was able to expand his originally planned hundred and fifty piece orchestra to two hundred and thirty-eight. When the youngsters arrived in Detroit they were given auditions and assigned to positions in their sections, and the first and second chair players were assigned the solo passages. Thirty states were represented. The town with the largest group was, of course, Joe's own Richmond. And of those nineteen Indiana students, thirteen won first chairs at the tryouts. The orchestra then rehearsed six hours a day as a group and two hours in sections.

One big and basic problem which might have been expected in the handling of two hundred and thirty-eight high school boys and girls, most of them away from home for the first time, was discipline. This problem was solved for Joe by his old friend and teacher, Giddings, who not only offered but insisted on relieving Joe of this part of the project. As a result there wasn't an extraneous sound, word, or movement during rehearsals. When Joe or Giddings spoke, the players listened. There was no extra horn tooting or chattering—no wasted minutes.

Ossip Gabrilowitsch refrained from associating himself with

the high school musicians until the final rehearsal. He sent his assistant conductor, Victor Kolar, to prepare the two works he was to conduct. Gabrilowitsch himself came to his first rehearsal just as the orchestra was playing the first movement of Beethoven's *Eroica*. He stood and listened. Most of the young members of the first National High School Orchestra had never read a symphony score before. In stunned astonishment, Ossip Gabrilowitsch proclaimed them the "music miracle of the century."

Interlochen

J OE'S first National High School Symphony Orchestra had a keen impact on the whole field of music education.

People in that Detroit audience of 1926 shed tears of emotion and enthusiasm when the concert ended, and news of this great orchestra, composed of young boys and girls, spread rapidly. Ossip Gabrilowitsch praised its wonders wherever he went. His seal of approval weighed heavily with professional musicians, who up to this time had scoffed at school music. School superintendents, also, had generally felt that music in the schools was a waste of taxpayers' money, and they too were impressed by Gabrilowitsch.

Joe was delighted when, within a week after his Detroit concert, he received a call from Dr. Randall J. Condon, then Superintendent of Schools in Cincinnati. Dr. Condon was President of the Department of Superintendence, the official organization of school superintendents. He asked Joe if he could assemble his National High School Orchestra again to play for a convention to be held in Dallas.

Joe lost no time accepting the invitation. Here was his chance to convince the superintendents and school boards of the nation as to the true value of music education. Here was an opportunity to show what young musicians could accomplish.

Dr. Condon gave Joe a free hand in organizing the group and promised full cooperation. It was impossible, however, to assemble the same orchestra that had played for the astonished audience in Detroit. Most of those students had been seniors and had graduated in June. For the convention in Dallas, therefore, Joe had to form a new orchestra. Dr. Condon's influence helped. So did Joe's orchestra committee of interested music directors and superintendents.

School boards were urged to support the project by sending the best local players and helping to bear their expenses. Arrangements were made to house the candidates in the homes of Dallas high school students without cost. With box lunches, specially reduced railroad fares, and the generosity of the hosts in Dallas, it was estimated that a student from Detroit, for example, could make the trip for about eighty-seven dollars, or a student from St. Louis for about sixty-three dollars.

When the second National High School Orchestra assembled for the Dallas convention that February, it numbered two hundred and sixty-six players from thirty-eight states. There were ninety-eight violins, thirty-two violas, twenty-six cellos, nineteen basses, twelve flutes, eight oboes, ten clarinets, seven bassoons, ten horns, eleven trumpets, ten trombones, six tubas, twelve harps, five percussionists. There was also one organist. And in all some fifty music educators had helped Joe with organization and training.

The program was selected and parts sent to the youngsters ahead of time, with their bowings and fingerings marked. Joe purposely chose works that expressed contrasting moods and had power to affect the sensibilities of an audience. And he hoped, of course, at the same time to affect the still somewhat withdrawn sensibilities of school superintendents toward music in the schools. He chose Mendelssohn's *Overture to Midsummer Night's Dream,* Beethoven's *Eroica,* Tschaikowsky's *Sixth Symphony* (the *Pathetique*), Rimsky-Korsakov's *Capriccio Espagnol,* Schumann's *Warum?,* Bolzoni's *Minuetto for Strings,* and Handel's *Largo.*

In Dallas the two hundred sixty-six young students, who had never met or played together before, rehearsed eight to ten hours a day for five days in preparation for their concert. Part of this time was spent with the complete orchestra; some was devoted to sectional rehearsals for strings, wind instruments, brass, or small ensembles practicing in separate groups. The enthusiasm of the youngsters for playing music throughout each long day startled the school administrators, but they were even more awed by the polished performance at their concert. In fact, Dr. Condon, who was presiding at the convention, experienced such astonishment during one number that he almost disrupted the performance by walking out onto the stage.

It happened during the *Capriccio Espagnol,* a work featuring solo cadenzas for violin, flute, and clarinet, and climaxed by a harp cadenza. During rehearsals and tryouts, eighteen year old Henry Siegel from Detroit had won the most coveted place in the orchestra—first chair violinist and concertmaster. With this, of course, went the honor of playing the *Capriccio* cadenza. But when Henry came late for the final rehearsal, Joe—the Giddings-trained disciplinarian—demoted him to last chair, forty-ninth in the first violin section. When it came time for his cadenza, Henry stood up and played it beautifully—from the back row in the sea of violinists.

Dr. Condon, meanwhile, had been standing backstage. He

peered out, startled both by the skill of the player and by his position in the orchestra. When the cadenza started, Condon unconsciously stepped forward. At the clarinet cadenza he moved forward still more. And during the harp cadenza he completely forgot himself, walked as if in a daze across the stage, and stood spellbound watching the twelve harpists execute their passages. Condon finally realized what he had done and hurried back into the wings as the cadenza ended, and the enraptured audience, too absorbed to have paid more than passing heed to the bemused wanderer in full view on the stage, broke into spontaneous cheers for the boys and girls who had made them experience the rapturous understanding that flows from beautiful music beautifully played.

From the time of this concert, the dream for which Joe had worked so stubbornly began its movement toward actuality. Music and the meaning of great music would at last be made available to the young people of America during their formative years. Often during the time of struggle the dream had seemed hopeless. Joe had met sneers, incomprehension, and opposition—and yet had stood fast by what he knew to be feasible and right. Now he saw the tide at last start its turning, and the long-awaited opportunity for his students begin to open before them.

The Department of Superintendence passed the following resolution which became the open door for music education in America: "We would record our full appreciation of the fine musical programs and art exhibits in connection with this convention. They are good evidence that we are rightly coming to regard music, art, and other similar subjects as fundamental in the education of American children. We recommend that they be given everywhere equal consideration and support with other basic subjects."

Henry Turner Bailey, Director of the Cleveland School of Art, wrote a review which was distributed to schools everywhere. Entitled *I Heard America Singing,* it expressed the feelings of a man who had been deeply moved. Describing the Dallas convention, Bailey said, "For five days the education of the children of our country had been discussed. On this last evening . . . the auditorium was packed with school officials from every state in the union. When the curtain rose . . . against a background of old gold and copper-colored silk . . . (there) appeared . . . two hundred and sixty-six boys and girls with their handsome instruments. When their leader appeared he was welcomed with happy faces and a clapping of hands, soon lost beneath the tumultous applause of the big audience. When his baton was raised, every eye was upon it; when it fell every tone was there on time. . . . The orchestra rendered the music with a precision, an enthusiasm, a vitality seldom achieved by professionals who play for money. Oh, it was a delight to watch those young faces, faces having the features of every nation under heaven, but alight with the common joy of cooperative achievement!

"They swayed the emotions of the audience like wind across a field of wheat. They held them for two hours, fascinated with beauty. From the first violinists at the front of the stage the musicians rose rank on rank to the twelve golden-harpers, high over all. And from that perfect harmony of color, a perfect harmony of tone poured over the audience its witchery of delight.

"In that orchestra boys from Wisconsin sat next to girls from Florida; girls from Texas next to boys from California. The children from Maine and Utah, from Nebraska and Georgia, from Oregon and Massachusetts, all looked equally beautiful and played equally well. There were forty-six from Michigan, twenty-four from Pennsylvania, nineteen from Ohio, sixteen from Kansas, but no human eye could have segregated them. They were all America's own. . . . No one who saw these young men and maidens and heard them play will ever forget it. It was like a vision of the world that is to be—a glimpse of the company out of every nation and kindred and tribe, before the throne of God, whose anthem of praise is like the sound of the sea. . . . And I heard the great true heart of my country singing as never before, and the harmony was as rich and deep as human brotherhood itself. . . ."

The effect of the orchestra demonstration in Dallas was apparent immediately. Throughout the country, school administrators no longer resisted efforts of music educators to establish music classes during school hours and with school credit. School boards could no longer refuse support for music education on the grounds that it was unessential, no proper part of education, a mere "frill." The superintendents of the entire nation had recommended that music be given equal consideration and support with *other basic subjects.* Three decades later there would be nearly four million school children playing in orchestras and bands, singing in choirs—and getting school credit for music as for Latin and algebra.

It had been a long pull and no one man could be given all the credit for the final achievement, but Joe, Giddings, Condon, and the many others who worked with them in the early struggle could each justifiably feel a sense of personal pride. Music was no longer a scorned exile; it was "accepted" by school officialdom.

Joe was closer to the young people than anyone else. He was the one who had selected the players and guided them through the five days of rehearsals that brought about the great achievement. He had insisted on discipline, conducted the orchestra . . . and now his student players seemed to him almost his own children. He had lived with them and worked with them, and he loved them.

But the concert was over.

Disbanded, the marvelous young orchestra would now simply go home, and Joe, his task ended, would return to Ann Arbor.

There was a farewell party in the school gymnasium, but an air of celebration was lacking. The young people nibbled at refreshments. They danced half-heartedly to the music of the hired band. In their ears were still ringing the glorious melodies they themselves had played. And now they must go home to their embryo school orchestras, which would never satisfy them again. The new friends they had made, the great accomplishment they had achieved together—all that was ended. The farewell party took on such an aspect of separation and sadness that some of the youngsters began to cry. Joe attempted to encourage them. He made a short speech telling how they were all to go back to their own schools and strive to spread the great privilege of understanding music.

Consolation, however, was in vain. Overwrought, and feeling a sense of inexplicable privation, the group found the sobs of its youngest and most emotional members becoming contagious. Finally an older boy in the back of the room called out urgently, "Mr. Maddy, why can't we get together *somewhere* this summer and play all the music we want to play—all day long?"

The boys shouted and whistled. The girls clapped and crowded pleadingly around Joe Maddy. All young eyes were fixed on him eagerly demanding an answer.

Joe climbed one of the gymnasium ladders affixed to the wall, and hanging there by his elbows, looked out on the sea of young faces. He understood their spirit, and he knew in that instant that his answer could not be a hasty "no." He made a rash promise— he would try to find for them a place where they could come together and play—"all day long," if that was their wish.

The gymnasium resounded with cries of joy. The pall lifted from the farewell party, but Joe, still hanging on the ladder by his elbows and mobbed by the excited throng, felt panic. *What* had he let himself in for?

"When?" they cried. "How soon?" "Where?" "How long?"

Grasping at memories of his own boyhood in Wellington with its summer camping trips, he told the youngsters that he would find them a "summer music camp." He didn't know yet exactly where or when, but it would be as soon as possible. He carefully refrained from telling them that he didn't know exactly how, either.

2

Joe went back to Ann Arbor feeling a combination of fiercely determined energy and helpless bewilderment. Having promised, he must keep his word—that was necessary in any good teacher. One did not allow youthful hope and enthusiasm to form, only to disappoint it. But how, he wondered, was he going to bring about this "summer music camp?"

His total financial resources were represented by his University of Michigan salary. And when he spoke to his friends about the notion of a music camp for boys and girls, he met only ridicule. There were recreational camps at the time, but never had boys and girls been sent to the same area at the same time. The very idea was shocking—in fact, immoral!

As for music, even musicians argued that Joe's tentative plan for an eight weeks summer session was absurd. How could you keep a group of high school students interested in music for that long a period? How many would be willing to give up their vacation for study? In the minds of most of Joe's fellow educators, even some who had the greatest faith in him, his idea of a music camp was considered nothing more than an unworkable chance scheme.

However, there was no malice in the skepticism. People were merely incredulous and pessimistic. Joe Maddy's character was beginning to be understood, his tenacity in assembling his two national high school orchestras was recognized, and it was felt that if Maddy had now decided to start a summer camp for students, he would probably do so. It would of course be a hopeless failure, they predicted, and the poor young professor would probably find himself in bankruptcy.

Meanwhile Joe typically found his resolution hardening in the face of opposition. And he discovered that he had two friends with enough confidence in him and his purpose to dig into their pockets and help. One was C. D. Greenleaf, the band instrument manufacturer who had backed Joe's *Universal Teacher*; the other was Giddings.

Giddings had felt deep personal pride at Joe's successes. And he did not think that keeping young people interested in music all summer long was impossible. Far from it. Furthermore, as a dedicated teacher, he believed that a promise must be kept. Having made his commitment, Joe *had* to build that camp.

Giddings told Joe that he must first arouse the interest of philanthropic foundations. Then he pulled out his own checkbook and gave Joe the money to go to New York and get in touch with them. Joe found, however, that the foundation officers listened with only mild interest. Some indicated they might be willing to support his project at some future date, if it proved worthwhile.

Music publishers offered to donate publications, but not funds. There was one exception: Carl Fischer, Inc., gave Joe twenty-five hundred dollars for scholarships. Such evidence of confidence deeply encouraged Joe. The Aeolian Company offered to print and distribute announcements, if and when the project actually started. It was then that Joe went to C. D. Greenleaf, the president of the National Association of Band Instrument Manufacturers who had successfully put his band instrument firm into the publishing business with the Maddy-Giddings *Universal Teacher.*

Although the band instrument manufacturers as a whole were not well disposed toward Joe because they felt he had exerted a disrupting influence on their business by revising band instrumentation, Greenleaf was an exception. He had been impressed when Joe presented his music camp idea to a meeting of the National Association of Band Instrument Manufacturers. Joe was dismissed immediately after his proposal to await their decision, and he was sure the answer would be a refusal, but he was wrong. Greenleaf brought him word that the Association had agreed to lend ten thousand dollars.

Joe was sure it would be easier now to get other contributions.

One vote of confidence backed up by financial support would inspire others.

But again he was wrong. No one believed his music camp could ever be self supporting. What could he do with ten thousand dollars? He needed money to buy land and construct buildings. He needed funds for endowments. And no one was inclined to contribute toward endowments—not for a project that existed only on paper. And Joe didn't yet even know *where* he was going to build.

But meanwhile Willis Pennington, a native of Michigan and a pioneer operator of summer camps in the north woods country, had heard about the project. He invited Joe to look over his property, a five hundred acre wooded site near a whistle-stop called Interlochen, sixteen miles southwest of Traverse City. The minute Joe and Giddings saw it, they knew it was the ideal location. On the property were two beautiful lakes, Wahbekanetta and Wahbekaness, half a mile apart, with an old resort hotel between them. There was a private boys' camp on one lake and a private girls' camp on the other, both operated by members of the Pennington family. Joe could envision a music camp that someday would include smaller children—and, in fact, he did later annex both those camps as part of his own.

At the time, however, the site was surveyed with the immediate aim of building cabins for high school girls on the lake front near the already existing girls' camp, and cabins for high school boys near the camp for younger boys already there; and to provide instruction facilities between the two camps somewhere near the hotel.

Since coeducational camps were unheard of in those days, the close proximity of the two lakes, with sandy beaches, pine woods, and plenty of room for building in between, seemed made to order for Joe's promise. Pennington, whose camps were prospering but who was losing money on his hotel, agreed to exchange sixty acres of lake shore property for the exclusive right to board all music campers at a fee of two dollars a day—or the cost of food and service plus eighty per cent of the profit during five years. The deeds to the land were placed in escrow to be delivered to camp officers when the terms of the contract were met, and Joe guaranteed that two hundred campers would board at the hotel after the first year. A non-profit corporation was formed with Joe Maddy, Willis Pennington and C. M. Tremaine as incorporators. An agreement between Willis Pennington and the newly formed National High School Association was drawn up and signed in the New York office of Joe's old friend Tremaine, who later became treasurer and one of the trustees.

Although Tremaine had always been one of Joe's stanchest supporters, he was as skeptical about the camp as most others. Nevertheless from the beginning he offered the help of his office staff and mailing lists.

Joe drew up plans for twenty-five cabins, each to accommodate twelve campers and one counselor. Confident that summer concerts would draw large audiences, and that the gate receipts would help financially, he also designed an outdoor music shell for rehearsals and performances. He reluctantly agreed to three hundred dollars tuition for each student, a fee which to him seemed exorbitant and "entirely unwarranted," but which his advisers thought necessary. He convinced himself that he could use the first year's income to pay for needed buildings and equipment. Then he could lower the fee to around a hundred or a hundred and fifty dollars.

The financing of the project seemed simple to him: two hundred and fifty students paying three hundred dollars each would bring in seventy-five thousand dollars. Board and room would take about twenty-eight thousand, which Joe thought much too high; and instruction should not cost more than fifteen thousand at the most. Concert receipts might bring in about twenty-five thousand. These were, however, the calculations of a musician, dreamer, and optimist—who then turned right around and let many of his students come on scholarships, paying for nothing but their transportation and their laundry. Joe, therefore, immediately went out begging for more scholarship money.

For a full symphony orchestra he needed players of oboes, bassoons, French horns, string basses, tubas, and harps—all expensive instruments and rarely owned by individual students. Players of popular solo instruments were plentiful. As Joe well knew, most parents did not wish to pay two hundred and fifty dollars for a huge bass fiddle for their son to lug around laboriously, and then have to lend him the family car to drive forty or fifty miles for the nearest available lesson, when for a fraction of the cost they could buy him the finest trumpet or saxophone, with instruction usually available in the next block. Such facts were among Joe's major problems in trying to form a well balanced group.

The Music Educators' National Conference again asked Joe to assemble an all-American orchestra, this time for its Chicago convention in the spring of 1928. Joe took up the assignment eagerly for he saw in this the chance to raise scholarship funds for his still non-existent music camp. He decided to stage two concerts at the convention, one for the public and one for the music educators. He would charge admission to the public concert and use the proceeds as a nucleus for his fund. He invited Guy Maier to contribute his services as soloist, and Dr. Frederick Stock and Howard Hanson to serve as guest conductors. He also persuaded Walter Damrosch and John Philip Sousa to put in appearances during rehearsals. The distinguished names generated a great deal of enthusiasm among both players and educators, but did little for the camp scholarship fund.

In the first place, while a severe blizzard kept hundreds of the visiting music educators in their hotel rooms on the night of the first concert, the weather cleared the next night when the concert was scheduled for the public only. And hundreds of music educators therefore jammed the concert auditorium that evening demanding free admission, saying that the orchestra had been assembled at their request, and for their benefit. They were the sponsoring organization. They should have free admission.

They did—while hundreds of others who would have bought tickets had to be turned away. Joe's scholarship fund might have had a start that night with six thousand dollars. As it was, he made six hundred—enough for two students.

During the following spring, however, Joe managed to beg about twelve thousand, five hundred dollars for scholarships for his camp, plus liberal donations of music and the loan of many musical instruments. But Joe, of course, meanwhile began to promise more scholarships than could be financed by the pledged funds. There was the little girl from Bloomington, Indiana, for example, whose mother couldn't afford the child's fare. But the girl played English horn and she wanted to come. Joe gave her a "scholarship"—out of his own slim pocket.

Music clubs and civic groups contributed part of the expenses for some campers. And many students earned some of their own tuition by working after school. For instance, there was Arthur Spalding, son of a country doctor in North Dakota, who earned his tuition by spending his after-school hours collecting old, out-lawed accounts for his father's services. And there was Lillian Friedman of Schenectady, who gave a private recital and sold tickets for it from house to house. Then, fearing that admissions would fall short of the needed amount, she sold program ads and collected enough cash for her camp fee.

But for every pupil who managed to pay, there were at least forty who had to ask Joe to find the money for them.

Joe had been too busy begging money for scholarships to worry very much about paying for the physical facilities at his camp. With his ten thousand dollars from the band instrument manufacturers he had started construction of the cabins, a camp hospital, an outdoor stage to be known as the Interlochen Bowl, and water and sewage systems—a total of forty-four thousand dollars. The down payment was twelve thousand. Joe borrowed two thousand from his scholarship fund, and expected to make this up and pay off his construction costs with advance tuition payments.

And so, on the picturesque site in the north woods, Joe and his friend Giddings watched the dream take shape, all with bor-rowed money and on land they didn't own.

The money ran out by the middle of May, with the buildings only half completed. One by one all the prospective donors lost courage and withdrew. Joe went back to C. D. Greenleaf and asked that the band manufacturers' association increase their loan by five thousand dollars. Greenleaf, still faithful, gave Joe his personal check for the amount. Joe then persuaded a group of Traverse City bankers to match the loan—but only for thirty days.

With ten thousand dollars in the bank, construction was resumed. And Interlochen's first season opened on the twenty-fourth of June, only fifteen months after he had swung by his elbows and made that rash promise to the students thronging around him in the Dallas high school gymnasium.

The camp opened with plenty of music but no music stands; fine teachers but no classrooms; two big lakes for swimming and boating, but no boats or canoes. No matter. More than ever Joe had confidence in his dream.

There was even a radio control room—but no broadcasts. Nearly everyone who saw Joe's blueprints of the Interlochen Bowl chuckled secretly at the space labeled "Radio Room." How could anyone be foolish enough to think radio programs could be broadcast from this remote spot? Little did they know that Joe would one day be operating his own stereo FM educational radio station from Interlochen.

Opening day of Joe's music camp came off with a great rush of joyful excitement. The young campers arrived, filled with enthusiasm and ambition.

There was only one thing wrong. Joe had miscalculated in his figures.

Instead of the two hundred and fifty to three hundred he had expected, only a hundred and fifteen campers had finally managed to find funds to come for the summer. Almost half of these were on scholarships. Total tuition receipts amounted to only twenty-eight thousand instead of the seventy-five thousand Joe had counted on. This was barely enough to pay the board bill for students and staff.

The Traverse City banks decided the camp was an unsafe financial risk and refused to renew their loan. The Sunday evening concerts were well attended, but at a twenty-five cents admission price, they netted only a little more than nine thousand dollars— far below the twenty-five thousand Joe had hoped for. And finally the camp wound up its first season with a deficit of forty thousand dollars.

Despite its poor financial showing, however, the camp was proclaimed an astounding and significant success by visiting musicians and educators. In addition to the orchestra, Joe organized a band and choir. Giddings taught the course in music methods. The faculty was composed largely of music educators who served as counselors as well as teachers, and taught composition, conducting, ensembles, drama, and of course the various band and orchestral instruments. Recreational activities included water sports, hikes, and overnight camping trips.

Far from becoming bored by eight weeks of music, the enthusiasm of the students increased every day. The thrill of performing in full the world's great works of music, the symphonies of Beethoven, Brahms, Tschaikowsky, Schubert, Franck, and Dvorak, kept them in a state of exultation all summer. In fact, it soon became necessary to establish some rules about—of all things—taking time off for recreation. While most parents have trouble making their children practice, Joe found that in the proper setting and with the right kind of incentive, young people will voluntarily practice more than is good for them. One of his biggest difficulties was to get them to observe recreation and rest periods.

Discipline was the least of his problems, despite the warnings of so many of his friends. Giddings took charge of this aspect of camp life, and he and Joe established the atmosphere of the camp that very first summer. This was to be a workshop, not a playground, and their sensible rules and high standards were based on their awareness that strict, impeccable discipline was paramount. But as it turned out, disciplinary problems were rare. The students loved camp life, became devoted to their teachers, and were far too busy to get into trouble. The spirit of Interlochen was established.

The boys' camp was located on the shore of Lake Wahbekaness, and the girls' division on Lake Wahbekanetta. The students met on the campus near the hotel for classes and concerts. Otherwise the two camps functioned as separate organizations. There were three important camp visitors that first summer. One was the Detroit Symphony conductor, Ossip Gabrilowitsch, who was so impressed that he said Interlochen ought to operate all year instead of only in the summer. Another guest was Percy Grainger, the famous Australian pianist, who later became a regular member of the faculty. A third was Howard Hanson from the Eastman School of Music who gave his official blessing by commenting, "The camp will prove a great step in the development of music in America."

With the first music camp season thus acclaimed, Joe naturally felt that someone would soon come along to help pay the bills.

For that, however, no one came.*

---

* Cash loans for the building of the camp included the $15,000 from C. D. Greenleaf and the band instrument manufacturers, $5,000 from the Traverse City banks, and $2,500 from T. P. Giddings. Scholarship contributions had come from Carl Fischer, Inc., the Juilliard Foundation, Willis Music Co., Oliver Ditson Co., G. Schirmer, George Eastman, Theo. Presser Co., C. C. Birchard Co., Teachers' College, Columbia University, and the University of Michigan School of Music. Music and other materials and supplies had been contributed by the Sinfonia Fraternity, the Aeolian Company, the Boston Music Co., Grinnell Brothers, Lyon and Healy, and the National Bureau for the Advancement of Music.

At season's end the music camp's assets were: twenty-nine cabins, one hospital building, one clubhouse for boys (donated by Sinfonia music fraternity), the Interlochen Bowl, and about eleven thousand dollars of music and miscellaneous materials and equipment—all this on land which the camp didn't yet own. It would become camp property only after four more years of successful operation—and payment of board to Willis Pennington.

Joe couldn't borrow money on this kind of assets.

The first season of the Interlochen Music Camp had been a great educational and artistic success. It had created a notable new appreciation of music and a spirit whose value—Joe felt—was inestimable. His young people had gone home enchanted, bearing new skills and great new hopes. The only trouble was that Joe Maddy was personally some forty thousand dollars in debt.

3

No one could convince Joe—though many tried—that he should surrender and give up the idea. Instead, he conceived the idea of issuing debenture bonds to cover present debts.

Despite the skepticism of the Traverse City bankers who refused further loans, Joe sold to a group of public-spirited citizens fifteen thousand dollars worth of debentures, payable in five years with seven per cent annual interest. He persuaded musicians and friends from other parts of the country to take up an equal amount. He was thus enabled to meet most of the pressing debts, and extended payment on the balance for another year. The subscribers to the fund in the Grand Traverse region elected a Board of Control comprised of businessmen, to supervise finances until the debentures could be repaid. Meanwhile the Michigan Highway Department, interested in a venture of such obvious advantage in bringing tourists to the State, paved the roads leading to Interlochen.

That winter Joe had an opportunity to spread the news of his music camp on a wider scale. He was asked to organize and conduct at least half a dozen all-state high school orchestras, as well as an All-Southern, an All-Southwestern, and a North Central group. In each locale he brought the message of Interlochen, and found it enthusiastically received. His second season opened with an enrollment more than double the first. There were two hundred and thirty-two boys and girls from forty-two states, plus Hawaii, and Alaska.

Fifty-one were enrolled in the college division, courses offered at Interlochen for credit by the Cincinnati Conservatory of Music, the University of Michigan School of Music at Ann Arbor, and the Teachers' College of Columbia University in New York. Thirty of the high school students came on scholarships provided by friends of the camp. Evidence of the need felt everywhere for such a program was that more than half were helped by local funds or benefit programs in their home towns.

The season opened with a welcoming address by Michigan's Senator Arthur Vandenberg who called the music camp a "benediction to America."

Opera and oratorio were added to the courses available. A day-by-day calendar, published in that season's yearbook, *The Overture,* vividly evokes the enthusiasm of this early crop of Interlochen campers.

MONDAY, JUNE 24: First orchestra rehearsal! Grand thrill as we attempt Beethoven's *Eroica*. We'll be an ensemble yet!

FRIDAY, JUNE 28: Tryouts! 'Nuff said. We read the *New World Symphony* and are thrilled.

SUNDAY, JUNE 30: Our first concerts. Everyone agrees, "It's wonderful."

MONDAY, JULY 1: *Odysseus* is introduced and we are told to be like the German who couldn't pass an opinion on *Tannhauser,* as he had played it only nineteen times.

TUESDAY, JULY 2: Who said there weren't any harps in Hades? We read Tschaikowsky's *Fifth Symphony.* Delighted.

FRIDAY, JULY 5: We read the Beethoven *Fifth Symphony.*

TUESDAY, JULY 9: We read the *Pathetique Symphony.*

FRIDAY, JULY 12: We read the Brahms *First Symphony.*

SUNDAY, JULY 14: Tschaikowsky's *Fourth Symphony.* Another wonderful concert.

TUESDAY, JULY 16: We sight-read Cesar Franck's *D minor Symphony,* and Sowerby's *Prairie,* dedicated to our camp. . . .

SUNDAY, AUGUST 4: The Northern Michigan Festival Chorus joins us in *Elijah.*

MONDAY, AUGUST 5: We begin work on *Prairie* and are introduced to seven and one-half quarter time.

WEDNESDAY, AUGUST 7: Our first opera, *Pirates of Penzance,* is produced with great success.

THURSDAY, AUGUST 8: Much suspense—solo contests. Thrills and heartbreaks as the winners are announced in the Bowl.

FRIDAY, AUGUST 9: Mr. Maddy wins bets on the orchestra's ability to read a Brahms symphony at sight.

SUNDAY, AUGUST 11: Audience and orchestra join in a wonderful performance of Bloch's *America.*

WEDNESDAY, AUGUST 14: Snow and colder. No concert. We go to bed to keep warm.*

THURSDAY, AUGUST 15: Despite the frigidness, a large audience turns out for our benefit concert. The orchestra freezes but plays on. Beulah-Benzonia Commercial Club [in neighboring resort community] announces gift of a clubhouse for girls.

---

* The summer of 1929 was marked by freakishly cold weather in Michigan.

SATURDAY, AUGUST 17: Last inspection. Wild packing. We begin to realize it is all over. . . .

SUNDAY, AUGUST 18: The season closes with *Les Preludes.* Then, *Au Revoir.*

This simple diary not only shows the spirit and enthusiasm of the early music campers, but it also gives insight into the scope and magnitude of their musical achievement. Most had never seen a symphony score before their arrival; and at Interlochen they were being introduced to the difficult music of the masters— not just one of them, but many: Beethoven, Brahms, Mendelssohn, Tschaikowsky. . . .

Eight professional symphony artists were added to the faculty that historic summer. Among them were Vladimir Bakaleinikoff, then assistant conductor and solo violist with the Cincinnati Symphony Orchestra; Walter Heermann, solo cellist for the Cincinnati Symphony; Mihail Stolarevsky, violist with the Cincinnati Symphony; Wendell Adair, Chicago Little Symphony; Louis Greene, former member of the Metropolitan Opera and New York Philharmonic Orchestra; Neil Kjos, Assistant Director of the University of Illinois band.

Praise was heaped on both Joe and his music camp. In a speech to the students Neil Kjos said, "It is through you that we will have a singing America. It is you who will inspire others to do better, and it is you who will lead them in this great renaissance of music as visioned by our genius, Mr. J. E. Maddy." Vladimir Bakaleinikoff said, "In the World War, the revolution and famine, we Russians lost everything and I thought I would never smile again. But the days I spent at the camp cured me and I became again happy." He predicted that the camp would "create great American musicians, composers, and audiences." Walter Heermann commented, "The material for our great symphony orchestras and bands is being shaped and developed right here in this camp. There will be more and better musical organizations in this country as a result of the work here." And Mihail Stolarevsky declared, "Nothing I have ever experienced would parallel the type of work done at this camp."

Howard Hanson awarded a number of scholarships to the Eastman School of Music to students who won solo contests during the final week of camp.

By the end of the second season there wasn't the slightest doubt in anyone's mind that Joe Maddy's Music Camp was a brilliant success—educationally and artistically.

But to Joe's great consternation he learned at season's end that he had had yet another financial disaster. The outgo of funds had exceeded the intake from tuition and contributions, and the highly successful season, instead of putting him out of debt, had bogged him deeper into the mire than before. All the gloomy warnings of his most pessimistic friends again seemed on their way to fulfillment. Joe was now sixty-seven thousand dollars in debt.

4

Well, as Joe often said later, what would *you* have done?

Musically, artistically, socially, educationally, the camp was a far greater success than anyone—except Joe and Giddings— ever dreamed it would be. No one now had any doubts about Joe's genius with young musicians, nor his ability to open a whole new world for them in their short eight weeks together. As for

Joe, he was more determined than ever. After two summers with his eager, talented youngsters, he knew that somehow, some way, he had to keep Interlochen going. Joe gritted his teeth and went out begging again. He talked people into buying more debentures and persuaded creditors to take long term notes to carry the enterprise until it could reopen in June. And in fact the winter did bring good news and brighter prospects. The Department of Superintendence again asked Joe to organize another National High School Orchestra as a feature of its 1930 convention, to be held in Atlantic City in February.

Dr. Frank Cody, Superintendent of the Detroit Public Schools, had been elected president of the school administrators, and he asked Joe to take full charge of all music. He told Joe to have music on each one of the meeting programs, and he gave him a free hand to fit his youngsters into the schedule in any way that was agreeable to the meeting chairmen. His only admonition was: "I want every music program to start and finish exactly on time." He appointed Arthur Searle of the Detroit School Music Department to assist Joe, and freed Searle from his other duties so he could devote most of his time to the music planning for the convention.

Exactly thirty-nine programs of music—all beginning and ending on time—were given for the various units of the convention by the three hundred and fifteen young musicians of that year's National High School Orchestra. From this group, Joe also formed smaller groups: a band, a string orchestra, plus dozens of string quartets, and small ensembles. One concert by the whole gigantic assembly was given with Dr. Walter Damrosch as guest conductor. Programs were broadcast over CBS and NBC.

When the convention closed, a selected orchestra of a hundred and eighty-two players, most of whom had been members of the previous summer's music camp, went on tour, giving concerts at the Metropolitan Opera House in Philadelphia under the auspices of the Philadelphia Civic Music Association; at Carnegie Hall in New York, under the management of Arthur Judson and sponsorship of the Juilliard School of Music; and at Constitution Hall in the nation's capital, under the sponsorship of Mrs. Herbert Hoover, and Senator and Mrs. Arthur H. Vandenberg.

In New York, Joe's music campers participated in a Damrosch Music Appreciation broadcast, performing Wagner's *Siegfried's Rhine Journey,* in which a fifteen year old horn soloist distinguished himself by playing the famous horn passage perfectly, thus winning the admiration of Dr. Damrosch and the members of his New York Symphony Orchestra.

The youngsters also were guests of the Cunard Line aboard the Steamship *Aquitania,* where they played for newsreel photographers for picture distribution throughout the world. For their Carnegie Hall concert, Ernest Hutcheson, dean of the Juilliard School of Music, was guest soloist; and the Juilliard School entertained the campers at a midnight reception afterwards.

In Washington, the orchestra played for President Hoover and other officials, and gifted young Betty Vandenberg, the Senator's daughter, appeared as piano soloist. Betty had been an Interlochen student the summer before.

The Atlantic City convention and tour was only half the story. Another Music Educators' National Conference convention had been scheduled in Chicago only three weeks after the Department of Superintendence convention in Atlantic City. And as usual the MENC insisted on having the National High School Orchestra as its drawing card.

In making his preliminary arrangements, Joe couldn't be sure how many concerts might be requested on the eastern tour, nor how long the tour would last. The only safe thing to do was to organize not one, but *two* National High School Orchestras simultaneously, one for the eastern trip and one for the Chicago convention. So he did.

As soon as the eastern trip was finished, Joe hurried to Chicago to start rehearsals with his second orchestra, another gigantic group—three hundred and fifteen eager young players, representing nearly every state in the country. The guest conductors were men of fame and distinction—Dr. Damrosch, Howard Hanson, John Philip Sousa, and Dr. Frederick Stock.

The effect of having two great youth orchestras giving successful and successive concerts in the short space of a few weeks, and in four of the largest cities, was immediately apparent. It resulted in nationwide broadcasts, national publicity, and great good will for Joe and his young people—and indirectly for the music camp at Interlochen. It also resulted in the offer of a radio broadcasting contract over CBS from the Grigsby-Grunow Company, sponsors of the *Majestic Hour,* an offer of sixteen thousand dollars for eight one-hour Sunday evening broadcasts from Interlochen. In the camp's financial need, this would be a life saver.

And then, suddenly, there were new and unexpected difficulties. The Interlochen orchestra would be displacing a seventeen piece union orchestra that had been employed regularly on the program. Joseph Weber was then president of the American Federation of Musicians. Joe went to see him and asked permission to broadcast, with the understanding that the union orchestra would receive its usual pay and would accompany a singer, who would present one or two solos.

Weber flatly refused.

Joe then went to Washington to confer with William Green,

president of the AFL, but Green offered him no encouragement. Senators, representatives, and even the Vice-President all referred Joe to the Secretary of Labor—who offered no help.

The first broadcast was set for early July—if the Union would give its consent. The annual convention of the American Federation of Musicians was scheduled for the first week of June in Boston. Joe's only chance was to present his case to the convention delegates, many of whom had children who played in school bands or orchestras. He also grasped at one more straw. Why not ask the students who had enrolled at Interlochen for the coming summer to use their influence on local delegates before the Boston convention?

He promptly wrote a letter to all prospective campers. He explained the situation, outlined the broadcasting plans and the camp's need for funds, and urged every student to write or go to see local union officials, who in turn should urge their convention delegates to support Interlochen's cause. Then Joe left for Boston. Time was running out. It would take two or three weeks to install proper wiring into the camp in the event the broadcasting was approved.

Joe didn't even know how to go about getting a hearing at the convention; he wasn't a delegate, and he had no official business there. He didn't dare telephone President Weber; Weber had made his position clear. At Joe's arrival in Boston, therefore, he simply sent a friend into the Executive Board meeting to ask if he could be given a hearing. The friend returned with the startling reply that the Board was asking for Joe Maddy; and in fact was expecting him. When Joe entered the room, he was greeted with "Hello, Joe," in chorus. Then before he could even state his case, the Board informed him that they had approved the broad-

• 207

casts—with the understanding that the seventeen piece regular orchestra be paid and that each program should carry an announcement that the program was "in the interests of living music with the approval of the American Federation of Musicians."

Joe's faithful Interlochen students had carried out their assignment of reaching the union delegates well indeed. But this peaceful settlement of an initial controversy was to prove deceptive. Actually it had been merely a minor storm—a warning of hurricanes pending, which if Joe had foreseen might have made his indomitable spirit shrink from what was to come.

It was during this same month, June of 1930, that Joe, who had started his life's work with only a ninth grade education, received his first important scholastic recognition. The Cincinnati Conservatory of Music conferred on him the honorary degree of Doctor of Music in recognition of his services to the youth of the nation. He was now entitled to be called Dr. Maddy. Joe, however, continued to identify himself as plain "Mr. Maddy," or more frequently, just "Joe Maddy." Nevertheless the recognition had deeply pleased him. It gave him more confidence, and more stature in the eyes of his colleagues in the field of music education. And now it seemed easier for Dr. Joe to tell the world—by gum—that he wasn't "educated" than it had been to make this admission before he got his first honorary degree.

It was with light heart and the brightest hopes yet that Joe opened his third season. There was a higher enrollment, and the camp for the first time engaged professional members of the nation's symphony orchestras to coach each section of the camp band and orchestra. College courses again were offered by Columbia

University, the Cincinnati Conservatory of Music, the University of Michigan School of Music, and the University of Wisconsin. A choir of sixty voices put on a performance of *The Messiah* with civic choruses from all over northern Michigan. They also produced the opera, *The Mikado,* in addition to regular programs and services.

The outstanding event of the season, however, was the visit of John Philip Sousa, and a concert by massed school bands from Michigan, numbering six hundred players, under Sousa's direction. This performance drew an audience estimated at ten thousand, many of whom had to stand on cars, fence posts, and tree stumps, as the woods filled with music from the Interlochen Bowl.

A new contribution to music education during the 1930 season was the establishment of drum-majoring classes for high school students, and a marching band tactics course for college division students under the direction of Raymond Dvorak. Until this time, drum majoring had been a matter of individual training, with no established techniques or standards. The mode of training begun at Interlochen soon spread, and universities everywhere began offering similar courses.

Several Interlochen students again won scholarships to Eastman and other schools of music. Faculty and visitors once more raised a chorus of praise. Sousa said, "The whole thing is wonderful." And Percy Grainger wrote Joe a note when camp was over, saying, "You have hatched a dream that, in my opinion, is the fairest hope on the American musical horizon."

Best of all, the camp had finally made enough money to pay off some of its debts!

In an expansive mood Joe pronounced the camp—for the first time—"a brilliant success, *financially.*"

During the winters, of course, Joe was still teaching at the University of Michigan. At the same time, however, he was in great demand to conduct all-state, regional, and national high school orchestras and to run state and national school band and orchestra contests and festivals. Since it was necessary for him to keep his classes going, he engaged at his own expense two of his former students, Walter Welke and Orien Dalley, to substitute for him when he was carrying on other activities.

Soon after the fall term opened, Joe was asked to report to the office of the University's president, Dr. Alexander Ruthven. He had no idea what Dr. Ruthven wanted. Was he about to be accused of shirking his classes, of not spending enough time at the college? Instead, Dr. Ruthven after a few pleasant opening comments told Joe his work outside the University had attracted so much attention that many were beginning to regard it as a significant development. The University, said Dr. Ruthven to his astonished professor, sent archeological expeditions at State expense to far-away parts of the world; why should it not send a man into the different parts of America in the interests of good music? The University had a grant from a foundation that could be used for precisely this purpose. From now on, concluded Dr. Ruthven, Joe was free to do as he pleased and travel where he saw fit—as long as he was promoting good music.

Joe could hardly believe his good fortune. He would retain his position, his professorship and his salary, and yet be relieved of his teaching duties in order to promote music throughout the nation. Early in 1928 the Carnegie Foundation had donated a hun-

dred thousand dollars to the University to be used for the further-
ance of the fine arts, twenty thousand dollars a year for five years.
It was under this grant that Joe had been chosen for his new
assignment, at six thousand dollars a year.

A man of vision, the president of a great University had put
his official seal of approval on Joe's work. In the final summing
up of those who lent him moral support, it was probably Dr.
Ruthven who gave Joe the most at a time when he most needed it.
Ruthven cleared the way for Joe to devote full time to a great
project and laid the groundwork for a step that would immeas-
urably enhance the prestige of the music camp: affiliation with
the University of Michigan.

With his new honorary doctorate, President Ruthven's personal endorsement, and money to pay off his camp's outstanding
debts, Joe's dream now seemed so close to becoming a reality that
Joe may have felt his struggle was all but over.

Then the bomb fell. The crash of 1929 was reverberating in far
off Wall Street. The Big Depression had hit.

As the winter went on, contributions to the music camp dwindled to practically nothing. Promotional opportunities for the
camp were curtailed, because most state and section festival
groups, contests, and conventions were either "postponed" or
abandoned. Nevertheless, Joe did not surrender his project. Instead he inaugurated music lessons by radio from Ann Arbor in
an effort to keep music alive in communities where teachers were
being dropped for lack of funds.

And he opened his fourth Interlochen season as usual. Enrollment was down. He had only two hundred and thirty students.
Piano manufacturers, suffering from the depression, could no

longer lend pianos, so Joe had to buy forty-five of his own. He also added a library building and a radio studio. Six sustaining programs were broadcast by NBC that summer—at no financial profit to the camp but at no loss either. It was not surprising that the camp failed to make any further reduction in its indebtedness during the 1931 season; what was remarkable was that it maintained its footing and went no deeper into debt.

The following winter was the bitterest period of the panic. Thousands of banks were forced to close their doors, business firms went into bankruptcy, millions of people lost their jobs and their savings, and the national income shrank by more than half. This time coincided with the fifth and final year of Joe's contract with Willis Pennington. If the terms of the contract were met, the Interlochen Music Camp would receive the deeds to the sixty acres on which its buildings had been constructed. But the contract stipulated that except for the first year there must be at least two hundred campers receiving board annually or the contract would be void.

Joe lowered the tuition fees in order to attract more students, but even by mid-winter that year it became obvious that only a miracle could save the camp from being washed away in the terrible financial tide that was sweeping so many of the nation's assets into nothingness.

In a flash of inspiration Joe decided that the only possible salvation was to buy out Pennington, his hotel and all his property, including the four hundred acres surrounding the camp. Even though he didn't have the remotest idea of what he could use for money, Joe went to Pennington to inquire how much he would take for his property. The asking price, Pennington told him, was a hundred and fifty thousand dollars. Joe would have been hard pressed to come up with a tenth of that amount, but he began bargaining.

Pennington realized it was to his advantage to sell. If the camp became forfeited to him, what could he do with it? He was not in the music business, and he could hardly have summer tourists sleeping on the stage of the Interlochen Bowl—supposing that there *were* any tourists that desperate year. He owed the camp four thousand dollars due to an error in his bookkeeping that had resulted in an overcharge of that amount for the campers' board the previous season. And he owed the banks forty thousand dollars, largely for additional facilities provided to accommodate Joe's students, and the banks were pressing him for payment. He and Joe agreed on a price of a hundred and four thousand dollars. Pennington inserted the condition that Joe bring him a ten thousand dollar down payment by March first.

That was January. Joe went out begging as he had never begged before, realizing that the entire future of his project depended on his ability to make the down payment. It was of course the worst possible time to be asking anyone for money. Two of the biggest donors, the Juilliard and Carnegie Foundations, had already withdrawn their support of Interlochen for the coming season. This was a serious blow; it had been difficult to get their interest in the first place.

Joe had first approached the Juilliard Foundation in 1928, when he had tried to see its president, Dr. John Erskine. He was refused an appointment. A short time later, however, he learned that Dr. Erskine had a speaking engagement in Ann Arbor on a certain date. So Joe went to New York and made a reservation on the best train back to Ann Arbor at the proper time. He had guessed right. Dr. Erskine *was* on that train! Joe managed to sit with him in the dining car—and to tell him about the music camp.

He didn't ask for money—then. Instead, he invited Dr. Erskine to come to Interlochen and play a piano concerto with full orchestra accompaniment. After Dr. Erskine's visit, the Foundation began to contribute twenty-five hundred dollars each year for scholarships. Similarly, the Carnegie Foundation contributed five thousand for the same purpose. But both donations were cancelled in 1932 because of the depression.

Joe knew the camp could not survive without their help. He made another urgent appeal. Both refused.

In desperation he offered each Foundation in turn his whole music camp as a gift. They again refused. He then offered it to the Traverse City banks. They too rejected it. Joe's scheme of course was to find some one who would take over the camp and keep it going, and he was willing to sacrifice his own stake in it. But his scheme didn't work. He was tense, haggard, and sometimes at low ebb in those days. But he was indestructible.

One day during the winter, while Joe was serving as guest conductor for the Illinois All State High School Orchestra meeting at Urbana, he learned that the National Board of the National Federation of Music Clubs was meeting in Milwaukee. This gave him an idea. Perhaps the Federation could afford to give financial assistance. He called one of the officers and was granted the opportunity to speak at the meeting.

The only way Joe could get to Milwaukee and back in the brief interval between rehearsals of his orchestra in Urbana was to fly. He engaged a private plane, operated by a University of Illinois student, to take him to Milwaukee early in the afternoon and back to Urbana right after his speech. But Joe's carefully arranged timing didn't work out as he planned. The Federation program was behind schedule and Joe had to wait until late afternoon to address the group. It grew so late that his young pilot was afraid to attempt the flight back after dark because he had no landing lights. They had no choice but to stay overnight in Milwaukee and return the next morning.

It was a cold gusty winter day. They were flying over Deerfield, Illinois, when suddenly the plane's radiator cap blew off. Steam shot out and froze over the windshield and cabin. Then the motor stopped, frozen. It was a water-cooled engine and the pilot had neglected the anti-freeze.

They had been flying at about two thousand feet. Below was a golf course and a plowed field. The golf course looked more inviting, but knowing about bunkers and other hazards, the pilot chose the field. They came down without injury, clipping the top off a small tree in the process. Several workmen rushed to them to find out whether anyone was injured, and Joe learned that he was on the estate of Mrs. J. Ogden Armour.

Joe at once composed a note to Mrs. Armour, explaining that he had landed accidentally on her grounds while on a trip seeking funds for his music camp. He dispatched the note by one of the workmen. The result was an invitation to come inside for a visit, and a check for two thousand dollars. Mrs. Armour took an instant liking to Joe and a warmly sympathetic interest in his story. In addition to her own gift, she persuaded her friend Samuel Insull to duplicate the amount. In fact, Insull promised two thousand dollars a year for the next ten years—a promise he couldn't fulfill since he was bankrupt at the time. His personal check to Joe was possibly the last money Insull gave to anyone.

Through the years Joe Maddy was to fly literally millions of miles, but this was his only plane mishap. And the forced landing in the frosty plowed field helped save his music camp.

With four thousand dollars in his pocket, Joe's confidence grew, and he pocketed his pride along with the money, to go out hammering on doors again, mainly the same doors that had not been slammed in his face when he had been selling debentures. Interlochen's only hope, Joe felt, was to sell more debentures to friends who already had an interest in the survival of the camp. It was they who would suffer most financially if the enterprise failed. He must show them it was to no one's advantage to let this happen, that not only was the opportunity for many young people at stake, but the monetary welfare of all the investors. His friends responded. Some traded in their Liberty Bonds; Joe himself borrowed on his life insurance; and his revered teacher and kindest friend, Giddings, at the last moment bought the final twenty-five hundred dollars worth of debentures.

On March 1, exactly on schedule, Joe delivered eleven thousand dollars in government bonds—instead of the ten thousand minimum—to Willis Pennington as a down payment on the property and buildings. The camp was to pay five thousand a year on the principal, plus interest at seven per cent, a total payment of more than nine thousand annually, until the mortgage was clear. In addition, there was three thousand annual interest due on debentures. This meant the camp would have to raise twelve thousand dollars each season *above* operating expenses to meet all obligations—a seemingly impossible feat for an institution operating only eight weeks every summer, and in the worst years of the depression.

The camp was now a hundred and forty-five thousand dollars

in debt! Anyone who knew the circumstances was apt to shake his head and feel grateful that he wasn't in Joe Maddy's shoes.

5

There was, however, sound logic behind Joe's action in acquiring the property from Pennington. Not only had he rescued the music camp and his investors, at a time when investments everywhere were disappearing, but there were other advantages. The camp could save itself Pennington's profit on boarding the students, which had amounted to some ten thousand a year. It could retain the profit made by the hotel, and the hotel could be operated largely with college students working part time and paying tuition. And, of course, everyone was expecting the depression to end. *It couldn't go on much longer!*

But only a hundred and forty-seven high school students and a hundred and five college division students were able to enroll for the camp's next season. But the spirit of experiment and love of music was even higher than before. One important innovation was the assembling of an All-State High School Orchestra, Chorus, and Band, each for one week at a time for a short concentrated session. The All-State groups were comprised entirely of young musicians from Michigan. The members of these organizations were given instruction by members of the camp faculty and they had the privilege of using the camp's recreational and musical faculties. Their organized activities included full and section rehearsals, ensemble study and concerts under the direction of music camp faculty and guest conductors.

Although superimposed upon the regular Interlochen program, the All-State groups soon became an integral part of the music camp. The All-State organizations served as feeders for college bands and orchestras and as demonstration groups for classes in music education, so it wasn't long until most colleges and universities offered summer training in music for high school students.

The University of Michigan became the sponsor of the Michigan All-State high school bands, orchestras and choruses in 1942. Then their terms were extended to two weeks, one group moving in as another group moved out. By 1960 there were six all-state music groups, representing more than 600 Michigan high schools, spending two weeks of each summer in intensive training under the National Music Camp faculty and under the supervision of music camp counseling staff and University of Michigan "Counselors-in-training" personnel.

The groups included all-state high school band, intermediate band, high school orchestra, intermediate orchestra, high school chorus and piano institute—nearly a thousand students in all.

At the end of the 1932 season Joe was able to meet his property payment, as well as the interest on debentures and the land contract, though some accounts had to be carried over.

The next year, however, he went into debt again—in order to finance a trip for his young musicians to the Century of Progress in Chicago. This was not—as might appear—a reckless action, but a move aimed at bringing both benefit to his students and financial help to their enterprise. The preliminary publicity regarding the proposed trip, plus a reduction in tuition to a hundred and seventy-five dollars, brought the largest enrollment to date: two hundred and twenty-one high school and one hundred and forty-two college students.

That year, 1933, was to be remembered as the "barter" year,

the time when money was so scarce that stations were established where merchandise could be exchanged in lieu of cash. Following the trend of the times, Interlochen offered to accept advertising space in the camp weekly program, *Scherzo*. The response was overwhelming. The booklet had to be increased from thirty-two to sixty-four pages in order to carry all the advertising. The camp's music library grew by leaps and bounds, and a great many musical instruments, materials, and supplies were obtained. Also as a measure of economy, the boys' mess hall was closed, and men and boy campers ate at the hotel, which had been reserved previously for the women and girls, a plan that proved so popular it was permanently adopted.

Meanwhile Giddings again dug into his pocket and donated funds for a much needed new chorus building. It was named Giddings Hall. He also financed and supervised long-overdue landscaping of the grounds around the hotel. In spite of the atmosphere of struggle, hopes were high and growth went on. One of the most important achievements of the season was the addition of the Eastman School's distinguished Dr. Howard Hanson to Interlochen's Board of Directors. But the crowning event of course for the students was their trip to the Century of Progress during the final week of camp.

Joe had been appointed by the Fair management, on recommendation of the Music Educators' National Conference and other music and education groups, to take charge of all music education demonstrations during the Exposition. It was an important assignment, and he accepted only after the Fair's management agreed also to engage a hundred piece union band for its entire duration—a demand of the American Federation of Musicians.

It was planned to invite music groups from every part of the country to participate in state, city, and other special "days" at the great Fair. For example, "Michigan Day" would feature the Interlochen groups, and other organizations representing that state's school and community music activities. "Detroit Day" would feature the Detroit Symphony Orchestra—and so on, for all states wishing to participate.

Exposition authorities promised to provide a suitable concert shell with safe storage for instruments. They would also furnish proper equipment—music stands, risers, lighting, and the rest. Elaborate plans were drawn up for a Music Building that would provide sleeping quarters for three hundred. All music groups were to pay their own expenses to the Fair, although they would be admitted free to the grounds during the days on which they were scheduled for programs.

By March, three months before the opening of the Chicago Exposition, Joe had made arrangements for more than three hundred school and community bands, orchestras, and choruses to appear on their own appropriate state or city "days." Then, without warning, the Exposition authorities, fearing a financial collapse of the undertaking because of the unexpected continuing severity of the depression, suddenly abolished the Music Committee, abandoned plans for the Music Building, and canceled the contract for the hundred piece union band. In the haste and panic typical of the times, they failed even to notify Joe of the change. He learned about it through the newspapers. Stunned, he tried immediately to reach the Fair officials, and was refused an audience.

Partly because of the Fair officials' attitude, and partly because he had no desire to get in trouble with the powerful Musicians

Union, Joe promptly wrote to all the music groups he had booked, urging them to cancel their plans because of the Exposition's refusal to meet its pledge to the hundred union musicians. But it was too late. The music groups had made their arrangements for housing and for participating in their special "days," and already had raised the funds for their trips to Chicago.

They arrived, right on schedule, to present more than two hundred free concerts and demonstrations, without the employment of a single paid musician by the Chicago Fair. Joe faced a difficult decision. Either he must disappoint his Interlochen students by canceling their appearance, or he had to do as the others were doing and go to Chicago in spite of the obvious injustice the Exposition had put upon the union professionals. As usual, his concern for his students won. Two hundred and seventy Interlochen campers, including counselors, nurses, and a physician were booked into special trains. Joe knew he might incur the enmity of the Musicians Union but he hoped for understanding. No less than they, he was angered by what the Fair had done, and he had protested as strongly as he was able.

The Fair's schedule for the Interlochen students was full of opportunity and excitement. It scheduled a four day series of concerts, including afternoon and evening performances, with such special events as an appearance by Senator Vandenberg's daughter, Betty, as soloist on a broadcast over NBC and a featured appearance at Soldiers' Field in connection with the gigantic Chicagoland Music Festival. Senator Vandenberg appeared at one concert and gave a talk on Interlochen's contribution to music. Dr. Howard Hanson was guest conductor for the National High School Orchestra in a performance of his *Romantic Symphony,* which he had composed at Interlochen. All programs were sent by loud speaker throughout the fairgrounds, so Interlochen was heard everywhere—a background to the swish of the roller-coasters, the shouts of Midway barkers, and the commercialized bedlam of the Exposition.

The music campers were treated well. They were housed in dormitories at the University of Chicago, with special trains to transport them back and forth. They had breakfast at the University, and all other meals at the Montgomery Ward cafeteria on the fairgrounds. Exposition officials gave them special attention, even providing half a circus tent for their performances, complete with a wooden stage and a few benches for the audience. The benches were a rare treat. Hundreds of the Fair's visitors were collapsing in the summer heat every day because there were so few places to sit down. The managers also gave Interlochen the use of a building, equipped with cots and chairs, where the students could relax and rest and lock up their instruments.

For the Interlochen young people, the final and crowning event was their appearance in the Chicagoland Music Festival at Soldiers' Field, before an audience estimated at a hundred and thirty-five thousand. Included on this program was a seven hundred piece union marching band—hired by the Chicagoland Festival, not the Century of Progress Exposition. It was led by James C. Petrillo. The program opened with the seven hundred unionists straggling across the field playing a march, with Petrillo walking ahead. The Interlochen Orchestra was stationed at the north end of the field, before the microphones for the stadium's public address system broadcast, in which the young players were the featured group.

When the union band completed its march, Petrillo came over
to Joe, sat down, and began talking to him—apparently in high
spirits. "Your kids play okay," he said, "because they play only
a few pieces that they've been practicing all year. When you
want real music, you gotta get my boys. They know how and can
play anything, any time."

Joe was non-plussed. He had expected a hot reproof from the
union boss for his part in the Exposition. But here was Petrillo,
praising Joe's young orchestra and showing no anger at the ava-
lanche of free music provided by Interlochen and other groups—
anger with which Joe would have been prepared to sympathize.
It was, however, a moment Joe would recall later. Was James
Caesar Petrillo, beneath his jovial manner, an expert dissembler?
Or did he simply change his mind later? Whatever may have
been the case, Joe would before long begin to suspect that the
union czar was a man with a long memory.

The Century of Progress project was both difficult and complex, but everything went exactly as planned. Not one student
was late for any rehearsal or concert. No one became ill. Only
one left the fairgrounds against rules, and he merely had to pay
seventy-five cents to get back in, which in those money-scarce days
was probably penalty enough.

An unusual demonstration of camp organization and discipline
occurred on the night the special train was scheduled to take the
students back to the University of Chicago after their final program at Soldiers' Field. It was around eleven o'clock. Some hundred thousand people were crowding for trains in the Illinois
Central station, with the Interlochen music campers mingled in
the throngs. There was a train every minute, each stopping only

briefly. When the Interlochen Special arrived and was called, the milling crowd made it seem impossible that all the young campers could disentangle themselves in time. But each student had been assigned to a certain car and each car had a counselor to check in the students. When the train stopped to unload, counselors reported that not only was every camper accounted for, but each one had been in the proper place!

That year the National Music Camp season, climaxed by the Century of Progress concerts, could again be called a success—except financially. The trip to Chicago had eliminated an important source of revenue, for it had been made during the final week, one normally profitable because of large audiences at final concerts, and also because of the large number of paying guests, usually parents, in the hotel. And, in addition of course, the Chicago trip had been financed entirely by the camp.

Again Joe had to put off his creditors, and when he opened the following June it was to the bleakest season he had yet encountered.

He had very little in scholarship funds. Enrollment had dwindled to a hundred and twenty-seven high school and a hundred and twelve college students, and nearly all were relying on part time employment at camp, which meant a substantial reduction in income from normal tuition.

Joe was advised to scale down the debts by offering to settle for fifty cents on the dollar, a course widely followed at the time. But he refused to do this. He felt too deep an obligation to those who had supported his project and, in purely practical terms, there wouldn't be enough money even then to pay all the bills.

It was Tremaine, as camp treasurer, who came up with the idea that brought temporary respite. He devised a plan whereby the camp could save fifty thousand dollars in ten years by reducing interest rates from seven to three per cent, and extending the principal for that time—*if* the creditors could be persuaded to agree.

Such a program could not succeed without the written consent of all creditors, and these included more than a hundred debenture owners scattered throughout the country. Tremaine spent weeks getting in touch with these people and trying to convince them that there was a fair chance of getting back their investment if the interest was reduced. Three per cent was the normal rate in those years, and it was perfectly plain that the creditors would get little or nothing if they refused and threw the camp into bankruptcy. Tremaine obtained universal agreement. He then persuaded Willis Pennington to cut the annual property payments from five thousand to three thousand dollars for the ten years, and to reduce the interest on the purchase contract also to three per cent.

The result of Tremaine's reorganization was to assure the camp a decade more of existence—provided the current operating expenses could be met, plus the three thousand dollars a year property payment and four thousand interest charges. Thus Interlochen got a new lease on life, but it carried with it an absolute necessity of making both ends meet.

Joe set himself a stern new policy: he would not grant any more scholarships from camp funds. Naturally, however, he promptly forgot all about it as soon as the new season opened. There were too many promising youngsters who simply couldn't pay. After all, he told himself, he had to obtain proper instrumentation for his orchestra. And a symphony without string basses and bassoons would have ruined the camp as an institution

of music. When string bass and bassoon players needed scholarships, Joe saw that they got them. But otherwise he did, with
the greatest reluctance, hold scholarship help to a minimum. As
a result he was able to reduce substantially the camp debt.* A
music convention attended by a hundred and fifty delegates
added revenue, as did summer productions of Gilbert and Sul-
livan's *Pinafore* and excerpts from *Aida* and *Der Freischutz*.

In April the following year Joe was elected president of the
Music Educators' National Conference. In spite of his promotional activities and his money raising struggles, he had found
time to complete a major research project for the MENC, which
served as guideposts for the construction or remodeling of music
classrooms, and for standards in equipment and materials for
teaching music in the schools. The study included recommendations for everything from type of chairs and music stands, to
number and quality of instruments that should be provided to
suit various school enrollments.

Joe's election to the presidency of the MENC, a two year
term, came partly as a result of his success with his research
project. But it was also a nation-wide endorsement of the ideals
he had set for himself and others in music education. And it
served as a vote of confidence for Interlochen. It was another
tribute to Joe's ability, and it heartened him to face his financial
reverses.

During his two year term as President of the Music Educators
National Conference Joe undertook a major project. He believed
that music instruction in American schools should carry over

---

* To a hundred and thirty-eight thousand dollars, of which thirty-nine thousand,
eight hundred was owed for debentures, and eighty-seven thousand was due on the
land contract.

into adult life and become an integral part of American culture. He worked out a plan to make a nation-wide survey of community and neighborhood orchestras, bands, choruses and other functioning music groups, then, when these facts became known, to develop plans to promote group music participation systematically throughout the United States as a major function of the MENC.

Working through existing affiliated state and regional music education organizations Joe succeeded in establishing a "Committee on Music in Community Life" in each state, whose chairman would serve as a member of a regional committee, whose chairman, in turn, would serve as a member of the national committee which would serve under the guidance of the president of the MENC—Joe.

The survey never materialized however, because the MENC executive committee thought the expense of postage and mailing too great at the time. Now that a quarter-century has passed since Joe's attempt to promote participation in community music activities by people whose musical talents were developed in our schools, there has been a tremendous advance in such participation, but far less than would have been possible had he been able to finance his project. Fourteen hundred symphony orchestras in the United States are proof that the music education in our schools is producing magnificent cultural results.

The music camp was now gaining a reputation from coast to coast, and the summer of 1936 brought it increased recognition by two notable events. One was the convention of the American Bandmasters' Association which brought some fifty of the most prominent band directors to Interlochen for four days. Two camp bands were placed at their disposal and five programs were presented, with forty guest conductors. There were three broadcasts over NBC, one in the form of a bandmasters' frolic featuring Herbert L. Clarke, Frank Simon, and other national figures in the role of comedians. Before it closed, the Bandmasters' Convention presented the Interlochen young people with funds for a new building, to be used as a much needed camp store, selling concessionaire supplies—anything from toothpaste and writing paper to Melody Freeze dips and popcorn.

The other outstanding event of this season was Damrosch Day at Interlochen on August sixteenth. It was the first and only visit of the venerable Dr. Damrosch to the music camp, and the Interlochen Bowl was filled to overflowing for the performance of Walt Whitman's *O Captain, My Captain,* to Damrosch's musical setting. Dr. Damrosch echoed the enthusiasm of other eminent visitors. During broadcasting of the program he said, "To me this orchestral camp is one of the great revelations that the American musical world has seen and that Americans have accomplished. I consider it to be one of the epoch-making developments of music in our country, and I cannot imagine anything that can contribute more to the American youth in the knowledge of music than this brave and noble experiment which Professor Maddy and his associates have started. I have nothing but praise for these young people and wish them happiness in the future and continuous pursuit of their musical profession. . . ."

For the young people of Interlochen the following season, it began to seem that Dr. Damrosch's wish for them was beginning to come true. Joe's travels in connection with his office as President of the MENC had taken him all over the United States— from New York to Tampa, to New Orleans, San Antonio, San Francisco, Portland, and points in between. And of course wherever he went, for whatever purpose, he did his best to let students know of the camp. Business conditions were improving and Joe felt able to raise camp tuition from a hundred and seventy-five dollars to two hundred. He booked a convention of Delta Omicron, national educational fraternity, into the hotel a week before camp opened. This would mean welcome added revenue.

The camp was regaining its financial equilibrium as a result of Tremaine's well-timed reorganization. With characteristic optimism Joe launched a pre-season program in which he ordered the repairs and remodeling necessary to make the camp hotel, dormitories, and cottages adequate for the needs of his anticipated heavy registration of both convention delegates and camp students. It proved to be an expensive project. Then on the opening day, the water system, also long in need of repairs and replacement, finally gave out. Joe had to buy new wells, a new pump house, and new machinery.

And when the season closed, Joe and Giddings had to dig into their pockets again to carry the camp through. Giddings loaned more than five thousand dollars. Joe mortgaged his life insurance again to come up with a little over three thousand dollars. And the music camp survived once more.

In the summer of 1938 Olin Downes, music critic for the *New York Times,* paid a visit to Interlochen and was overwhelmed by what he found. "Having been a music critic in New York all my life," he wrote, "I had to come west to find the real music of the United States." Soon after this Downes was appointed Music Director of the New York World's Fair. One of his first acts was to invite Joe and his National High School Orchestra.

The Interlochen young people went to the World's Fair during the final week of the following season, and gave fourteen concerts. One was presented at the special invitation of Mayor

LaGuardia. The students' blue knickers attracted attention: some Fair visitors thought Interlochen must be in Switzerland; others were soon joking with the youngsters about their "Swiss costumes," and the knickers became a pass to almost any form of the Fair's entertainment.

One result of the New York World's Fair trip was a movie contract with a Hollywood studio to film a story based on Interlochen. It was called, *There's Magic in Music*. Unfortunately, it turned out not to be a very good movie, but the camp was paid five thousand dollars for the rights. The picture was released in the spring of 1940, and that summer Interlochen had to assign six full time guides to escort visitors and curiosity seekers around the camp grounds.

Visits by the venerable conductor of the Chicago Symphony Orchestra, Dr. Frederick A. Stock, in 1940, 1941 and 1942, provided unforgettable inspiration to the members of the high school orchestra and to all campers who were privileged to observe rehearsals and performances under his direction.

"Don't play notes, play music," he admonished them time and again when the players reverted to back-home music.

When Joe thanked him as he was leaving Interlochen following his third and last visit as guest conductor, Dr. Stock replied, "Don't thank me. Thank those wonderful young people for giving me such a great inspiration."

The publicity resulting from the World's Fair appearance and the Hollywood movie gave Interlochen two banner years, in which the camp not only was able to meet its annual payments but finished with a small operating surplus*—the long-awaited

---

* End of the 1940 season showed a net operating surplus of $13,824.98. The camp's total indebtedness had been reduced to $102,931.69.

achievement at last! In 1941 the camp had a total enrollment of three hundred and sixty-eight, the largest number yet. For the first time it became necessary to turn away students because of overbalance in some sections of the orchestra. And the biggest concert crowd in Interlochen's history turned out for Paul Whiteman's guest appearance with his twenty piece orchestra in the Interlochen Bowl. But the most important development of that season, and perhaps one of the most significant events since the music camp had opened, was the culmination of proceedings making it officially an affiliate of The University of Michigan. All college courses offered at the National Music Camp would now be given as campus courses of the University. The University had been accepting credits earned at the camp, but this new and direct affiliation meant that actual University of Michigan courses could now be taken at Interlochen.

During the 1941 season, University officials had visited the camp and watched the educational, recreational, and business procedures. The following November, the Board of Regents approved a plan whereby graduate as well as undergraduate studies would be offered for credit. It was a significant tribute to Dr. Joe and his faculty.

The camp's financial position also continued to improve. The summer ended with an operating surplus of more than thirteen thousand dollars.* In accordance with the terms of the original contract, Pennington gave over the deeds to the entire property after the close of that season, and the camp gave a mortgage in the amount of the balance still due.

---

* Liabilities of the camp at the close of the 1941 season amounted to $92,700, of which $50,850 was still due on the land purchase contract—payable at the rate of $3,000 annually—and $33,400 represented outstanding debentures payable in 1943.

Joe had started Interlochen with nothing more than a dream and a promise—to those youngsters in Dallas on that long ago day. By 1941 he had invested more than two hundred and ninety thousand dollars in land, buildings, and equipment; and he had paid off nearly two hundred thousand in only fourteen eight-week seasons of operation, despite the agonizing struggle during the years of the depression. There was still a long road ahead, and it would not be until 1956 that Joe would make his final payment and the property would be fully deeded to the camp; but the danger that the camp would die in its early years was now behind.

Meanwhile, there was the achievement itself, a dream shaped by the courage of one man, helped by his friends who believed in him and impelled by the vision that did not forsake him. Joe Maddy's dream was now a splendid shining reality, an enchantment that would become part of thousands of lives.

"Tit Willow, Petrillo"

I

THINGS appeared to be going well for Joe and his music camp during the early days of the next summer. For the first time in his fourteen year struggle to bring his dream to fulfillment, he could indulge in a feeling of accomplishment and a sense of security. He had fought the battle for Interlochen's existence, and won it. He had brought it through bankruptcy and a depression; he had steered it onto solid financial ground and into the hearts of every music loving person in America. Joe felt he could relax. The worst was over and the future bright.

Then another bomb fell—not the lethal kind, such as those exploding elsewhere in the world that war-time year, but one that seemed to Joe the sort of thing that could destroy the very principles for which Americans were fighting. And like other bombs before and since, it meant war: Joe's war, an all-out effort that made his previous struggles pale by comparison, and, before it ended, was to involve not just Joe and Interlochen but countless thousands all over the country.

The bombshell which shattered the tranquility of Interlochen came in the form of a telegram, delivered to Joe one Friday night, just as he was rehearsing the two hundred and sixty-five members of the world's youngest symphony for the next day's

coast-to-coast broadcast. This was to be the first of eight scheduled programs and would mark the camp's thirteenth season of
regular weekly network music.

The strains of Beethoven's *Eroica* Symphony were filling the
woods, and the rehearsal was only half over when a blue-knickered student-messenger came to the podium and handed Joe the
telegram. He read it quickly. Then he read it again, more carefully. For a fleeting second he considered halting the rehearsal.
But only for a second. As his youthful musicians played on, not
one of them knew that a part of Dr. Joe's world had just crashed
down upon him.

When the rehearsal was over, Joe made a quiet announcement:
"This message is from NBC. Mr. Petrillo won't let us broadcast
tomorrow."

The telegram said a great deal more than that. But Joe couldn't
bring himself to tell his youngsters the whole bitter story all at
once. Not only one but *all* scheduled and future radio programs
from Interlochen were canceled on order of James C. Petrillo,
now the new President of the American Federation of Musicians,
the same man who had said at the Chicago World's Fair that
Interlochen competition did not bother him. Petrillo's telegram
further stated that if the order were not obeyed, he would call a
strike in which all union musicians employed by NBC would
leave their posts.

Dr. Joe's students, most of whom never had heard of James C.
Petrillo, were bewildered. They assumed this must be the result
of some misunderstanding, and with youth's typical optimism
they concluded they could help clear it up. They bombarded Petrillo with letters and telegrams explaining that they were at

Interlochen to learn, not to cheat union musicians out of work. They invited him to come visit them, to hear and see for himself. Their letters, telegrams, and invitations received no replies.

Dr. Joe by this time, however, knew Petrillo—not personally, for the two had come face to face with one another on only two occasions and had not exchanged more than a dozen words. But Joe understood him, well enough to know that he had a battle royal on his hands.

Joe's first encounter with James Caesar Petrillo had been in 1928. That year the Music Educators' National Conference convening in Chicago, had asked Joe to assemble his National High School Orchestra to play for the convention, and arrangements were made to broadcast the program over NBC. This was not intended as a commercial venture but as a demonstration to show the music educators and the people of the nation what young, serious music students could achieve.

Petrillo at that time was head of the Musicians Union of Chicago and was already demonstrating the measures he intended to use to promote both his union and himself. Joe felt the sting of his ruthlessness when he arrived in Chicago and learned that Petrillo had issued an ultimatum: either a fifty piece union orchestra would have to be employed at twelve dollars per player to stand by while the students gave their broadcast, or the High School Orchestra would not be allowed on the air.

Only a heartless man could have endured to cancel that radio program and Petrillo knew Joe's reputation for being anything but heartless about his students. The young people had already gathered, full of expectancy. Their families and friends back home were looking forward to hearing them. Rather than disappoint them, Joe scraped together the necessary six hundred dollars to pay the union standby orchestra, mostly out of his own pocket—an action which presented a ludicrous contrast. Joe at that time was earning an annual salary of three thousand dollars from his post at The University of Michigan, while Petrillo, as president of the Chicago Musicians Union, was being paid twenty-five thousand a year and had an armored car and a chauffeur supplied to him by the Union.

Joe Maddy was not a man who would accept without protest such an injustice as the one put upon his students in Chicago. He let it be known that he intended to air the facts of the case during the broadcast, and neither Petrillo nor any members of the Union could stop him.

Petrillo did try to stop him. He telephoned Joe and hinted broadly that Joe's health might suffer if he said anything about the case during the broadcast, and an official at the radio station got in touch with Joe and informed him that a technician might "accidentally" drop a pair of pliers during Joe's speech and cut the program off the air.

These threats and maneuverings failed to shake Joe. A union man himself, he intended to tell the public about what he regarded as a flagrant abuse of union rights and privileges. But the directors of the MENC convention did have the power to stop Joe from speaking out, and they became alarmed. A worried official confronted him, "If you give this talk you could antagonize union leaders all over the country against music educators, and we don't want that."

"I paid six hundred dollars, partly for the right to talk, and I think I should," Joe replied.

"We're going to reimburse you. We would rather do that than take the risk. We want you to keep quiet, Joe."

Joe realized that there was more at stake than his own personal feelings about what he saw as an abuse of power, and he agreed to say nothing during the broadcast.

What Joe did not realize at the time was that a pattern was set by this episode, a pattern to be duplicated repeatedly in later years.

Joe persisted in his belief that radio offered one of the best media for developing and encouraging the young talent in America. The broadcasts by his students showed other students what could be accomplished, it proved to the public what young people could do, and Joe refused to give up use of the medium. Petrillo's insistence that all radio music should be played by his union musicians, Joe regarded as simply unfair. Petrillo had an obligation to *all* musicians, Joe felt, not just to those who were currently paying dues into his Union. These young people were the rising generation, and Joe insisted that to hold them back was not right.

That the students might be his own union members of the future did not seem to occur to Petrillo. His harassment tactics continued. All during the years when Joe was conducting radio music lessons over NBC, with the programs originating out of Chicago, a payment of twenty-five dollars to Petrillo's Union was demanded each time a radio pupil played a few notes over the air as part of the instruction.

During these years Joe was also in charge of an NBC sustaining or non-commercial program called *Music and American Youth*. Its purpose was to demonstrate the achievements of school music groups in various sections of the country. Each demonstration originated in a different city. When it was scheduled for Chicago, the Petrillo order went out: no student instrumental musician could take part.

Joe chafed under the treatment, although he was not and would never become anti-labor. Joe had joined the Union twelve years before Petrillo himself became a member, and Joe had worked conscientiously for policies aimed at obtaining maximum employment for the Union's musicians.

Ironically, one of these very endeavors had cast him in the role of a union musician battling school authorities, although he never resorted to Petrillo-type procedures. Joe's argument with school officials resulted from a practice, which he believed to be far too prevalent, in which people engaged high school bands—because they were free—for functions which were not demonstrations and more appropriately called for the services of professional musicians. Joe believed that school officials should prohibit this practice. At one time his campaign became so vigorous that he angered a number of men in his own teaching profession, but he drove home his point: that there was a type of function proper for school music groups and another for professional musicians. Joe's contention was that *neither* should endanger nor try to usurp the rights of the other.

The troubles with Petrillo still further convinced Joe of this fact, and he renewed his campaign to prove that the areas of the two groups could be delineated with justice to both sides, and they could live in peace to their mutual benefit and to the benefit of music in America.

In 1937 Joe's campaign took him to Louisville, Kentucky, and a meeting of the International Executive Board of the American Federation of Musicians. Having become president that year of the Music Educators' National Conference, Joe had worked out with members of that group a carefully detailed proposal, or "code of ethics," listing the limitation as well as the prerogatives of student musicians on the one hand and of professional musicians on the other. It was designed primarily to protect union musicians from competition from school bands and orchestras, and described the functions of both groups as follows:

The field of entertainment is the province of the professional musician.

Music education may include demonstrations and certain other activities which are not in conflict with the interest of professional musicians, such as school functions, community functions organized strictly for educational purposes, occasional broadcast demonstrations presented for the sole purpose of acquainting the public with the type of music instruction offered to the children, benefit performances for charity, and educational or civic occasions which have been mutually agreed upon by school authorities and representatives of the union.

The members of the AFM's International Executive Board were extremely receptive to the music educators' proposal. Joe left the meeting feeling encouraged for the first time in over a decade. Progress was being made; peace was in sight—or so he thought.

Three weeks later, however, a brief and matter-of-fact telegram informed Joe that the AFM Board believed the matter was one for individual locals to decide, and the Board was taking no action. Joe was never able to find out exactly what happened during those three weeks but he was told, unofficially, that Petrillo, who had just become a member of the AFM Executive Board, had brought about the reversal of opinion. Instead of progress and peace there was to be stalemate and discord.

Throughout these turbulent years radio audiences across the country tuned in on NBC and enjoyed the weekly summer broadcasts from Interlochen, unaware of the price that was being paid to bring them about, a price not only in financial difficulty, but in strain upon the principles for which Joe had fought all his life. During the first year of the broadcasts when the Grigsby-Grunow Company paid the music camp two thousand dollars for each hourly program, Joe felt this was too tempting a sum to refuse at a time when his camp was in such desperate need of funds. But when the Union demanded that salaries be paid a seventeen-piece stand-by union orchestra, and that each program carry the announcement that the broadcast was "in the interests of living music in cooperation with the American Federation of Musicians," Joe found that such action placed too great a toll on his convictions. After that first year, he never against sought a sponsor for his Interlochen programs. The following year NBC took them over on a sustaining, non-commercial basis and although the music camp received no money, NBC bore the costs. One of the expenses: payment to a union orchestra to stand by in NBC's New York studios each time Interlochen went on the air.

In the summer of 1941 Petrillo saw his chance to strike another blow, and at the same time maneuver his thirteen-year battle against Joe's students out of his own Chicago bailiwick and onto the grounds of the National Music Camp. Paul Whiteman had arranged to bring his band to Interlochen, at his own expense, for a benefit performance to raise money to help pay off the camp's indebtedness and put it on the road to financial solvency. Three days before the scheduled concert, Petrillo notified Whiteman's manager that Whiteman would not be allowed to donate the services of the band.

"There are too many benefit performances," Petrillo declared. "They must be stopped."

As was usual, the order's timing created maximum difficulty. The program had been widely advertised and ticket sales were well underway. Rather than cancel the concert, Joe arranged to pay the members of the Whiteman organization the union scale fees for such an engagement, which were in addition to the weekly salaries paid by Mr. Whiteman. When Petrillo learned of this arrangement, he immediately decreed that the National Music Camp must pay the Whiteman band members *three times* the union scale, and insisted that a written contract be executed and a copy delivered to him personally.

Joe signed the contract, not wishing to place the Whiteman musicians, all union members, in jeopardy.

But he did it only after he reached by long distance telephone two members of the International Executive Board of the AFM. He asked for a rational explanation of Petrillo's order, because he himself could think of none. The reply from both Union officers was simply that the matter was in Petrillo's hands and they themselves had nothing to do with it.

On the night of the concert, Joe insisted that his youngsters play a number with the Whiteman band, a move which was in direct defiance of all Petrillo-made orders. This unquestionably brought Petrillo's long-seething anger to the boiling point.

These were the events preceding the union bombshell which finally barred Interlochen from the air in 1942. Petrillo became president of the American Federation of Musicians that year, and his new office armed him with the power he needed to issue the ban. It climaxed a fourteen-year war between Joe and Petrillo, and marked the point at which Joe resolved to stand his ground and yield no further compromise between the dictatorship of James C. Petrillo and his own strong convictions and principles.

2

"Maddy and all other music educators are murderers. They are training musicians to take the bread and butter from union musicians, causing them to starve to death."

With this description Petrillo explained his reasons for issuing the ban on Interlochen broadcasts. A wave of indignation swept the country. The United States Senate, acting on a resolution from Michigan's Senator Vandenberg, whose daughter had been a student at Interlochen, ordered an investigation. Back at Interlochen the disappointed youngsters plastered pines and hemlocks with hand-drawn signs reading, "Tit-willow, tit-willow, down with Petrillo."

The Federal Communications Commission conducted a separate investigation. Commission chairman James L. Fly demanded an explanation from Petrillo and received the following reply: "It is easy to understand that the more free music the radio stations receive, the less need for the professional. That is the primary reason for opposing the broadcasting of the concerts from Interlochen. . . . Interlochen is not in as good a position as other school bands and orchestras because Interlochen is a commercial proposition. . . ."

Was Interlochen indeed a "commercial proposition?" To find out, the FCC and the Department of Justice conducted a study of the music camp. From their findings an official report was issued: "The camp is a non-profit educational institution in the strictest sense of the meaning of the term."

Petrillo, however, remained unmoved and unperturbed in the face of both government investigations and public condemnation. He extended his broadcast ban to include all student music groups. Among these were the radio programs presented by students of the famed Eastman School of Music and the Cincinnati Conservatory.

As Petrillo continued to cut a wide swath through the hopes of the nation's young musicians, the Senate was bogging down in its investigations of his tactics and purpose. Joe was bitterly disappointed when the Senate hearings, after dragging on for almost a year, were considered closed; and members of the investigating committee expressed the opinion that "from a legislative standpoint there is nothing that can be done." One of the senators wrote to Joe and suggested that he communicate with Petrillo and work out "some sort of agreement which would be reasonably satisfactory."

Joe's reply to this suggestion was contained in a pamphlet— one of many he was to publish at Interlochen and circulate all over the United States as he went into his desperate battle on behalf of his young musicians. "I have not communicated with Mr. Petrillo," Joe wrote. "I am not interested in a 'reasonably satisfactory arrangement.' Chamberlain and Hitler worked out a reasonably satisfactory arrangement at Munich—with the final results which we all know too well. I would prefer never to broadcast educational programs, than to do so only with the permission of Petrillo or any other dictator.

"It matters little whether we broadcast again from Interlochen. But it is of the utmost concern of every American that the use of radio, the greatest avenue of communication and culture ever devised by man, shall not be denied our children.

"It is incredible that the Congress would ever by law deny education the use of radio for non-commercial purposes, yet that is exactly what a union dictator has done by fiat. It seems outrageous that one union boss has been permitted to do that which the Congress could not and would not do."

While Joe's words were well-spoken and undoubtedly expressed the opinions of a large portion of the American public, they nevertheless had little effect in spurring Congress into action. Fortunately, however, Petrillo himself by ill-timed remarks of his own, unwittingly accomplished Joe's mission for him when he boasted: "There are no school bands or orchestras on the networks, and there never will be without the permission of the American Federation of Musicians." This braggadocio so angered members of the Senate that the subcommittee hearing was reopened, again spearheaded by Senator Vandenberg, who termed Petrillo's action "a raid on the school children of America." He introduced a bill to prevent interference with non-commercial radio broadcasts that were not in competition with professional talent.

With the Senate again interested, Joe flew into action. He circulated his pamphlets more vigorously than ever, offered to appear at congressional hearings, challenged Petrillo to cite one single instance within the past ten years when the broadcasting of any school band or orchestra had deprived any union musician of a dollar of income. He urged all Americans to write to Congress and insist on passage of the Vandenberg bill.

And now Joe's voice was heard. It was heard first by school children. Led by present and former students of the music camp, indignant students in schools throughout the country entered the fight. They circulated petitions and wrote their congressmen. Seventeen hundred music students participating in a Youth Festival at Wichita in June, 1944, drafted the following petition which became the basis for congressional action: "Whereas, we the music students of Kansas, in common with all music students of America, have been denied the right of the use of the air in broadcasting; therefore we demand of the Congress of the United States that the Bill of Rights be enforced by enactment of legislation that will prevent interference with the broadcasting of non-commercial programs when presented by academically accredited, tax-exempt, educational institutions not in competition with professional talent." This resolution became the war cry not only of the students but of their parents and friends. Members of Congress were deluged with letters, telegrams, and petitions demanding action which would free American boys and girls from the music czar's domination.

The following January Senator Vandenberg's bill passed the Senate by unanimous vote. A similar bill was immediately introduced in the House by Representative George Dondero of Michigan, and was referred to the House Committee on Foreign and Interstate Commerce.

But the passage of Senator Vandenberg's bill, while bringing Joe his greatest victory to date in his battle against Petrillo, also brought him the greatest personal disappointment of his career. Petrillo, obviously seeking revenge against Interlochen and its young musicians for their part in bringing about the passage of the Vandenberg bill, evoked the most drastic and punitive reprisal at his command: he placed the music camp on the National Unfair List of the American Federation of Musicians. He also decreed that students could no longer receive instruction from any member of the Musicians Union and that union members who had been teaching at Interlochen could no longer continue as members of the staff, on the threat of expulsion from the all-powerful Union. The decree also meant that great artists such as Percy Grainger, Howard Hanson, Walter Damrosch, Frederick Stock, Edwin Franko Goldman, and John Philip Sousa could no longer inspire students as guest conductors and that if Joe Maddy ever again raised his baton to conduct another concert on the grounds of the National Music Camp at Interlochen, he would automatically lose his membership in the Union.

Contracts for the coming season already had been signed, virtually all of them with union musicians, the regular faculty members who had been coming to the camp for years. When students, parents, and teachers read in the newspapers that Interlochen had been blacklisted, they were sure this was the end. No school could operate without a faculty. Petrillo had finally succeeded in destroying Interlochen. Or so everyone thought. Everyone, that is, but Joe Maddy.

After only a moment's hesitation while he considered, then disregarded, his personal plight in the matter, Joe hurriedly began to canvass America's high schools and colleges for a substitute non-union faculty. On such short notice it was an enormous undertaking and a frantic race against time. And one large and imposing question loomed in Joe's mind: would the loss of prominent guest conductors and teachers keep students away? Since much of the camp's reputation had been built on the attraction of famous conductors and outstanding professional symphony men as teachers, would the lack of such people ruin the camp's enrollment? Everyone told Joe it would.

But they underestimated the loyalty of Interlochen students. Letters and telegrams flooded Joe's office. Students pleaded that the camp not be allowed to close. Many offered to bring their own teachers. Former students even resigned from the Union in order to come to Interlochen and teach. The rest of the faculty was drawn from the staffs of the nation's high schools and colleges, where only about half of the instrumental music teachers were members of the all-powerful AFM.

When Interlochen opened in 1945 it had the largest enrollment in camp history—and an all non-union teaching faculty many of whom had been former symphony men.

Furthermore, the "Czar of Music" had turned out to be not Interlochen's destroyer but its best press agent.

As Joe Maddy lifted his baton on opening day, he knew that his thirty-seven years as a member of the American Federation of Musicians was over. But he also knew that now Interlochen could survive anything; his young people through all the seasons since the camp's struggling beginning were back of him.

Even former faculty members, including many of the celebrities who had brought glamour to Interlochen, could not stay completely away. Prohibited by order of Petrillo from setting foot on Interlochen's grounds, they rented cottages nearby, and from this distance would listen to the concerts. They would walk as far as the camp's entrance to send messages via the students to Joe, congratulating him and wishing him luck. Musicians whose names were famous the world over, were seen quiet and alone in the deepening twilight, standing safely outside the gate, to listen while their former students performed.

The Union didn't notify Joe of his own expulsion until November, but this was not due to an oversight.

Petrillo was following his usual policy of waiting and watching, playing the game of cat and mouse for which he had now become famous, with his eye this time on the House Committee on Foreign and Interstate Commerce. The Committee was still considering legislation which had begun as Dondero's bill and which had been revised and was now known as the Lea Act. It called for an amendment to the Communications Act of 1934 in order to curb interference with non-commercial, cultural or educational broadcasts by schools. When in November the Committee passed the bill and reported it favorably to the House, Petrillo pounced. In his typical fashion of seeking retaliation whenever he or his union suffered a set-back, he placed three measures into effect.

First, he issued an order which seriously impaired the development of frequency modulation broadcasting and television.

Second, he placed a ban on the broadcasting in this nation of music programs originating in foreign countries.

Third, and finally, he sent Joe his official notification to appear at a meeting of the International Executive Board of the AFM to answer charges that he had violated the laws of the Union by teaching music to the young people at Interlochen.

Joe appeared at the meeting with his attorney in the hope of finding the real reason for the "unfair" ruling placed against the National Music Camp. But during the five-hour "trial" he received none of the information he sought. Excerpts from the board members' recorded remarks: "We are under no duty or obligation to bring before us organizations, or corporations, or institutions, whom we declare to be unfair. We owe no such obligation to anybody. . . . It would be highly improper to permit an inquiry into the actions of this board because it has the right to put anyone on the unfair list it wants to and you have no right to question our ability to legislate or pass a rule. . . . The man or organization against whom our Federation has acted has no right to come in and demand the reasons for it."

Petrillo was not present that day, but there was little doubt he had penned the words that were spoken.

It was shortly after this, in response to the demands of an aroused public becoming increasingly more resentful of Petrillo's ever-spreading dictatorship, that Congress by overwhelming majorities in both houses passed the Lea Act, which was signed by the President on April 16, 1946.

Petrillo followed his well-established pattern. He retaliated this time by calling a strike at a Chicago radio station which had refused to submit to union demands that it employ twice as many record turners as it needed. Petrillo's purpose this time was to test the legality of the Lea Act. His strike call, as he had intended, forced the Federal Court to order him to stand trial. And, as if Petrillo had been writing the script, the trial resulted in the Chicago court declaring the Lea Act unconstitutional.

Petrillo, therefore, continued to hold the upper hand.

The case went to the Supreme Court. There, on June 23, 1947, more than a year after Congress voted the passage of the Lea Act, the decision of the Chicago Federal Court was reversed and the constitutionality of the Act was upheld.

This should have been the end of Joe's long battle and the termination of the ban on the Interlochen broadcasts. But it was not.

Several months before the Supreme Court decision, a disturbed

Congress, aware that nothing it had done so far had improved the nation's labor situation, began a study of labor-leader activities to determine if still further legislation was needed to protect the public from continued abuses by labor dictators. First on its agenda was an investigation of Petrillo's domination of American music. Heading the House Subcommittee in charge of the investigation was Congressman Carroll Kearns of Pennsylvania, a member of the AFM, a former music teacher, and a man who thoroughly understood Petrillo's high-handed interference with music education.

Joe welcomed the investigation, never dreaming that Kearns' activities would end in frustration and disappointment. In the beginning Kearns relied heavily on Joe's help in preparing material to be used as evidence of Petrillo's strong-arm methods. Kearns asked Joe to be the key witness against Petrillo in the educational phase of the investigation, and on the evening before the hearings were to open, he invited Joe to his home to go over the procedures for the following day.

But Joe never got to the witness stand. Other witnesses were heard, people who testified that they had endured abuses from Petrillo and his union. A confident Petrillo also took the stand, but he was noticeably more subdued after two days of constant questioning from members of the Committee. After the second day Kearns suddenly gaveled the session into adjournment, much to the surprise of everyone present.

Then Kearns called Joe into his office and there recounted a strange tale. Petrillo had approached the Congressman just before the afternoon session started. He said he understood that Joe Maddy was present and asked if he was to be called as a witness. When Kearns replied that he was, Petrillo asked him not to let this happen. Petrillo then told Kearns he was willing to make any "reasonable concession" if "that guy from Interlochen" could be stopped from testifying against him.

Kearns asked Joe to let him handle the matter in his own way, with the understanding that he would induce Petrillo to remove the music camp from AFM's unfair list and reinstate Joe in the Union. He asked Joe to say nothing, either at the hearings or to the press. Joe agreed.

He returned to Interlochen without testifying and without making any statements for publication. And there he waited.

Nothing happened.

Joe tried to reach Kearns by telephone, to no avail. He sent telegrams and wrote letters. These received either no replies, or very brief ones, asking Joe to be patient.

In July of 1947, exactly one month after the Supreme Court upheld the constitutionality of the Lea Act, Joe was surprised to pick up his newspaper and read the front page headline, "PETRILLO LIFTS BROADCAST BAN AGAINST STUDENT MUSICIANS." The story was date-lined Washington and quoted Kearns as saying that James C. Petrillo "has agreed to steps which will let school children-musicians participate in civic functions and broadcast music festivals." In disbelief Joe realized that Kearns was giving Petrillo the credit for lifting the broadcasting ban, when actually the ban had been lifted a month earlier by the Supreme Court's action in upholding the Lea Act.

The newspaper stories indicated that the National Music Camp had not even been mentioned at the meeting. Questioned by reporters and asked specifically if the Interlochen ban would be lifted, Petrillo made the following statement: "They're not school children at Interlochen. They don't belong to any school when they're out there. We didn't go into it, and I don't want to go into it."

This was Kearns' way of "handling the matter" himself. This was Petrillo's "reasonable concession!" This was Joe's thanks for not going on the witness stand against Petrillo! It seemed to Joe that the immense power of the "Czar of Music" could still affect even the Congress. And he was to learn that it extended no less effectively into other areas.

Two months later the officers of the Music Educators National Conference, along with the officers of the Department of Super-intendents of the National Educational Association, arranged a meeting in Chicago with Petrillo to work out a "code of ethics" patterned after the one Joe had authored and presented to the Union's Executive Board meeting ten years previously and which had first been approved, then rejected, after Petrillo took office as a member of the AFM's Executive Board. Joe had been invited to this Chicago meeting and then denied admittance when he arrived—without explanation.

When this "code of ethics" was adopted and given widespread publicity, the question naturally arose as to its effect on Inter-lochen. The Music Educators and National Association officers refused to comment on this but Petrillo issued a statement that "Interlochen does not come under this agreement because it is a commercial institution."

This, in spite of the fact that the federal government had estab-lished four years earlier as a matter of record that the camp was a non-commercial, non-profit institution "beyond any doubt of the meaning of the phrase!" That Petrillo's power could force the members of MENC to let Joe down was a bitter blow.

He thereafter had to limit his student broadcasts to educational stations. Fortunately for Interlochen, these were becoming numerous. He also noted that the number of radio stations employing union musicians was steadily diminishing, and there was nothing the Union could do about it. Petrillo could undoubtedly begin to feel the ground growing slippery under his feet, but he undertook bitter and final strokes of vengeance against Interlochen by expelling a number of musicians who had defied his "unfair" ruling and had either taught or performed in concerts at the camp.

Then in 1958 the man whose music career had consisted mainly of performances as a trumpet player with the Chicago Newsboys' Band, and whose own union members called him the world's worst trumpet player, withdrew as head of the Musicians' Union. He was retiring, he said, "in tears" because he was tired of fighting. Some strongly suspected, however, that other factors forced him out. Good musicians all over the country had become exasperated by the high taxes the Union was taking from their incomes, particularly since these funds had not been used to create more employment for good musicians, as Petrillo claimed, but to help poorer musicians become officers of local unions. As a result of the spreading dissatisfaction with the AFM, other groups were being formed, such as the Musicians Guild of America, and these were gaining steadily in power. Petrillo and his henchmen had led the AFM perilously close to disaster, and now one by one they faded into retirement.

That same year, the National Music Camp was removed from the Union's "unfair" list. It was agreed by Union officials that the camp was not a commercial organization and should not be discriminated against.

Thus single-handedly Joe had waged his angry battle against

one of the toughest bosses in the nation's history. He always said, "These young musicians of today will be the union leaders of tomorrow." And throughout all of his long publicized war with Petrillo, no one could fairly charge, either that Joe Maddy was "anti-labor," or that his young music students had caused hardship to any of the nation's professional musicians.

Joe's Other Battles

In a backhanded way Petrillo's blow at the young musicians may have been one of the best things that ever happened to Interlochen.

The news made headlines everywhere and millions of people who would never otherwise have heard of the National Music Camp now knew about it.

Not only that, but most of the public was sympathetic. It is human nature to fight for the underdog, and especially when the fight involves a nation's youth. People everywhere rallied to the Interlochen cause. Women's clubs started campaigning for funds to give talented youngsters a season at the music camp. Teen-agers around the country formed anti-Petrillo clubs.

In the period when Petrillo was putting Interlochen in the spotlight, its enrollment more than doubled. And it continued growing. Joe never again needed to worry about having enough students. His future problems concerned where to put them. In the post-Petrillo years the music camp began to have a waiting list; it began for the first time to have to turn numbers of students away.

Joe fought for more funds for his camp—he fought for its soundness and its growing reputation, and these efforts began increasingly to involve him in controversies. In the spring of 1948, for example, he decided to test the effect of the Lea Act. He wrote NBC, which had carried the Interlochen broadcasts for twelve years, and suggested that since the constitutionality of the Act had been upheld by the Supreme Court, the broadcasts might be resumed. In return he received a letter from an NBC official stating that no network would consider carrying the Interlochen broadcasts as long as the camp was on Petrillo's "unfair list."

However, Joe also had submitted the idea to the Mutual Broadcasting Company. Less than an hour after reading the letter of rejection from NBC, he received a telephone call from Mutual in New York, telling him that Mutual would be glad to broadcast the concerts that summer. During the telephone conversation, Joe was asked whether he had "cleared the matter" with Petrillo. He replied that it was not necessary to "clear with Petrillo," because the Lea Act prohibited union interference with educational, non-commercial broadcasts. Mutual then scheduled the program, and Joe released the statement that the Interlochen broadcasts would be resumed.

As might have been expected, the story was featured by every newspaper that had taken an interest in the Petrillo controversy. *The Chicago Tribune* carried a story conspicuously headlined:

PETRILLO LOSES TO INTERLOCHEN . . . . MBS TO AIR
CONCERTS BEGINNING JULY 5

The world famed National Music Camp at Interlochen won its long battle against James C. Petrillo today when the Mutual Broadcasting System agreed to take the teen-age symphony on a nation wide hookup despite the camp's blacklist status with the musicians' union. . . .

Dr. Maddy's only comment on his victory over the music union's boss was: "I'm glad there's one network that has the courage to give more importance to the law than to a union leader's edict."

Newspapers throughout the country carried the story that at long last Maddy had won his fight against Petrillo. Then, less than a week later, Mutual suddenly canceled the broadcasts. In a statement to the press Philips Carlin, then vice-president in charge of programs for Mutual, said that when the agreement for the series had been made a week earlier, "we were not aware of the six year controversy and that Interlochen was on the unfair list."

Said the *Chicago Tribune,* "He (Carlin) did not explain how a nationwide broadcasting organization would fail to take such a development into consideration. . . . Carlin's statement today attacked Dr. Maddy, charging that, in talking to the press in connection with announcement of the new series, he 'took undue advantage of us.' We booked this program merely to get the music,' Carlin said. 'We were interested only in the music. Maddy used the story as a means to further his own controversy in which we did not want to be a part. It is not our object to become involved in a controversy between him and the union."

It was never explained how an organization such as the Mutual Broadcasting Company could possibly have been unaware of the Interlochen-Petrillo controversy, nor how any national network could expect to take on the Interlochen broadcasts without making headlines. It seemed obvious to Joe that in spite of the constitutionality of the Lea Act, no radio network was willing to incur Boss Petrillo's displeasure.

In the early years of Joe's fight with Petrillo, he also had another, less publicized, battle on his hands, this time with United States government officials. These were the war years. Music was not vital to national defense and there were many who simply took it for granted that Joe would disband his camp. Joe, as usual, entertained no such notion. Thanks to Petrillo, Interlochen's reputation was growing, and success was making Joe Maddy more determined than ever not to give up a single inch of ground he had won.

There were times when it seemed impossible to everyone except Joe that Interlochen could survive the war period. There was the nearly insurmountable problem of obtaining supplies, equipment, and labor to operate a "non-essential" eight weeks summer camp which was contributing nothing to the war effort. Joe's argument that music is the language of peace held little weight with members of the War Production Board and other government agencies charged with the responsibility of rationing materials and supplies.

One of the first major difficulties arose when Joe tried to get meat for his campers. Interlochen, like other institutions, was given ration points, of course. But then, for no reason Joe could see, he was not permitted to buy the quota of meat allowed by the points. Joe found this incomprehensible. After all, the youngsters would be eating, whether they were at camp or at home. Nothing was to be gained for the war effort by denying them their ration of meat.

Joe decided, by gum, to buy his own herd of cattle. He fattened them and was about ready to butcher, when a government official called on him and informed him that he couldn't do this. He would have to ship the cattle to Grand Rapids to be butchered.

It was a penitentiary offense to butcher his own cattle, Joe was told.

Joe was forced to obey the regulations—but at least his campers had meat.

The next round came when Joe decided to mill his own lumber. During the war years lumber was almost impossible to get, and Joe had no intentions of attempting any large-scale building or expansion. But he needed lumber for repairs. Therefore, he bought a sawmill, cut down some of the trees on the camp's property, and proceeded to make his own lumber. It seemed to him a highly sensible measure. Interlochen wasn't drawing on the nation's lumber supply nor depriving anyone of materials essential to the war.

One day, however, a stranger appeared and asked for Joe Maddy. He introduced himself as an official of the War Production Board and said he had come to investigate "this sawmill business." He asked how many feet of lumber Joe's "business" was putting out and what it was to be used for. He also asked numerous other questions which Joe secretly felt were none of his affair, but he answered them all politely and offered to take the man on a tour of the camp.

The man wasn't interested in a tour. He was interested only in the sawmill, he said. Moreover, the purpose of his visit, he explained, was merely to notify Joe that he would have to cease his sawmill operations immediately—or be subject to a penitentiary sentence.

By this time Joe was becoming weary of being threatened with penitentiary sentences for activities in which he not only could see no wrong but was sure were right and good.

His Maddy blood was boiling. "It's our sawmill and our trees, by gum! We'll make our own lumber here whenever we need it." He stopped—just long enough to fill to the popping point with indignation—and then he popped: "Just try to stop us!"

He waited, expectantly. Would he be handcuffed? The WPB man merely glowered silently, then stalked out, and never came back. Joe went on sawing up Interlochen trees.

2

Interlochen had survived the depression, the war years, near-bankruptcy, and Petrillo-ism, but there was more to come. It must have seemed to Joe at times that the whole world, or at least a good portion of it, was intent on destroying the peaceful little music kingdom. And why?

In the Grand Traverse area there were some who felt that Joe Maddy was becoming too sensitive and overly protective toward his music camp. He was apt to rare up unnecessarily or prematurely, they thought, on the slightest provocation. In the minds of many, Joe was becoming headstrong whenever anyone or anything posed a potential threat to his camp.

One summer, for example, the Michigan Highway Department began construction of a new highway that was to run through the Interlochen area. The new highway would not only destroy the privacy of the girls' camp but it would restrict the future growth of the entire Interlochen project. Joe filed an injunction to prevent the highway from being built. He finally had to spend ten thousand sorely needed dollars to buy the fourteen acres involved in the proposed plan and add them to his own campus.

A couple of years later the Michigan Conservation Department and the Correction Commission decided to develop the Interlochen State Park, adjacent to the music camp grounds, and to employ convict labor for the project. Joe was out of town at the time. When he returned he found working crews building a convict labor camp within three and a half miles of the music camp. The convict labor camp force would be living within walking distance of Interlochen. Joe began vehement protests immediately, but was told that it was too late because the State Legislature had approved the site and work was well underway, too far along to be stopped.

Joe then appealed to the women of Michigan, who could understand the hazards that the presence of unguarded convicts would have for a camp of young boys and girls located miles from police protection. Seventy-five thousand members of the Michigan State Federation of Women's Clubs and the Michigan Federation of Music Club launched a militant campaign in an effort to force the State's Correction Commission to remove the convicts to a distance of fifteen miles or more from the camp.

In Traverse City, however, the anti-convict campaign met with some resistance. Local officials had planned to use the prison labor also to clean up the lakefront, but did not wish the convicts housed in the city itself. The belief locally was that the prisoners were mere first offenders convicted only of minor crimes, and therefore not dangerous to the community.

Then, however, three of the convicts strayed into town, and robbed and kidnapped a Traverse City family. For Joe the event's timing couldn't have been more perfect. The people of Traverse City rose in wrathful indignation and demanded that the prison labor camp be moved out of the area. It was. The convict dormitory was torn down. Its T shaped concrete foundation still stands, grown over with tree ferns and shaded by pines.

For many years there were also strained relations between Joe Maddy and some of the leading citizens over the matter of Interlochen's participation in the Traverse City Cherry Festival Parade. Traverse City had always taken great pride in its reputation as the nation's cherry growing capital. In spring the surrounding hills and countryside came alive with the tremulous beauty of cherry orchards in bloom, and in summer the fruit stands popped up everywhere with heaping boxes of big, ripe Michigan sweet cherries.

In summer, too, came the Cherry Festival, three days of festivities climaxed by the crowning of the Cherry Festival Queen. It was a time of community spirit and pride and traditions that had become as meaningful to the people of the Grand Traverse Bay cherry regions as the spirit and pride and traditions of Interlochen had become to Joe Maddy.

If tempers sometimes flared between Joe and his community neighbors, they usually cooled quickly. For although Joe might not admit it, his Interlochen music camp was in fact a source of pride to most citizens of the area. Interlochen, in spite of that stubborn, pugnacious, "ornery cuss" at the head of it, had brought distinction to northern Michigan. And those who regarded Joe with anything less than warm affection were usually at least resigned to him.

But his snubbing of their Cherry Festival Parade was almost

too much. There were some who would probably never forgive him.

For several summers Joe did take his band to march in the Cherry Festival Parade. And then he stopped. Some of the townspeople were infuriated, some were indignant, some were hurt. The Cherry Festival was the most important event of the year, and its success was a matter of civic pride. Other communities and other school bands always participated. Why shouldn't Interlochen? It was easy to understand why Traverse Citians were piqued. The fame of Interlochen had spread, and what city wouldn't be proud to have an Interlochen band marching in its parade? The youngsters, in their blue knickers and shirts, were popular with Cherry Festival crowds, and many would be disappointed not to see Interlochen represented in the colorful Cherry Festival Parade of marching bands.

Was the cancellation of the Interlochen band in the parade just another sample of Joe Maddy's orneriness?

Joe's answer, which no one in the heat of the controversy would believe, seemed perfectly simple and logical to him. During the first seasons of the music camp, when he was taking his band to march in the parade, there were basically only three camp activities: orchestra and choir in the morning, and band in the afternoon. In those days, taking the band away from camp for an afternoon meant missing only one band rehearsal—and holding two or three marching practice sessions to teach the players how to march properly, because many came from schools not having a band.

But when the camp grew to several hundred students and developed a class schedule that continued all day and every evening, circumstances changed. Afternoon classes then included composition, conducting, music theory, chamber music, and numerous other activities under faculty guidance. An afternoon away from classes was in Joe's mind an unfair demand on the young people who had paid their fees for class and private lessons. In addition, the NBC broadcast sometimes fell on the evening of the Cherry Festival, and players who had marched were tired or had sometimes injured their lips from a misstep while marching.

But even worse, so far as Joe was concerned, was the fact that the students who marched in the band sometimes brought back mumps, measles, and chickenpox and spread these diseases among other campers. Joe had made every effort to cooperate with the Community's Cherry Festival promotions, but when polio came into the picture he called a halt. Dr. Mark Osterlin, a Traverse City physician and for many years a member of Interlochen's Board of Trustees, not only advised but strongly urged Joe to cancel the Interlochen Band's participation in Cherry Festival parades. The Festival was always held in hot-weather July, and this, combined with the strenuous activity of playing and marching in a parade, could possibly create a polio epidemic at Interlochen.

All this, however, seemed nonsense to Cherry Festival committees, who failed to see why Interlochen musicians should be any more susceptible to mishaps than others who continued marching in their parades.

The result was a breach that took a long time in healing, but meanwhile it gave Joe an opportunity to establish what to him seemed the only sensible course for Interlochen: no more interrupting of class schedules for benefit performances anywhere, parades, festivals, county fairs, or other local events. He could not begin to accept all the invitations that were beginning to pour in to Interlochen, and if he had, there would have been no time for music. Whatever the people in the area might feel about him, there would be no more marching in the Cherry Festival parades. And there was not.

Joe was constantly besieged by requests to bring a band, orchestra, choir or ensemble group to furnish music at all kinds of local events, from club meetings to county fairs, in the surrounding communities. His policy was to refuse.

However, he received one in the spring of 1957 which he decided should be an exception. It was an invitation for an Interlochen band to perform at the dedication of the new Mackinac Bridge. Joe knew this would be an important event for the state of Michigan. He not only accepted the invitation but he commissioned composer Don Gillis to write a march dedicated to the opening of the bridge.

Soon after Joe accepted, he was told as politely as possible, that the invitation to the music camp would have to be withdrawn. The reason: the president of the Detroit Musicians' Union had informed the president of the Detroit Edison Company, who had issued the invitation, that if the music camp band went to Mackinac, the union would send up pickets.

Under normal circumstances Joe would not have cared one way or another about an invitation to the bridge ceremonies. In fact, he had deliberated at some length before accepting the invitation, and if it had been withdrawn for any other reason he probably wouldn't have given it a second thought. But he was incensed at the continued interference from the musicians' union. He flew to Washington and got a hearing before a House Labor Sub-committee, with the result that the invitation was re-issued and the Interlochen band went to the dedication. The title of the dedication march was changed from "The Mighty Mac" to "Mr. Big," in a light poke of fun at the union boss who tried to cancel the trip. There were no pickets present. And it was the same union boss, the president of the Detroit Musicians' Union, who only a year later helped remove the music camp from Petrillo's blacklist and cordially welcomed Joe Maddy back into the AFM.

Even more spectacular than Joe's long war with Petrillo, during which public sympathies were generally on Joe's side, was his tangle with the politicians over the establishment of a jet air base near Interlochen. Joe's protests touched off one of the stormiest controversies in decades, and at times it seemed that nearly the whole of northern Michigan was ready to tar and feather him. Investors lost money, politicians lost votes, friends stopped speaking, and communities started feuding. Newspapers in the area were filled with scathing editorials and blistering letters from angry citizens. Merchants and owners of restaurants and taverns were particularly bitter over the loss of anticipated income from the thirteen-million-dollar jet air base which they believed would certainly have been located in their area if Joe Maddy had not stepped in.

Actually Joe wasn't the only one who objected to the jet base; he was only the first and most vocal. Moreover, he stood ready to withdraw his objections if the Air Force would give him a guarantee that the jets would not interfere with the operations of his music camp—a guarantee no one in his right mind would make. If the noise from the jets became intolerable, he would have to move his music camp to another location, and this would cost well over five million dollars, an expense which Joe insisted should be borne by the Federal Government.

When Joe first heard the news on the radio of the proposed jet base—to be built in the exact area formerly but briefly occupied by the convict labor camp—he went uninvited to a Chamber of Commerce meeting in Traverse City and recommended another equally suitable site for the base near Kalkaska about thirty miles away, far enough away to reduce the noise from jets so that neither Traverse City nor Interlochen would be seriously disturbed, but close enough for the city to benefit economically.

Joe realized that the community relied heavily on two seasonal industries, cherry farming and the tourist trade, and he could understand the desire of local businessmen to improve the town's economy. But his recommendation of a different site for the jet base was received with the scorn that practical men reserve for a bumptious idealist, and Joe was told to go home and keep quiet.

This, of course, was not the proper technique to use with Joe Maddy. He telephoned the secretary of the Air Force, Harold Talbot. He told Mr. Talbot all about Interlochen, and how even an ordinary two-motor passenger plane passing within a mile of the music camp often disrupted concerts, broadcasts, programs, and rehearsals. He explained that the younger children had a rest period each afternoon, and this rest period would be useless if interrupted by jet planes passing overhead. "I understand," he added, "that the planes to be used at this base are of the noisiest type."

A sub-committee of three members of the Congressional Armed Service Committee visited the area, escorted by officials of the Traverse City Chamber of Commerce who promoted the

Long Lake site, three miles from Interlochen, and failed to mention the Kalkaska site.

Joe flooded the Pentagon with packets of literature, concert schedules, and miscellaneous vital statistics to prove that his camp was an educational institution of the highest caliber, and he invited Talbot and his Air Force officials to come out and see for themselves. The upshot was that they did. Soon after their visit came the official announcement from Washington that the proposed jet base site near Traverse City had been rejected by the Air Force—and would be moved instead to Kalkaska.

Joe had committed the worst crime of all—he had been right. The Air Force officers, on Joe's recommendation, had investigated the Kalkaska site and decided it was just as suitable as the one near Interlochen.

So far as Joe was concerned his active role in the jet base controversy was over. He could relax and await the next crisis. But the fighting and feuding were far from finished. The Michigan jet base issue became a political football of the stickiest kind. No sooner had the people of Traverse City adjusted to the proposed official relocation in Kalkaska than Representative Ruth Thompson from Michigan's Ninth Congressional District began voicing her protests. Kalkaska was not in her District.

This triggered a fresh outburst of bickering. Dozens of Michigan towns all the way from Alpena to Beaver Island decided they might as well bid for the jet air base as long as the location was still doubtful. Finally a delegation from Traverse City flew to Washington to apprise Secretary Talbot of the distinct advantages of their area, and Talbot was later quoted in the press as saying, "I am awfully fed up with the Traverse City area. I am disgusted with the people up there. . . ."

The controversy finally reached the floor of Congress where the members voted to locate the jet air base at the so-called Manistee County site, a few miles south of Interlochen—in Ruth Thompson's district. This action angered the Air Force officials whose objective was protection, not politics.

After two years of bitter community rivalry over the air base, the Air Force announced another change in plans. It was 1956, and by that time the rapidly developing missile program had reached a stage where jet bases of the type proposed for the Michigan area were no longer considered effective, so the entire project of a jet air base was abandoned, saving the nation some thirteen million dollars.

But these facts were not recognized, and it was Joe Maddy whom angry citizens blamed for the loss of their coveted base. Joe himself wasted no time on personal bitterness. He knew that Interlochen in its quarter century of existence, had touched more lives, shaped more careers, and entered far more hearts than the ugly controversy over the base.

Money Beggar

To THE young students at Inter-lochen Dr. Joe Maddy became a legend and a symbol, and the most idolized figure who ever walked the campgrounds.

Famous conductors could come and go and the young musicians always thrilled to the opportunity of playing under them, but it was Dr. Joe the youngsters stomped and cheered for the loudest at the beginning and the end of each camp season. Toward the end, when it came time to order their memory-book pictures, it was Dr. Joe's picture they wanted, to take home with them.

It was Dr. Joe who had *cared*. It was he who made the littlest camper feel every inch as big as the high school and college musicians. It was he who knew the students by name, who was never too busy to stop and talk with them, who was always popping in on classes to watch them perform. It was Dr. Joe and Mrs. Maddy who regularly came to the junior campers' campfires, and to every student recital, no matter whether the youngster was a mere beginner or a child prodigy.

It was always more important to Joe that every student should have the opportunity to perform than that he perform with perfection. When a boy or girl hit a sour note, Joe was quick with his reassuring smile, that said, "Don't worry. You'll get it next time."

There were many who understood the meaning of Joe Maddy's music camp and wanted to be a part of it. Even when they had to accept low pay and difficult working conditions, faculty and guest artists returned loyally year after year. They returned not only because they loved children but also, in a way, because they loved the stubborn genius named Joe Maddy.

Joe was the first to admit that Interlochen could never have survived without the help of its dedicated workers. He would be swift to say that he couldn't have done it single-handedly. But the fact was that he had come as close to that feat as any man could.

For the truth was quite simple: it was Joe Maddy who had cared enough to spend most of his life begging the money to keep Interlochen going. That had been the most difficult job of all, and the most important. On the staff, for example, who could say that they cared enough to work without pay, or believed enough in Joe's dream to help him finance it? That was Joe's own problem. No one knew it better than he. No one was more aware of both the passive and active resistance he met at every turn—until he had the money to pay the bills.

If, after going out and begging the money, Dr. Joe felt entitled to run things his own way, who could blame him?

Joe had known nothing about fund raising. Begging so that young people could have music was in many ways humiliating to him. Yet, he had been forced to spend much of his time doing it. He had tried many expedients. Some worked; others did not.

For example, when he was teaching in Ann Arbor, he had proposed that the school buy two thousand dollars worth of instruments and rent them at reasonable rates to the students. He was sure the plan was good, but only after he threatened to operate a rental business himself would school officials agree to invest in the instruments, which were still in use after thirty-seven years.

On the other hand, at a later period, he went into debt trying to manufacture aluminum violins which he hoped would bring the camp through its financial crisis. He thought there would be a market for aluminum violins. His own campers could use them, and any profit he could make would help pay some of the bills during the depression years. But it turned out that no one wanted aluminum violins. In 1962 Joe's garage attic was still full of the plain, serviceable aluminum instruments he had manufactured to help save Interlochen.

At another point Joe decided, finally, to take the advice of others and hire a professional fund raising firm. He had been urged for several years to do this, and after the close of the nineteen thirty-eight season, he engaged a firm to put on a three weeks campaign in Traverse City and Chicago to raise money to help pay the camp's debts. The promoters charged five hundred dollars a week for their services. After spending another five hundred on photographs and brochures, they were ready to start work.

Joe learned a lesson. The fund raisers didn't raise funds. They merely managed—or tried to—his own labors.

It was Joe, not the fund raisers, who had to go out raising the money. For three bitter weeks he went from house to house, from store to store, doing the job for the professional fund raisers. One apparently good prospect, a wealthy woman who owned the best shoe store in town, kept telling Joe to come back the next day. The fund raisers had set a goal of fifteen thousand dollars. Joe was hoping the shoe store lady, who kept encouraging him to come back, would make a generous contribution. After five calls, she finally gave him five dollars.

Three leading merchants agreed to contribute two hundred and fifty dollars each, provided the other two contributed equal amounts. Those were the three largest pledges. Most contributions averaged between five and twenty-five dollars. Some pledged twenty-five—payable in five years.

In three weeks Joe managed to beg enough to pay his fund raisers and fire them. He never again hired a professional fund raiser.

There were other types of outside help, however, that were successful, and also helped restore Joe's faith in human nature. For instance, one local volunteer fund raiser who did a great deal to boost Joe's morale as well as the camp's net worth was Mrs. Maud Miller Hoffmaster, a well known artist who lived in Traverse City and for many years taught art at the music camp. She was a woman of keen convictions and strong energies, and in 1944 she put them to work leading a campaign of the Michigan Federation of Women's Clubs to collect fifteen thousand dollars for an art building at Interlochen. Other women's clubs and music organizations followed suit and began contributing various amounts for building programs.

When Joe wasn't out personally knocking on doors, he was bombarding friends of Interlochen with letters asking help in reaching individuals who might contribute. One of these was Mrs. Edith Rhetts Tilton, for many years Educational Director of the Detroit Symphony Orchestra and a strong supporter of Joe's music camp. She induced two Detroit men to give a thousand dollars each. One was Gerald Webber, president of the J. L.

Hudson department store. The other was Stanley S. Kresge, president of the Kresge Foundation.

Mr. Kresge was willing to meet Joe and hear about Interlochen. Joe went to his office, carrying a projector and a film of the camp. Mr. Kresge was both moved and impressed. He gave Joe a check for two thousand dollars, twice the amount he originally had pledged.

This encouraged Joe. He went back again to see Mr. Kresge, this time with a bigger project. He was hoping for a new assembly hall with a roof that would extend over part of the audience. The estimated cost was thirty thousand dollars. The trustees of the Kresge Foundation approved the plan and pledged the money, to be paid as construction progressed. This was the largest single contribution Joe had been given so far. But the year was 1945, a time when the War Production Board was still in existence. The board refused the camp permission to build the Kresge concert stage because of the scarcity of building materials.

The ban was maintained until 1947, when Joe suddenly learned that bowling alleys and bow and arrow factories were being built with governmental approval. Indignantly he went to Washington to register his protest against such discrimination. How could the WPB approve bowling alleys and bow and arrow factories but not permit construction of an educational building?

Joe's congressman Albert Engel, then Chairman of the House Appropriations Committee, was also angered. He called the WPB office and suggested pointedly that the board have written approval ready for Joe in ten minutes. It was. And Joe learned later that the board's absurd position in regard to the Kresge Assembly Hall had helped substantially toward the final congressional dissolution of the WPB.

By that time, however, construction costs had almost doubled. Work on the Kresge Building was to start in the fall and be completed for the opening of the 1948 season. The money ran out. In a meeting with his Board of Trustees, who by this time had replaced his Board of Control, Joe was urged to write to Mr. Kresge and tell him that unless he contributed more money, the half finished building would stand as a steel skeleton. In fact, the trustees themselves had already written the letter. They handed it to Joe to sign and send to Mr. Kresge. To Joe such a letter seemed offensive and totally unfair. He tore it up. He was sure that it would have alienated Mr. Kresge and his Foundation officials for all time.

Later Joe simply got in touch with Mr. Kresge and invited him to come up and go deer hunting. Stanley Kresge saw for himself the plight of the building, and after his return home the Foundation sent Interlochen a check for forty-five thousand dollars to cover additional costs. And through the years the Kresges continued to be one of the camp's most generous and warmly appreciated contributors.

2

On the final day of the 1941 camp season, Joe opened an envelope addressed to him, and out fell a check for twenty-five hundred dollars. With it was a short note from Mrs. R. B. Canfield of Ann Arbor, who had just left after a few days visit. Mrs. Canfield, widow of a doctor and a patron of the arts in Ann Arbor, had visited Interlochen several times and had been impressed by what she saw. In her note she told Joe to use the money in the way he thought would benefit the camp most.

Joe knew that his Board, which he then still had, would insist that the money be applied toward retirement of debentures. After much deliberation he decided not to tell his Board about the money. Instead, he conceived the idea of using the money to build a guest house which he hoped Mrs. Canfield would rent during the camp season. The rental income would be used for scholarships.

So the Canfield Scholarship Lodge was built that winter. And it was rented by Mrs. Canfield each summer as long as she lived. The rent she paid covered the cost of one camper for a season at Interlochen. Canfield scholarship students came to see Mrs. Canfield during her stay at camp and expressed their appreciation. She enjoyed the students, and she enjoyed spending her summers in the guest lodge that was built with her money and named for her.

Thus the idea proved highly successful, and Joe finally told his Board that he intended to build more scholarship lodges. "Someday," he said, "we're going to have fifty like this one." The Board members were anything but enthusiastic, but their opposition was relatively mild. They expected the additional scholarship lodges to continue to exist nowhere but in Joe's mind. Just another of his ideas, they thought.

By 1963, however, Interlochen had forty-four endowed scholarship lodges bringing in more than thirty thousand dollars in guest rentals each summer. Many of the lodges were duplexes, with three or four rooms for rental. In addition, many donors "bought" rooms in the student center and dormitories. The dormitory rooms and lodges were named for the donor or anyone designated by them. Many were contributed by various state, national, or federated music clubs, with the rental income designated for scholarships to students from a specified state or town.

The endowed scholarship lodge plan which Joe conceived and started with Mrs. Canfield's check developed into a sizeable scholarship fund. By 1963, some hundred twenty-five of America's finest young musicians, artists, and dancers had attended Interlochen on the scholarship-lodge funds which had mushroomed from Joe's "idea."

And the debentures got paid off as well—in 1943, with each holder getting every cent of his money back, plus interest.

By 1950 it could be said that the music camp was solvent, or it would have been if Joe had let well enough alone. But his dream was not yet complete, and no one, not even his stanchest supporters, could believe in its newest unfolding. There was only one exception, Joe's beloved teacher and old friend, Giddings. Of all those who spasmodically put their trust in Joe, it was Giddings who never wavered. Of all who tried to hold Joe in rein, it was the cryptic, crusty old music master, the demon of discipline, the purist in teaching methods, the hard shelled vigilante of Interlochen, who invariably loosened the reins and said, "Go ahead." It was Giddings who understood that Joe's dream was big—bigger than either of them, bigger than the music camp, bigger than anything one man alone could achieve.

He knew why even Joe's most loyal supporters viewed the newest development of the dream with at least tolerant amusement. He knew why they refused even to listen or discuss the idea with Joe. He knew why some felt that Joe Maddy had now really completely lost touch with reality. He knew, too, that even if he could give Joe everything he had, it could not now really help get his dream off the ground. Giddings was not a rich man. He was a school teacher. And he was getting old.

He thought about it a great deal the summer before he died. He remembered the first summers—the time when Henry Ford's assistant had sent up four car-loads of miscellaneous surplus supplies and equipment, while Mr. Ford was in Europe. There were things like army cots, bedsteads, some outdoor lanterns, slop jars, and toilet bowls. They had put most of the things to use. The slop jars made nice flower pots. The toilet bowls were used for boat anchors. If only Joe could persuade the Ford Foundation—or someone! "What you need is an angel," Giddings told Joe, and his merry eyes had a touch of sadness as he added, "But don't worry. You'll find one."

Even Giddings with all his faith was appalled at the scope of what Joe now planned to do. He intended to turn his eight weeks summer camp into a year round private boarding school for students gifted in the arts. He would start on the secondary level but someday he would have a great University of the Arts. How many men would even dream on such an impossible scale? And where, in Heaven's name, did he expect to find anyone to contribute so much as a dime to the school he planned?

Nevertheless, Joe knew what he was doing and quietly, unobtrusively, he set out toward his goal. In 1945, less than a year after the music camp had paid off its debentures, he started a remodeling and winterizing program with his year around school in mind. The debentures, of course, weren't the end of his financial worries for the camp, for the camp was still heavily in debt. Few of its buildings were fully paid for yet.

But this didn't bother Joe. Bit by bit and penny by penny, he began remodeling. He started on the hotel. First the kitchens and dining area, then a new wing of bedrooms, then another, then a lobby. Gradually, over a period of years, the old hotel completely disappeared and was replaced by a modern, fireproof, winterized student center.

No one thought too much about it, except to note that it certainly was an improvement over the old hotel which the staff had always worried about because it was such a firetrap. That was reason enough for Joe to build the new structure. No one took him seriously when he said it was the beginning of his school. Joe, as everyone well knew, was a visionary. Then, however, construction began on the new staff and faculty quarters. The Brahms, Beethoven, and Mozart dormitories replaced the ramshackle cottages on Faculty Row. Next came new student dormitories. All were modern, comfortable, and heated for winter. They were built with borrowed money.

By 1958 most of the music camp staff, and its trustees, realized that Joe was serious about turning Interlochen into a completely accredited school. They also knew that it was impossible! If Joe wanted students for a full school year, he would have to offer them science, mathematics, English, history, biology—all the normal requirements for college entrance. Where was he going to get the teachers? How was he going to pay them? Where was he going to get students who would be willing to come and live in a boarding school in the frozen northwoods? Most people felt that Joe must be protected from his own lack of realism. The majority of his staff and trustees at once embarked on a program of passive and active resistance.

And meanwhile Joe embarked on the most intensive money-begging campaign of his life. It was one of the most discouraging. No one wanted to give money to a school which hadn't started yet, which had no faculty, no buildings, no students, no guarantee that it would even open—except Joe's word.

Joe learned that Foundations had little interest in contributing to secondary education, that money was much easier to get at the graduate and post-graduate levels. From the standpoint of enlisting financial support Joe's proposed school had three strikes against it from the beginning. It was planned as (a) a high school, (b) a school emphasizing the arts, and (c) a school for exceptionally talented or gifted students. Philanthropic foundations and individuals were far more willing to help the handicapped or backward child than the gifted one, and they were far more generous in contributing to the study of science or nuclear physics than the arts.

By 1961 Joe had interested only three foundations* in his arts academy. Nevertheless, with the funds thus contributed, he started construction of a Liberal Arts classroom building. On the last day of camp, Joe held the formal hole-digging ceremonies, complete with band music, and announced as the first spadeful of sod was turned that on this site the first winter school classroom building would be finished in a few months and that the new Interlochen Arts Academy would open in September, 1962.

Not one soul believed him.

In the first place, the money he had begged couldn't begin to meet the cost of the hundred and fifty thousand dollar building. In the second place, he had plunged Interlochen head over heels back into debt. Only a few months before, in the early spring of 1961, there had been some question as to whether there was enough money in the bank even to pay the salaries of the camp's

* The Kresge Foundation; the Mott Foundation of Flint, Michigan; and The Lilly Endowment of Indianapolis.

small year-round staff. Joe had spent it all on the winter expansion program. And in the third place, his Board of Trustees had decided it must finally apply the brakes. Joe was told that he must have a three hundred thousand dollar guarantee for faculty salaries before his school could open.

Three hundred thousand dollars! That was more than Joe had been able to beg in all the years put together. It was a lot of money to raise in one year. Joe set out on another round of hope and quiet determination. . . .

Looking back, it seemed inevitable that Joe Maddy should meet W. Clement Stone.

Professionally they were poles apart but philosophically they were kindred spirits.

Stone was an insurance man, president of the Combined Insurance Company of America. Like Joe Maddy, Stone had risen from meager beginnings. And like Joe he had reached the pinnacle by one success formula: that which the mind believes, it can achieve. There was one great difference between them. Stone's application of the formula had brought him personal wealth.

Stone's book, *Success Through a Positive Mental Attitude,* had been given to Joe by a friend. Joe promptly decided to go to Chicago and see Mr. Stone. Joe had never consciously defined his own eternal optimism as "positive mental attitude"—which Stone called PMA. But all the way to Chicago and to Stone's house, where a friend had arranged their meeting, Joe remembered those letters, PMA. Would they work? They *had* to.

Mr. Stone had never been to Interlochen, had never seen the music camp, had never met Joe Maddy before that night. All he had to go on was some camp literature, a detailed financial report from Joe on his operating costs and needs, and a friend's word that Dr. Joe Maddy was a man he would like very much.

Joe, the money beggar, swallowed his pride again and inwardly prayed for a miracle.

The minute he walked into Stone's house that night there was a bond between them. In one swift glance Stone's sharp eyes took in everything about Joe: the firm handshake, the shoulders a little stooped with age but rared back as if in some grand defiance, the taut clenched look in his face but the flash and sparkle of his eyes when he talked about Interlochen, his neat dark blue suit and freshly polished shoes that gave him a professorial dignity when he felt compelled to use it, and the nervous, impatient tapping of his fingers on his briefcase as he waited, hoped, talked . . . and waited. . . .

Behind Clement Stone's success as one of the world's richest insurance men was a gentle and generous man with a yearning as great as Joe's. No one could define what it was. But many had felt it. There was his woodcarver's school in New Zealand, the boys' clubs all the way from Auckland to Chicago, the prisons and hospitals and schools and churches and people whose lives had been touched and changed by a name unknown to them. He had a poker player's face, a little manicured mustache, and swiftly cruising, penetrating eyes that could size up a man or a situation at a glance. Mr. Stone always wished to remain anonymous, yet the gifts he left along the way always seemed to multiply and spread and reap unknown harvests.

Joe Maddy knew none of this as he sat there that night banking his hopes on a man who had never even been to Interlochen.

Mr. Stone brought out the typewritten financial report Joe had sent, and gave it to Mrs. Stone to read aloud. They went over it point by point, with Mr. Stone interrupting now and then to ask Joe a question. Finally they came to Item Number One under the heading: Funds Needed for the Opening of the Interlochen Arts Academy. Mr. Stone said quietly to Mrs. Stone, "You can skip that part and go on to the next item. We're taking care of that." And Mrs. Stone went on reading.

Joe wasn't sure he had heard correctly. The Number One item was the one demanded by Joe's Board of Trustees, the faculty salary guarantee of three hundred thousand dollars!

The subject was not brought up again until the end of the evening when Joe was ready to leave, and Mr. Stone said, again quietly with no questions, "I'll send up written confirmation for your trustees tomorrow."

One of the wonders of Joe's life was that W. Clement Stone not only believed in him on first sight but that he *offered* his gift without subjecting Joe to the ordeal of begging for it.

Before leaving, Joe mustered his courage and asked Mr. Stone whether he would possibly consider serving on his Board of Trustees. Stone smiled and said, "I'd be happy to." He didn't even ask for time to think it over.

A month later Stone flew to Interlochen for the first time, to be present at his first trustees' meeting. The camp was not in session. The grounds were deserted and bleak. Stone arrived after dark and left immediately after the meeting the following day. He couldn't possibly know what Interlochen was like when it was alight with music and sun.

But in the meeting he had sensed that Joe Maddy was in deep

difficulties, even with his faculty guarantee. And Mr. Stone liked a man with indestructible faith in a dream that everyone thought was impossible.

In the trustees' meeting Stone offered another three hundred and fifty thousand dollars to get the new school going. And he did it with his customary easy simplicity that meant, Let's not dwell on this, but get on with the next order of business.

The trustees were astonished. One of them ventured, "How can you do this when you know nothing about our institution?"

Mr. Stone replied calmly, but with a firmness that left no room for argument: "I'm betting on the man."

Triumph of an Idea

I

ON SUNDAY night, August 16, 1962, the wooden benches were filled to overflowing with those who had come to hear and see the final concert of the season. Some sat in the trees and on the tops of classrooms and practice buildings.

On the stage of the Interlochen Bowl and in the ground pit in front more than fourteen hundred youngsters had assembled, proud as eagles, their instruments polished like Tiffany windows, their chins up and eyes shining in the spotlight.

The first part of the program was over. The hardest was still to come: the performance of Liszt's hauntingly beautiful *Les Preludes* which traditionally marks the closing of each Interlochen music camp season.

Dr. Joe long ago had chosen *Les Preludes,* the beginnings, as Interlochen's closing theme each summer to try to help his young campers, and probably himself, over the farewell hump. He always told them during the last week of rehearsals to remember on Sunday night that this last concert wasn't really an ending but a beginning for them, the beginning of a better and richer life through music.

Traditionally the final concert was the only one of the season which brought together the entire student body from their separate camp divisions, the junior and intermediate campers as well as the high school and college groups. Anyone who could play an instrument well enough was in the gigantic orchestra, and the art and drama students who were also singers joined in the chorus.

All sat poised and ready for *Les Preludes.* The lights blazed across a sweep of color—dark corduroys and scarlet sweaters— through a tracery of fourteen great golden harps lined end to end across the front of the Interlochen Bowl. The dancers in their long filmy costumes waited on either side of the Bowl for the cue for their entrance.

It was a spectacular picture, and a hush fell over the audience and on the fourteen hundred young people as they waited, expectantly.

In the shadows at one end of the Bowl, a tall slim girl reached into the cedar bushes and pulled out a white cork tipped basswood baton. She waited while Joe Maddy paused briefly, alone and hidden from view in the darkness of the cedars. His face was tense with unashamed emotion. He cleared his throat and stepped out of the shadows. Then Joe straightened his shoulders and hurried onstage, with a spring in his step and a smile for the young people he cherished. They jumped up spontaneously, all fourteen hundred of them, and stood cheering and clapping for the man who had given them Interlochen and all it would mean to them for the rest of their lives. It was ten minutes before Joe could quiet them.

Thirty-five summers had come and gone, thirty-five summers of saying goodbye with *Les Preludes,* of feeling the haunting finality, and yet knowing that *Les Preludes* was always the beginning. No one in the vast audience that night could distinguish in the white sea of young faces onstage that a little violinist in the back row was bent over quietly sobbing, or that one of the flutists was too choked with tears to go on with her part.

Outside, under the pines, the throngs of listeners could share the beauty of the music, and they could sense the poignancy that belonged to the world of Interlochen. But they knew it was not their world. For this was Interlochen's winged night, the witching hour, a tender moment suspended fleetingly from a great, smashing aurora borealis of music. And it could belong only to those who had been part of it. . . .

The tall slim girl who had given Joe his baton was still standing in the shadows when the youngsters came offstage. Not long ago she had been one of them. Melinda Dalley had worn the camp's blue knickers each summer for as long as she could remember. Her mother had been a cellist in Joe Maddy's National High School Orchestra in Dallas. She was there when Joe hung by his elbows in the school gymnasium and made that wild rash promise to find his young musicians a place where they could play music all summer long.

Melinda's mother and father had grown up with Interlochen and married after a romance that started in Joe's music camp orchestra. Later they became members of the Interlochen faculty. Gretchen Dalley was a cello instructor, and her husband Orien, a violinist, was made director of the University of Michigan's All State musical organizations at Interlochen. Joe had taught both of them, and then he had taught their children. The Dalley children had grown up in the world of music and Interlochen. They were music camp babies even before they were old enough to enroll as junior campers.

Melinda Dalley had started taking cello lessons from her mother at Interlochen when she was only five years old, before she was big enough to hold a full size cello. Dr. Joe had found a quarter size cello for her, and he had seen her grow up and work her way up through the junior and intermediate orchestras to first chair in the high school symphony, the same chair her mother once held.

Melinda's brother John was a violinist, like his father, and he, too, grew up and worked his way up from the younger orchestras to become concertmaster of the high school symphony. After Interlochen, John became an instructor at Oberlin, and then went on to greater recognition as a concert artist. He was one of the semi-finalists in the 1962 international Tschaikowsky competition, the annual event which a few years earlier had brought fame to pianist Van Cliburn.

Melinda Dalley had become principal cellist in the Amarillo Symphony Orchestra, but during summers she still came back to Interlochen. In the summer of 1962 she worked in the camp's music library, and it was part of her job to see that all scores were on hand and in order at concerts, and that the conductor had his baton when he went on stage.

Thus it was only a small, insignificant, routine act of duty for Melinda to give Joe his baton as he went out to conduct the closing night *Les Preludes,* but somehow it caught the quintessence of Dr. Joe's Interlochen—and of Interlochen's Joe Maddy. Melinda was twenty-one. Joe would soon be seventy-one. He had guided her mother and father through many Interlochen summers and many closing night *Les Preludes* before she was born. He had watched music take wings in their children, and he had seen the pride and abiding faith of a family, indeed many families, and their children in a dream they shared. It was young people like Melinda and those before her and the ones yet to come that made *Les Preludes* always a glorious new beginning at Interlochen.

And in this year, 1962, *Les Preludes* held a very special significance for Dr. Joe and for Melinda and for the others who had kept faith in his dreams. It was the end of a very special summer still enchanted by its memories of the White House and Van Cliburn concerts. But it was the beginning, the fulfillment, the reality of Joe's Big Dream, the one that had been almost twenty years in the making.

In a few weeks Joe's Interlochen Arts Academy was going to open. The faculty was hired, the students were enrolled, Joe Maddy, by gum, was opening his *SCHOOL*.

And on the mimeographed faculty roster was listed the name: Melinda Mary Dalley, instructor in cello and bassoon, former principal cellist Amarillo Symphony. Melinda was one of the first to give up her job and come home to Interlochen, to teach in a school that most educators and musicians said would never open.

2

There was an unusually solemn note in the autumn air of Interlochen on that early September evening in 1962. It was not at all like opening day of summer camp when the woods filled with the cacophony of a thousand and more exuberant youngsters tuning and tooting their instruments. The lobby of the Student Center was crowded with faculty, staff, and trustees, some long faced and somber, some misty eyed, and some just plain bleary from lack of sleep and physical exhaustion. "I've never been with a school that's just started," George Wilson said quietly. "I don't suppose many of us have."

The week had been one of the most difficult in the memory of those who had worked for Joe over the years. Getting a full fledged *school* launched and off the ground was quite different from opening an eight weeks summer camp. There were many new faces among staff and faculty, and some had to be indoctrinated gently but firmly into the Joe Maddy way of life. Faculty meetings had droned on all week with the scores of problems that were to be expected in the founding of a new school, as well as some that had not been anticipated.

Not the least of these, for example, was the problem of a school uniform. Joe seemed surprised that anyone would even question what the students would wear. Naturally, they were going to wear corduroy pants and knickers. What else? He had conceded, however, that they could change for dinner.

When it came to the question of what the faculty would wear, a battle raged long and volubly. The arts faculty, most of whom were former music campers, favored the corduroy uniforms. But members of the new academic faculty, unaccustomed to Interlochen tradition, were clearly horrified. "I simply can't see myself trying to teach William Blake in knickers," said Miss Claire Kleinschmit, head of the English department. Joe finally prevailed upon the faculty to try the corduroys for a month, and the month, of course, stretched into the full school term.

The corduroys, however, were conspicuously absent from the opening convocation of the Interlochen Arts Academy. This was a solemn and historic occasion. For the first time in thirty-five years Joe was presiding at an official function on his music camp grounds—out of uniform. He seemed quieter than usual and a little self-conscious in his dark blue suit, white shirt, and tie as he waited for the lineup to go into the art building for the convocation.

He could be proud. He was opening his school with one hundred thirty-three students. Six months earlier people had been sure that he wouldn't open with fifty—if the school opened at all. But Joe knew that private schools had opened with as few as ten students, and he counted on at least a hundred. As it turned out, he had over-reached his goal.

While the line was forming for the convocation a little girl in a starchy pink dress and long black braids ran up to Dr. Joe, reached high and flung her arms around him as he bent over and swung her up in his arms. She smothered his face with kisses. Then he put her down and she swirled over to her parents who were waiting to go in to the convocation. The child was Cynthia Raim, a ten year old piano prodigy from Detroit. She had played twice with the Detroit Symphony Orchestra, and music critics predicted a bright future for her.

Cynthia had spent two summers at the Interlochen music camp and she wanted to come to Dr. Joe's new Interlochen Arts Academy. But she wasn't old enough to enroll as a regular student, and her father in any case couldn't afford to send her. He had been a milkman. Recently he had gone into the furniture reupholstering business. He wanted Cynthia to have the special training she needed—but how?

With the permission and cooperation of her music teacher in Detroit and of her parents, Joe had given Cynthia a full scholarship to the Academy and arranged for her mother to live with her at Interlochen to supervise her training. He had also engaged private tutors to instruct her in her academic studies. Of course there had been the usual to-do about the "social adjustment" of a ten-year-old child thus singled out. Some feared the experience would limit her chances for "normal" development. But Joe knew there were thousands of schools geared to a child's "social adjustment" and "normal" development. He must have known, too, from the dancing lights that shone in Cynthia's brown eyes on the night the school opened that she would get along well at the Academy. . . .

The attention of the whole educational world was focused on Joe Maddy when he opened his Interlochen Arts Academy on that September evening in 1962. What he was doing had never been done. Private schools, yes, by the thousands; music conservatories on the college level; day schools for professional children; summertime arts centers; and some private boarding schools with special courses in the arts, but there had never been a boarding school that offered to students of high school age a full and balanced combination of the performing arts and academic, college preparatory training.

In Joe's school there would be no football, no fly tying, no cooking classes, no non-essentials. Students who didn't know how to bake a cake, brush their teeth, or drive a car could learn these skills at home—not in his school. Instead he would give them the music and arts they were denied in most secondary schools. They would have their basic academic subjects: science, mathematics, history, English, and foreign language. But they would have time to concentrate on music, art, drama, creative writing, and dance—activities that were still considered "frills" in many schools. The emphasis in Joe's Academy on music and the arts was in direct contrast to the curriculum of most high schools. And he could never let people forget that Einstein was once a musician, and so was Albert Schweitzer, and that artistic and academic abilities have always gone hand in hand.

In his blue suit and tie, Joe stepped to the podium to deliver the convocation address for his new school. He had no notes. It was his habit to talk from the heart, and those who had been with him a long time always knew pretty well what he was going to say. "Thirty-five years ago," he began, "the National Music Camp was established here without any money. We ended up our first season forty thousand dollars in debt. I was criticized for this. But artistic success and educational success are far more important than financial success. . . ." His trustees and his book-keeper-treasurer George Mackmiller sat sphinx-like as Joe talked on. It was clear to them, and to everyone in the room, that Joe had no intentions of changing his way of life economically.

On either side of him, for example, sat his new Academy faculty, a teaching staff of thirty-four for one hundred and thirty-three students, a remarkable ratio of four to one. And it was a faculty of the highest caliber. "These students are going to get the very best," Joe said. "The finances will take care of themselves." He had hired a harp teacher from the University of Illinois, as a visiting instructor for only two harp students. And he had persuaded Joseph Knitzer, one of the nation's finest violinists and head of the violin department at the Eastman School of Music, to be a visiting Master Teacher and Chairman of the Academy's string department. From Eastman, too, had come Knitzer's first violinist, Richard Kilmer, to teach at the Interlochin Academy; and Ramona Dahlborg had left the faculty of

Stephens College in Missouri to teach flute and fencing in the new Academy. There was also Marcia Weissgerber Palmer, who was to serve as Dean of Girls for the new school. Marcia first knew Joe Maddy when she was a little girl of ten back in Richmond, Indiana, taking class violin lessons for ten cents apiece.

Four of the five members of the Amarillo Symphony's well known Woodwind Quintet had left Amarillo for Interlochen, and with a fifth player they formed a new Interlochen Arts Academy Quintet which even in its first year was to become known as one of the finest in the music world. Under professional management in New York, they were to teach and perform at the Academy during the school year and continue their touring engagements between terms. Four of the five had once been students at the music camp. One, of course, was Melinda Dalley, the girl who had started at Interlochen on a quarter size cello.

Nearly all of Joe's arts faculty for his new Academy had been either students, teachers, or guest artists and conductors at Interlochen over the years.

And although Joe's first love would always be music, and he made no secret of that fact, he had overextended himself to please the skeptics who had worried about his ability to find an academic faculty for his school. The skeptics and accreditation officials were more than satisfied. Heading the Academy's science department, for example, was John Charles Runge, a graduate of Trinity College in Oxford, England, and former teacher at Phillips Exeter Academy in New Hampshire. The other academic teachers were of equally outstanding caliber. Thaddeus P. Giddings would have been proud of his favorite pupil that night if he could have lived to see it.

And as Joe stood there at the podium, no one could question

what it was that made the man and his dreams imperishable. "Someday," he told the audience, "there will be a great University here. . . . Our students are going to learn about sixteen times as much here as they would learn at any other high school in the United States. And after that, they won't be satisfied with continuing their education at an average college. But we'll have a college for them right here at Interlochen very soon. . . ."

When the convocation was over people gathered outside in the dark, some awed, some still fearful for the success of Joe's new school. "Well," Mackmiller sighed, "at least we've got money in the bank. Of course I still have to pay the bread bill and the meat bill and the power. . . ."

His comment marked the school's founding as a doubly historic occasion, for this was the first time in history that anyone had ever heard Mack say, even with qualifications, "We've got money in the bank." It was a good sign.

On Monday morning school started. There were still some very big holes in the ground that had not yet been filled in with buildings. But no matter, they would be. Meanwhile an old garage had been cleaned out, spruced up, and heated. Joe put up a sign: ORCHESTRA HALL, and there at eight o'clock sharp on Monday morning he started rehearsal of his first Interlochen Arts Academy Orchestra. Eighty-five of the hundred and thirty-three students enrolled in the Academy were in the orchestra. The first concert was scheduled for the following Sunday, and in spite of objections from his staff that neither he nor the students could stand the hard work of putting on a concert every week, Joe went right ahead and scheduled a concert a week. Later he could enjoy telling his audiences, "We're the only high school in America with a symphony orchestra that performs a concert a week."

There were, of course, a few details yet to be worked out. After his first rehearsal, for example, Joe hurried over to the student admissions office and ordered, "Get me another cello player right away. I want the best you can find and don't worry about the costs." In a month's time the orchestra had improved so much that Joe could say it was *almost* as good as the one that went to Washington, in spite of the fact that his Academy students had to spend part of their time on algebra and Latin.

The students themselves soon learned that a great deal more was expected of them in Joe Maddy's school than in schools they had been attending. Some who had been straight A students in other schools found it difficult to get up to a B or C at the Interlochen Academy. But at least by the end of the first term everyone who had worried over the success of Joe's big dream could relax. They knew at last what he had known all along.

There were only two more projects requiring Joe's immediate action. One of course was to go out and start begging for more money. The other was to find a set of bagpipes. He had been charged jokingly with gross negligence by one of his staff members for not having bagpipes for his students, and it all started with a pretty little fifteen year old girl named Mary Streeter from New Jersey. Mary was the joy and delight of the Academy faculty. She was a straight A student, even though she was carrying five hours of academic subjects, a heavier load than most others, and she played third chair bassoon in the orchestra which rehearsed two hours daily. She was taking private bassoon lessons, and she was editor of the school paper. After a few weeks, however, Mary's teachers were astounded to hear that she was also beginning French horn lessons. One of her teachers asked her, "Don't you think you're doing enough already, Mary, without taking on anything more?"

Unabashed, Mary replied, "Oh, it's easy. I have plenty of time." She hesitated a moment, as if about to make a confession, and then she did, quite seriously. "I'm not really sure I'm going to like the French horn so well," she said. "You see, I'm part Scotch and what I'd really like to learn to play is the bagpipes. I was a little disappointed to find they don't have bagpipes here."

Mary's complaint was duly reported to Dr. Joe, along with the naïve question, "But is there anyone who could teach her to play bagpipes if we did have them?"

"Sure," said Joe. "I can play the bagpipes. That's no problem. But I haven't seen any bagpipes around in a long time. I wonder where I could find some besides in Scotland. . . ." Never let it be said that Joe Maddy had disappointed a student. He sent out a call for bagpipes.